"Thanks for all your tips to clean up at home, while I try to clean up at the plate!"

—Luis Gonzalez, left fielder, Arizona Diamondbacks

"Linda Cobb, the self-styled Queen of Clean®, sweeps into the big time with spotless timing for a book on dirt. . . . *Talking Dirty with the Queen of Clean®* . . . has certainly cleaned up."

—*People*

"There's no stain Linda Cobb can't tame."

—*New York Post*

"We thought we'd heard all the dirty talk for the Queen until a bagpipe-playing listener needed to clean the silver balls on his bagpipe thingy. With her encyclopedic knowledge, the Queen was able to get 'em all cleaned up. Linda is more than amazing . . . she's 'clean-a-rific!'"

—*Beth and Bill in the Morning*, KESZ-FM 99.9, Phoenix

"The Queen of Clean® has dug deep into her cleaning pail to find those elusive cleaning solutions. With this new book I never again will have to worry about a stain on my reputation."

—Tara Hitchcock, *Good Morning Arizona*, KTVK-TV3, Phoenix

"In high school, I was the scrub on the football team. It wasn't a compliment. The Queen of Clean®, however, has made me proud because with this new book, I can scrub anything clean!"

—Dan Davis, *Good Morning Arizona*, KTVK-TV3, Phoenix

"There isn't any stain or cleaning problem for which Cobb doesn't have a solution."

—*The Arizona Republic*

The Queen OF Clean®

Clean Like the Queen

A Queen for All Seasons

The Queen of Clean® Conquers Clutter

The Royal Guide to Spot and Stain Removal

LINDA COBB

POCKET BOOKS

New York   London   Toronto   Sydney

POCKET BOOKS, a division of Simon & Schuster, Inc.
1230 Avenue of the Americas, New York, NY 10020

A Queen for All Seasons copyright © 2001 by Linda Cobb
The Queen of Clean®: The Royal Guide to Spot and Stain Removal
  copyright © 2001 by Linda Cobb
The Queen of Clean® Conquers Clutter copyright © 2002 by Linda Cobb

The Queen of Clean®: The Royal Guide to Spot and Stain Removal is
excerpted from *Talking Dirty with the Queen of Clean®* copyright © 1998
by Linda Cobb and *Talking Dirty Laundry with the Queen of Clean®*
copyright © 2001 by Linda Cobb

ISBN: 1-4165-0320-X

This Pocket Books paper over board printing May 2004

10 9 8 7 6 5 4 3 2 1

Manufactured in China

For information regarding special discounts for bulk purchases,
please contact Simon & Schuster Special Sales at 1-800-456-6798
or business@simonandschuster.com.

A Queen for All Seasons

A Year of Tips, Tricks, and Picks
for a Cleaner House
and a More Organized Life!

Thanks

John. You are soft-spoken; I am a chatterbox. You love to sing; I love to laugh. You sang will you marry me, and I shouted yes! You have made my heart smile every day since.

The Queen Mother. You continue to amaze and inspire me. The pride and love in your eyes when you look at me is all I will ever need.

Dad, I look over my shoulder and know you are still there.

Our kids and their families who put up with our crazy life. We love you—and even more, we like you.

Duane Dooling, who gifted me with the title for this book, you are and always will be, a friend for all seasons.

Zack, The Palace Pussycat. It's not easy to motivate a cat to put his thoughts down on paper. Once he got started he worked doggedly without a peep until he was satisfied with his work.

Brenda Copeland, my incredible editor. With me from the first word keeping Zack and I on track, motivating, sympathizing and lending moral support, a shoulder and a hug, while using a gentle editorial pencil.

Thanks

All of you at Pocket Books who make it happen, Judith, Karen, Tracy, Seale, Cathy Lee, Craig and Barry.

Nigel Stoneman, my rocket from Pocket, UK.

Win and Carolyn Holden, Alan and Debbie Centofante, Beth McDonald, Bill Austin, Christi Paul, Jim Ranaldo, Brian Gilbert, Lisa and Bobby Aguilar, and Mark Manley, you make being Queen a pleasure.

Chester, Spanky, Max, Peke-A-Boo, Phoenix, See-Aye-Tee, and Bubba for conferring with Zack.

Chris and Brian Centofante. May God always smile on you and keep you safe.

To all of you, remember, if I can be Queen you can be anything you want—it's never too late!

The Year Ahead

I've been at this cleaning business a long time, and still I'm surprised by the number of people who get hung up on what to clean and when. Seems that for some people, cleaning is a dirty word. They want to know how often to clean this, when to put away that—as if there's going to be a big test at the end of the cleaning semester. But life's not like that. Sometimes you win. Sometimes you lose. Sometimes your house is clean. Sometimes . . . well, let's just leave it at that, shall we?

I don't believe in keeping to someone else's schedule and someone else's rules. I believe in making my schedule work for me, and I have only one rule: IF IT'S NOT DIRTY, DON'T CLEAN IT. We're all busy, and we all have better things to do than clean house. No one but the marines wears white gloves these days, so we don't have to be concerned with the white glove test. That said, few of us are happy living in a home that's dirty or unkempt. It's hard to relax when the dust bunnies are having a rodeo in the corner of your living room.

Sit back and think for a moment. What does clean mean for you? How organized do you want to be? Are you the type of person who's just dying to rearrange the magazines at the dentist's office, the one your office mate runs to when she spills cola on her keyboard? Or are you the person whose idea of cleaning is to put the dirty dishes in the oven, whose laundry schedule is determined by *Can I get away with this another day?*

Chances are you won't have to think too much about this. You already know who you are. You know what makes you comfortable and how you like to live. I suspect that despite our natural tendencies, most of us flit between one group and another. There are times when we feel that things are ordered and under control, just as there are times when chaos rules. I'm not trying to get you to change teams, to convert you or give you a cleaning citation. I want you to find your comfort, to do the things that will get you there, and help you stay there.

And that's where this book comes in. I've started off with a list of things to think about, from everyday household tasks that you'd never overlook (like washing dishes) to those uncommon tasks and easy oversights, such as flipping your mattress and cleaning the gutters. I'd like to encourage you to find out what's right for you. Some people, for example, may like to change their sheets every week. Others may find every two weeks often enough for them. A schedule only works if it's flexible and realistic. Start with that in mind and you can't go wrong.

That's part of what this book is about. Establishing a routine that works for you. The other part? Fun stuff. Each month brings its own particular signature. February, for example, can be a time of high heating bills, but it's also a time for Valentine's Day and romance, and that can mean flowers, champagne and chocolates (for starters . . .). I'll let you in on the best ways to care for flowers, how to help keep the bubble in that bottle of champers, and what to do when the chocolate strays on to the furniture and bed linen. (Oh, don't tell me you've never eaten chocolate in bed!) Turn to April, and you'll find some fun, natural ways to color your Easter eggs, as well as how to get ready for allergy season. October contains some Halloween fun, and December, as you might imagine, rounds out the year with lots of holiday advice.

But that's not all. I've included a few recipes throughout the book (well . . . you *have* been asking), and I'm also including some recommendations from my four-legged co-writer: Zack The Palace Pussycat. Zack helped me with my last two books (mainly by sitting on the manuscript), and this time he wanted to contribute further, so look for his suggestions in THE CAT'S MEOW. Zack's segments provide advice from the feline point of view, and of course he reminds us that behind every successful woman there's usually a rather talented cat.

This is not your typical cleaning book. But then again, I'm not your typical Queen!

It's About Time

DAILY DUTIES

Personally, there are only two things that I do *every* day: kiss the King and feed the cat. I make the bed most days (it's so much nicer to come home to), and I do try to see that the dishes are done, but sometimes I'm just so busy or distracted that even the simplest tasks fall by the wayside.

We're all very busy. We all have too much to do. That's why I've kept this list of daily chores short. Carry out these few tasks on most days and you'll find your life running smoother than you could imagine. Miss a day . . . well, the dishes will still be there tomorrow.

- Make beds.
- Put dirty clothes in the hamper.
- Hang up clothes.
- Clean up spills.
- Wash dishes.
- Wipe counters and stovetop.

TWICE WEEKLY

I've kept this list gloriously short—only one item:

- Vacuum carpets!

You can get away with vacuuming carpets just once a week (six days is the average gestation period for dust bunnies), but vacuuming twice weekly will prevent the dirt from getting ground into the fibers, and will therefore prolong the life of the carpet.

WEEKLY

Weekends were made for more than housework, so try spreading these tasks out through the week if you can.

- Sweep hardwood floors.
- Dust hard furniture.
- Dust knickknacks.

- Do the laundry.
- Change sheets.
- Clean sinks.
- Clean showers and tubs.
- Clean the toilet.
- Clean bathroom mirrors.
- Empty trash cans, put out garbage. (Clean the trash can if odors remain.)
- Sweep porch, patio and doormats.

BIWEEKLY

- Vacuum stairs.
- Dust TV/VCR/stereos, etc.

MONTHLY

- Replace the bag on your vacuum.
- Vacuum upholstery.
- Clean makeup brushes and sponges.
- Clean hairbrushes and combs.
- Vacuum drapes.
- Clean mirrors.
- Vacuum or dust blinds and shutters.
- Dust ceiling fans.
- Dust woodwork and dust down any cobwebs.
- Wash kitchen and bathroom area rugs.
- Vacuum carpet edges.

- Check hard floors and re-wax heavy traffic areas if needed.
- Clean out the refrigerator.
- Spot clean the kitchen cabinet fronts.
- Clean the fronts of stove, refrigerator, dishwasher, etc.
- Check the furnace filter: change or clean if needed.
- Hose off entry mats.
- Sweep out the garage.

QUARTERLY

- Sweep or wash the walkways and driveways.
- Change or clean the furnace filter.
- Wipe off lightbulbs as you dust (be sure they are cool).
- Look over knickknacks and wash or thoroughly clean any that require more than dusting.
- Flip the cushions on chairs and sofas for even wear.
- Clean humidifiers and dehumidifiers.

TWICE A YEAR

- It's got to be done: clean the oven.
- Clean stove hood and/or exhaust fan.
- Check the contents of freezer for things that are past their freshness. Clean freezer.
- Turn the mattresses on beds.
- Wash any plastic, vinyl or leather furniture.
- Clean scatter rugs.

- Dust books on shelves, making sure to dust shelves under the books.
- Vacuum the heat registers and cold air returns.
- Vacuum under furniture.
- Check silverware and clean if necessary.
- Replace that little box of baking soda in the refrigerator.
- Dust all the things you haven't been able to reach all year long.
- Clean bedspreads and slipcovers.
- Clean closets as you change seasonal clothes.

ANNUALLY

- Wash blankets and comforters.
- Dust down walls.
- Wash walls (every two years).
- Strip any waxed floors and re-wax.
- Wash all windows and screens.
- Wash or dry-clean drapery.
- Move and clean under and behind large items.
- Wash blinds.
- Clean carpet and upholstery.
- Clean any areas you have avoided all year long.
- Have the air conditioner checked and cleaned.
- Have the furnace checked and cleaned.
- Sort through the medicine cabinet, clean it, and organize and discard old medicine.

- Clean out kitchen cupboards, wash and reorganize.
- Replace the batteries in smoke detectors and other safety devices.
- Check the batteries in flashlights.
- Clean rain gutters.
- Wash all exterior windows.
- If you have a chimney, clean it.

So there you have it. Your annual checklist. Now read on for some fun stuff.

January

It's January, a time of good intentions and new beginnings. We've made our resolutions and, with any luck, have recovered from our seasonal indulgences. We're ready for a fresh start. But first we have to clean up from last year. That means putting away the Christmas decorations and taking down the tree, storing the lights, and all that half-price wrapping paper that seemed like such a good idea at the time. So let's get to it. If we start now, we'll still have time to enjoy that Super Bowl party!

Let's Un-Deck the Halls

Putting up decorations can be a lot of fun, what with all the excitement of the holidays to look forward to. But there are few surprises after Christmas—unless, of course, you're talking about that mystery stain you've just discovered on the hall carpet. The best way to clean up after the holidays is to take a deep breath, roll up your sleeves, and get down to it. The sooner you start, the sooner you'll be finished. And isn't that what it's all about?

LIGHTS

If you just whip the lights off of the house and tree and toss them in a box, you'll hate yourself come next December when you find them twisted, tangled and broken. Wrap them around an empty paper roll instead. Take a large paper roll—one from wrapping paper will do fine—and cut a notch at one end. Tuck one end of the lights in the notch and start rolling them around the tube. When you get to the end of the tube make another notch to fasten that end of the lights. Do this to each strand, clearly labeling the tubes as you go—indoor or outdoor lights, tree lights or decorative strands, etc. Make sure you separate any lights that aren't functioning properly and mark those too, either for repair or scavenging.

Large lights or extra long lengths can be rolled in a circle, like a cowboy loops a rope. Delicate, expensive or special light strands can be stored in the type of inexpensive plastic food bowls that come with covers. The lights won't get crushed or broken, and they can be stacked for storage without damage.

CHRISTMAS TREES

Taking down the tree is really a two-person job, so try to enlist some help. A tree bag is your best bet, as it will prevent pine needles from being trailed through the house. Just make sure to buy a bag large enough to cover the base of the tree, and long enough to cover the height. The first step is to siphon off all the water that you can—a turkey baster works great. Next, lay a large covering, such as a plastic shower curtain, on the floor. Take a good look around to ensure that breakables are safe, and make sure you're well out of range of any hanging light fixtures. Loosen the tree stand, and gently tip the tree onto the covering, being careful not to shed too many needles or spill any remaining water left in the reservoir. (Remember the first rule of cleaning: If you don't make a mess, you won't have to clean it up!) Don't pull the bag up haphazardly, and don't tug. Be gentle and gradually unroll the bag up the length of the tree, something like putting on a pair of panty hose. (If you wear panty hose, that is . . .) Once you've got the tree into the bag, tie it tightly and drag it outside. You can, of course, carry the tree, but there's always the chance that you'll drop it, and that may cause damage.

Artificial trees can be stored fully assembled in Christmas tree storage bags. Simply open the bag, "fold" up the limbs on the tree as directed (You did keep the booklet that came with the tree, didn't you?), place the tree carefully into the bag and zip it up! Lack of storage space may dictate that you dismantle the tree and keep it in a box. If that's the case, just make sure to identify the branches, base and stem—unless, of course, you like jigsaw puzzles.

ORNAMENTS

First, make sure to dust the ornaments before you store them. Used fabric softener sheets are great for this job, but you will need rather a lot. Wipe the ornament with the used dryer sheet, then cover it so that the *other* side of the sheet touches the ornament. The fabric softener sheet will protect the ornament during storage, and the residue of softener will help to repel static electricity—and therefore, dust—when you hang it on the tree next year! Once you've wrapped the ornament, place it gently in a storage container, such as a shoe box or plastic storage carton. Those large metal canisters that once held popcorn are great, too.

Did you know?

Decorative candles can be cleaned quite easily with a cotton ball moistened with rubbing alcohol.

Whatever container you use, make sure not to overcrowd it or force the lid down, and try not to use tape to secure the box. Tape can ruin the box for future use and, if stored in an attic, can get sticky and gummy during the hot summer months. That can cause a real mess. A bungee cord hooked around the ends of the container will keep the lid firmly closed. Try that instead.

Once again, make sure to mark the storage container, and make sure to separate ornaments that are expensive or have sentimental value. Delicate elongated ornaments can be stored inside a toilet paper tube, and smaller items can be placed safely in egg cartons. Save silk balls that are starting to unravel by giving them a spritz with some hair spray or spray starch.

WRAPPING PAPER

The most important thing about storing Christmas paper is to actually remember that you have it so you don't go out and buy more next year! Either put the paper in an obvious spot so that it's the first thing you see as you start to take out the decorations, or make a note that you have *x* number of rolls on hand. It's not a bargain if you buy it twice!

I store my wrapping paper under the bed. Long plastic storage containers meant for this purpose work exceptionally well, and can be found quite inexpensively in dollar and discount stores. If you don't have a storage container, lay the rolls of paper on the floor and tie them together with some string or an elastic band. A bungee cord hooked into the ends of the rolls will hold the paper in a neat bundle. Just make sure to slip them into a large garbage bag to keep them clean during storage. Some people like to store their wrapping paper and ribbons in an old suitcase. That can work well, just as long as you remember which one you've used. You don't want to end up in the Bahamas with nothing to wear but Santa Claus wrapping paper and a big red bow! As I've said, labeling is important.

RIBBONS AND BOWS

• Store pre-made bows in a plastic storage or shoe box to prevent them from getting scrunched up. If you've bought an assortment of bows, tip them out of the bag and into the box. Those bags always seem to be too small to hold the bows, and so many of them wind up flattened and bent.

I hate it when that happens . . .
You've just found the perfect color bow at the bottom of the bag and, darn, if it isn't crushed! Not to worry. Crushed bows can be brought back to life by putting them in the dryer on air fluff (no heat) for a few short minutes. Presto! Good as new.

• Keep rolls of ribbon tidy by putting a rubber band or ponytail holder around the roll. You'll prevent unraveling that way.

BOBBLES, BANGLES AND BEADS—
IN OTHER WORDS, *MISCELLANEOUS!*

• Garland is usually too lush to be wrapped around just one paper roll, so fasten a few tubes together with a rubber band and wind the garland around that. Make sure you wrap the garland around the roll like a candy cane, side-to-side, and secure it in notches that you've cut in each end. Don't draw the garland from top to bottom—the strand could stretch or break.

• Dust silk flowers before storing them with a blow-dryer, set on cool.

• If you store Christmas dishes in plastic wrap or stacked in Ziploc™ bags you won't have to wash them before using next year.

• Make sure to launder Christmas tablecloths and napkins prior to storing. Old spills will oxidize during storage and can be difficult, if not impossible, to remove.

Save those empty baby wipe boxes. They come in handy for storing gift tags and those slivers of ribbon that are so handy for decorating small packages.

• Take care when storing the Nativity scene. Wrap each figure separately, either in tissue paper or a used fabric softener sheet. Paper towels don't work well for this job because their fibers can catch on any rough edges. If you do scratch a figurine, try touching it up with a child's colored pencil.

Delicate Christmas knickknacks can be stored in egg cartons.

• Artificial wreaths can be stored year-to-year in a large pillowcase (depending on the size of the wreath) or in a large plastic bag. Wrap some tissue paper around the wreath first, but be gentle when removing it—you don't want to damage any of the branches. If the ribbon on the wreath is flattened, just plump it up with a curling iron.

• Many charities make good use of discarded Christmas cards. St. Jude's Ranch, for example, is a nonprofit youth home that teaches kids a trade and a way to earn money by cutting off the verse and making the fronts into new cards. Entire cards are welcome, as are cards with the backs cut off. For more information call 1-800-492-3562, or visit St. Jude's website at www.stjudesranch.org.

MAKING A LIST, CHECKING IT TWICE

Make a note of what seasonal items you've stored, and *where* you've put them. If you make a list of what you think you'll need next year—wrapping paper, Christmas cards, extension cords, larger-sized pants—you'll be in a good position to pick up bargains. More importantly, you'll save yourself that last-minute flurry of panic when you realize that your tree lights don't reach the outlet. Remember: Excitement is good. Panic is bad.

It's Time for That Super Bowl Party!

I love Super Bowl parties. Everybody seems to be in such great spirits. Good friends, good food, and good fun. What could be better?

TOUCH-UPS AFTER TOUCHDOWNS

You wouldn't cry over spilt milk, so why shed a tear over beer? First thing to do for a beer spill on the carpet is to blot up all the liquid you can, then flush the area with club soda and blot, blot, blot again. Now turn to a great carpet spotter like Spot Shot Instant Carpet Stain Remover® and follow the directions carefully. Try to avoid carpet cleaners that contain stain repellents. If the beer doesn't come out during the first try, the repellent could lock in the stain and you could be left with a permanent mark.

Beer stains on clothes? Flush with cool water, work in a few drops of liquid dishwashing soap and launder as usual.

Salsa—the sauce, not the dance—tastes so good and stains so bad. For salsa spills, blot with club soda as soon as possible, then treat with Wine Away Red Wine Stain Remover™ or Red Erase®. Both are fabulous at removing red stains from carpets, upholstery *and* clothes.

Guacamole is my favorite, but what a cleaning disaster it is! Think about it: It's oily *and* green. Clean up guacamole spills on carpets and upholstery by scraping with a dull, straight edge, such as a credit card. (The one you used to pay for the party should do nicely.) Remove as much *gunk* as possible, then flush with club soda and blot, blot, blot! Let sit 10 minutes, then flush with cool, clear water. Once the surface is dry, apply a good carpet and upholstery cleaner according to the directions on the container. If you still have a green reminder, mix up a solution of ½ cup of hydrogen peroxide and 1 teaspoon of ammonia, spray on liberally, let sit 15 minutes, then blot. Continue until the stain is removed and then flush with club soda and blot until you have removed all the moisture possible.

If you happen to be wearing the guacamole stain, treat with Zout® Stain Remover or rubbing alcohol. Gently dab the alcohol on the stain and let sit for 15 minutes before pre-treating and laundering as usual.

If your house has that smoky, day-after smell, bring some white vinegar to a boil, then reduce to a simmer for about 30 minutes, being careful not to let the pan boil dry. Let the vinegar stand and after a few hours unwanted odors will be absorbed.

Did you know?

Simmering orange or lemon peels can give your home a fresh, natural scent.

If the upholstery smells like smoke, lay a clean sheet on the furniture and sprinkle it with ODORZOUT™. Let sit overnight, then remove the sheet and shake outside. ODORZOUT™ is all natural and won't hurt anything. For carpet odors, sprinkle directly, then vacuum in the morning.

Spilled ashtray? Don't reach for the vacuum—at least not right away. You could have a nasty vacuum fire on your hands, at which point you'll be wishing that a spilled ashtray was your only problem! Pick up any butts and dispose of them in an empty can until you are sure they are cool. Ash on hard floors should be cleaned with a broom and dustpan; ash on carpet should be vacuumed using only the hose—no beater bar, which could grind the ash into the carpet. If you're sensitive to cigarette odors, you may want to dispose of the vacuum bag or empty the canister. Never apply water to an ashtray spill. You'll have a black, gooey mess on your hands that's far worse than anything you started with.

Somebody break a glass? It's bound to happen. Pick up the large shards first, then use a cut potato to pick up the slivers. (Yes, a potato.) Just cut the potato in half and press down on the glass with the damp side. Vacuum the remaining small pieces, using the attachment hose to concentrate the suction, then vacuum the carpet thoroughly. Never use a vacuum with a beater bar to vacuum glass until you've picked up all you can with the potato and the attachment hose. The beater bar will only flip the glass around, making it harder to clean up the debris.

Let's Dish!

Guacamole is such a wonderful Super Bowl tradition. And now that you know how to clean it up, you can serve it with flair! Here's my favorite recipe:

Chi Chi's Super Bowl Guacamole

4 ripe avocados, mashed or pureed (can do in food processor)

½ cup canned diced green chilies

¼ cup minced onion

1 tablespoon salt

¼ cup lemon juice

Combine all ingredients, cover and chill. Serve with corn chips. Makes about 3 cups.

❤❤ February ❤❤

This is the month of cold weather and high heating bills. Thank goodness it's also the month of love. Offset the winter cold by snuggling with your honey. Let those Valentine's flowers remind you of spring, and brighten those long winter nights with some sparkling jewelry. And if Cupid does leave his mark, well, look no further for some quick cleanup tips.

Conservation for the Nation

Cuddling is an energy-efficient way to keep warm. Want to save water? Bathe with a friend! Of course there are other ways to save on your energy bill.

• Why heat an empty house? Lower the thermostat when your family is out during the day—try 65 degrees or so—and bring the heat back up in the evening. If you lower the temperature when everybody is toasty warm in bed, you'll cut your bill even further. A double setback thermostat can adjust the temperature according to your needs. It's well worth the money.

• Moist air retains heat, so invest in a humidifier (or adapt your existing heating system) and you could lower your thermostat by another 3 or 4 degrees. That can save you up to 12 percent on your heating bill!

• A gas-fired heating system should be professionally cleaned and serviced at least once a year to keep it working at maximum efficiency. Oil-fired systems should be cleaned and serviced twice a year. Those of you who have had the misfortune of a furnace backup *know* I'm giving you good advice. Cleaner is better.

• Shut the dishwasher off at the dry cycle and allow dishes to air-dry with the door partially open.

• Just cooked a nice roast dinner? Leave the door open a crack (once you've turned off the oven, that is), and let the heat warm the room as the oven cools. Don't do this if you have young children—nothing is worth a potential burn.

• Keep radiators, registers and ducts clean. Vacuum with the duster brush attachment; for hard to reach spots use a telescoping duster. Make sure they're clear of debris and free from obstructions, such as furniture and draperies.

• Replace furnace filters frequently. A clean filter will distribute heat more efficiently. Check filters monthly, say the first of every month. Vacuum to remove dust, and replace filters when vacuuming alone won't get the filter clean. Disposable filters should be replaced at least every three months.

• Heat can escape through air conditioners, so store yours if you can. If that's not possible, do your best to winterize the unit. Cover the outside of the a/c with cardboard cut to size, and then wrap it in a heavy-duty plastic. Drop cloths and plastic tablecloths are ideal. Secure the covering with a bungee cord, making sure to avoid corner flaps that might tear in the wind.

• Conserve energy in winter *and* summer by adjusting the rotation on your ceiling fan. A counterclockwise rotation will push the hot air from the ceiling down into the room—perfect for winter. A clockwise rotation will pull up warm summer air and replace it with a nice, cool flow.

• Conserve water by taking showers instead of baths. The average bath uses 25 gallons of water, whereas the average shower uses just 10 gallons.

• Don't leave water running while you brush your teeth. Turn it off until you're ready to rinse.

> *That "small load" setting may save water, but the washing machine still goes through the same number of rotations. Avoid washing small loads if you can.*

• Whenever possible, use cold or warm water for washing clothes. Always use cold water to rinse.

• Clean the lint filter on your clothes dryer each time you dry a load. Clothes will dry faster and more efficiently.

• That little black dress may be a hot number, but there's no reason to keep it warm. Keep closet doors closed.

Happy Valentine's Day!

Flowers, jewelry, candy? I'd love Valentine's Day even if it *wasn't* the day the King proposed!

PETAL PUSHERS

• Do your best to select the freshest flowers available. Look for healthy stems with unblemished leaves and petals. Flowers that are just beginning to bud will last longer than those in full bloom.

• Be sure to remove leaves that fall below the waterline. They can contaminate the water.

• Cut stems on an angle while holding them under running water, then immerse in fresh water. It's best to do this in the early morning when it's coolest.

• Coarse, heavy stems (you'll find them on flowers such as gladiolus, mums, pussy willows, forsythia, and even roses) should be split with a sharp knife before placing in water. This will encourage the stem to drink up the water. Pounding the base of the stem with a wooden spoon works well, too.

• Change the water every day. And for a longer life, add one of the following mixtures:

> A teaspoon of sugar and about a ¼ teaspoon of lemon juice
>
> Several aspirin tablets that have been dissolved in a little warm water
>
> A tablespoon of liquid bleach. That will stop the water from clouding; particularly useful when using a clear vase.

• Prolong the life of flowers by keeping them cool and displaying them out of direct sunlight.

• Remove anthers from lilies. Those long, pollen-bearing shoots can rub off on clothes, carpeting and walls and can be extremely difficult to remove.

Clean pollen stains from clothing by sponging with rubbing alcohol. Don't use anything with ammonia. That will set the stain.

ARTFUL ARRANGEMENTS

• Flowers too short for the vase? Place stems in plastic drinking straws before arranging.

• Vase too deep? Fill it with marbles prior to adding water and flowers.

• Wilted flowers? Snip about an inch off the ends and stand them in hot water for about 20 to 30 minutes before returning to a vase of clean, cool water.

• Make sure floral foam is saturated with water before adding flowers.

• Arrange large flowers first, then follow with smaller blossoms and greenery.

Did you know?

Tulips are the only flowers that continue to grow after they've been cut!

• Coffeepots, teapots and milk bottles make lovely imaginative vases.

• Plastic hair rollers are great for arranging flowers. Stand them upright in the bottom of the vase and place stems in the cylinders to keep them in position.

• Try to match the flowers to the vase. Hourglass shapes are good for single-bloom flowers like tulips, and urns are great for flowers that droop easily. Slim, cylindrical vases are best for tall flowers like gladiolus.

• Placing your arrangement in front of a mirror will double the impact of your flowers.

DIAMONDS ARE A GIRL'S BEST FRIEND

Who doesn't love to get a gift of jewelry? Who doesn't know how to care for it?

• Rubbing alcohol is great for cleaning costume jewelry. Pour a little rubbing alcohol over the piece—place the jewelry in a shallow dish or small container first—and gently brush with a soft toothbrush. A word of caution: Many costume pieces are glued, and soaking can loosen the glue. Try not to saturate. Finish with a quick rinse in cool water and wipe dry.

• Costume jewelry that doesn't contain glue can be cleaned with denture-cleaning tablets. Drop a few tablets in a cup of warm water and allow the jewelry to soak for 5 minutes or so. Rinse and dry well. For intricate pieces, dry with a blow-dryer.

• Remove dirt from intricate pieces by brushing with a soft bristle toothbrush and some white, nongel toothpaste.

Rinse by brushing with a clean toothbrush and just water, and dry well.

Restore the luster to pearls by buffing gently with a soft cloth moistened with olive oil.

• Clean diamonds by placing in a tea strainer and dipping them in a pot of boiling water into which you have added several drops of ammonia and a drop or two of dishwashing liquid. Immerse for a few short seconds and then rinse in cold water. For extra sparkle, dip the diamonds in a little bit of undiluted vodka or alcohol for a minute or two, then rinse and pat dry. This may be used for hard stones such as diamonds, rubies and sapphires. *Do not* use this method on emeralds.

• Emeralds are extremely soft. They can crack easily and absorb water, so buff them with a soft toothbrush or an ACT Natural™ Microfiber Cloth. Don't soak them or immerse them in water, and if you want a thorough cleaning, take them to a professional.

• Remove tarnish from silver with a paste of lemon juice and baking soda. Apply the mixture with a soft toothbrush, then allow to dry. Remove with a clean, dry toothbrush and polish with a clean, soft cloth.

• Jade can be washed in mild, soapy water. Dry immediately.

• Opals and turquoise are porous stones that should not be washed. Brush settings with a dry, soft toothbrush and shine with chamois-type leather or an ACT Natural™ Microfiber Cloth.

• Wash gold in a bowl of soapy water. A soft, gentle stroke with a soft toothbrush will help clean crevices, details and links. Dry with a soft, lint-free towel and then buff with a chamois or microfiber cloth.

I hate it when that happens . . .

Tangled chains got you in knots? Place a drop of baby oil on the chain, then gently untangle by pulling the links apart with two sewing needles.

• Always fasten a chain-link necklace before storing to prevent tangles. Chains that tangle easily can be slipped through a drinking straw. Cut the straw to half the length of the chain, drop the chain through and fasten the clasp on the outside of the straw. No more tangles.

The Valentine's Day Stain Chain

Love should last forever, not that chocolate stain.

• Chocolate on clothes requires special treatment. Scrape off all you can with a dull straight edge, taking care not to force the chocolate more deeply into the fabric. Gently apply some Zout® Stain Remover, allow it to sit on the fabric 5 minutes or so (don't let it dry), and then flush under a forceful stream of warm water. If a grease mark is still visible, sponge with any good dry-cleaning solution such as Engergine Cleaning Fluid®. For really tough stains, soak in Brilliant Bleach® by Soapworks. Follow package directions carefully.

• Chocolate on carpets should be treated immediately with your favorite carpet cleaner. Try Spot Shot Carpet Stain Remover®. For really stubborn stains, saturate the area with ½ cup of hydrogen peroxide, to which you have added 1 teaspoon of ammonia. Allow to sit for 20 minutes, then blot. You may need to repeat this process. Once the stain is gone, flush the area with club soda and blot by standing on old heavy towels. This should remove the moisture. Allow to fully dry before walking on the area.

You can keep the fizz in champagne for hours if you slip the handle of a metal teaspoon down the neck of the bottle. I don't know why it works, but it does!

• Champagne spills should be sponged immediately with club soda. The salt in the soda will help to prevent permanent stains and the carbonation will draw the spill from the fibers. Two remedies for the price of one!

• Dried alcohol stains will turn brown as they age, so quick removal is important.

• Champagne spills on clothes should first be blotted with club soda, then pre-treated with a good laundry stain remover.

• Champagne spills on carpets should be treated with Spot Shot Instant Carpet Stain Remover®. Just make sure to blot well with club soda first. Treat spills on upholstery the same way, drying with a hair dryer to prevent a ring from forming.

• Stains from pink champagne can be removed with Wine Away Red Wine Stain Remover®.

• Perfume stains can be avoided if you apply your fragrance *before* you get dressed. Make sure it's dry before putting on your clothes.

• Perfume is a combination of alcohol and oil—deadly to fabrics. Treat perfume stains with Zout® Stain Remover and launder as soon as possible. If the fabric is dry-clean only, be sure to point out the stain to your dry cleaner.

• Never iron an area that has been sprayed with perfume. You might set the stain, or worse, remove the color from the fabric!

• Perfume stains can be removed from sturdy fabrics with a lather of Fels-Naptha Soap® and warm water. Work well into the stain, let sit 15 minutes and launder as usual.

• Stains from massage oil can be removed with a good waterless hand cleaner, such as GOJO™. Rub it well into the fabric—*massage* it in if you'd like!—then flush with warm water. A paste of liquid dish soap and 20 Mule Team® Borax will also work. Launder as usual using your normal detergent and the hottest possible water for the fabric. One-half cup of 20 Mule Team® Borax will ensure that all residue is removed.

• Oil stains on carpets should be covered quickly with baking soda. Allow the baking soda to absorb the oil—this may take several hours—then vacuum it up using the attachment hose to concentrate the suction. Vacuum very well with the hose before vacuuming with a beater bar to remove all of the baking soda. Finish off with your favorite carpet cleaner.

March

It's spring! The flowers are blooming, the birds are singing, everything's fresh and new, and you can't wait to get started with your spring-cleaning. Yikes! Did I say spring-cleaning? That has no part in my spring fantasy. How about yours? Spring-cleaning was a necessity a long time ago when log cabins were boarded up to keep out the winter cold. The arrival of spring presented the first opportunity to clean out all the soot and grime that had accumulated during the long winter months—hence the term spring-cleaning. Those of you living in log cabins may want to continue this practice, but for the rest of us, well, there are better things to do.

That's not to say that there aren't certain times of the year when you'll want to clean a little more thoroughly. It may be just after Christmas, it may be right before Aunt Martha's next visit . . . it might even be spring. *When* you do it is entirely up to you. As for *what* to do, read on.

Spring Forward

DON'T CLEAN YOUR CLUTTER

The hardest part of cleaning is working around the accumulation of all those things you've somehow acquired. If you really want to streamline your cleaning process, take a few minutes, go room to room and take stock of what's in sight, as well as what's hiding in your cupboards. I'll bet my crown (the cheap cardboard one . . .) that you have things that haven't been used in three, five, ten years or more. Think carefully. Do you really want to keep that purple giraffe? Do you really want to clean it?

If you can't bear to part with your collectibles (I love cats and pigs—don't ask), consider storing some and displaying others, rotating your selection from time to time. You'll have less to clean.

If you have a lot of treasures, think about investing in a glass-fronted display cabinet. The glass will protect your ornaments from dust, and you shouldn't have to clean them more than once a year.

Are you really going to read all those back issues of *National Geographic*? Don't be timid. Throw them out.

If that cat figurine that Aunt Lucille gave you 10 years ago is missing a paw and part of its tail, look at it, smile at the memories and then say good-bye. Don't keep things that are broken and can't be repaired.

Think before you purchase the latest gadget. If you don't buy it, you won't have to clean it.

A WORD ABOUT CLEANING PRODUCTS

Gather all your cleaning products together in one container before you start your rounds—something with a handle is ideal. If you have more than one bathroom, think about purchasing a set of cleaning products for each. It may cost more at the time, but you'll save yourself the aggravation of toting products from one floor to the next.

Can't find any twist ties and the trash bag is full? Just use dental floss or a rubber band. Both are tough and water resistant, so you don't have to worry about the rain.

Make sure you have plenty of clean cloths and vacuum bags. If you anticipate throwing out a lot of garbage, make sure you have lots of good, strong bags. Check supplies of soaps and any all-purpose cleaners that you may use. There's nothing worse than starting a task only to have to stop halfway because you don't have what you need at hand.

The most expensive products are not always the best. Try store brands and homemade solutions—they can work just as well as their more expensive counterparts.

Try not to depend on harsh chemicals. Things like baking soda, white vinegar, 20 Mule Team® Borax, Fels-Naptha Soap®, lemon juice, salt and club soda work just as well and aren't harmful to your family or the environment. Baking soda is a great deodorizer and a wonderfully mild abrasive. White vinegar is a terrific cleaner, especially for soap scum and mildew. Borax is a never-be-without laundry additive, and Fels-Naptha Soap® is great for stubborn stains. And let's not forget the club soda, lemon juice and salt. Club soda works on all sorts of spills; lemon juice is a great natural bleach; and salt can be used on just about everything, from artificial flowers to clogged drains.

Be wary of using too many antibacterial products. Unless you're prepping for surgery, good old soap and water work just fine.

Look for odor eliminators instead of cover-ups. Make sure to purchase products without scent. Try using baking soda or a good, natural odor eliminator such as ODORZOUT™.

Don't forget to change that little box of baking soda in your fridge. Pour the old box down the drain, and chase it with a ½ cup of white vinegar, and you'll create a little volcano to naturally clean and freshen drains.

Smells in old trunks and drawers can be eliminated with a slice of white bread placed in a bowl and covered with white vinegar. Close the trunk or drawer for 24 hours, and when you remove the bread and vinegar the odor will be gone!

Fresh, dry coffee grounds will remove smells from refrigerators.

A pan of cat litter will remove musty smells in closets and basements.

Place crumpled newspaper in drawers to remove musty odors.

Put dryer fabric softener sheets in luggage, storage containers, closets and drawers to leave a clean, fresh scent.

FIRST THINGS FIRST

Decide on your approach and be consistent. If you decide to clean for an hour, stick to it. If you decide to clean one room now and another tomorrow, stick to that. Indecision and distraction can really affect how well you clean. If you start out doing one thing and end up doing another, you'll have a houseful of half-finished projects, and you won't feel as if you've accomplished anything. That can be very frustrating, to say the least.

I like to start with the room that requires the least amount of effort, and that's generally the one that's used the least. It may be the guest room, the living room . . . it may even be the kitchen. Hey—no judgments. Think of it as a sort of warm-up. Start with the lightest task and you'll see results fast. That will motivate you to keep going!

Generally speaking, work from top to bottom. Dust from the light fixtures, tops of furniture, etc., will fall onto the carpet and floors. So do floors last and you'll know that your house really is clean.

Remember: If it isn't dirty, don't clean it!

Don't backtrack. Finish one task before moving to another. Put on some high-spirited music to set the pace and keep you going.

LET'S GET STARTED

Dusting comes first. But don't just pick up any old cloth, and don't, for heaven's sake, use a feather duster. They may be some man's fantasy, but they just scatter the dust all around. Really, they're worse than useless. I strongly recommend washable lambs wool dusters. Lambs wool both attracts and contains dust, so it won't whisk the dust around from one surface to the other. Lambs wool is also washable, so it lasts for years. (You can buy lambs wool dusters in many varieties, including dust mitts and telescoping dusters, which are great for those hard-to-reach corners.)

Use a telescoping lambs wool duster to clean ceiling fans.

Don't just move ornaments while you're dusting. Make sure to dust them, too!

After you've dusted your electronic equipment, it's a good idea to give it a wipe with some rubbing alcohol. Apply with a clean, soft cloth, then buff dry. Make sure to turn the power off first, though.

Once you've dusted, give the upholstery a good going-over. Use the appropriate attachment on your vacuum cleaner—the small brush for cushions and arms, the long nozzle for crevices and hard-to-reach areas. If you own a sofa bed, make sure to open it up and vacuum the mattress. (Most sofa bed mattresses are one-side only, so don't try to flip it.) Don't forget to vacuum scatter cushions.

Climb the walls, I mean *clean* the walls, by tying a towel over the head of a broom and pulling it down the wall. Shake out the towel as necessary, and change it when it becomes soiled. Work up and down the wall—not side to side—and use strokes that are comfortable for you. Complete one room at a time.

Walls don't need to be washed every year unless you're a smoker. So don't wash walls that don't need it. If, however, a room looks grimy, a good wall wash could save you the effort of painting.

FLOORS

Grit can scratch wood floors, so they should be swept before washing. Use long, directed strokes, moving from the corners to the center of the room. Sweep all the grit—that means crumbs, cat litter, and all that unidentifiable stuff—into a dustpan.

Now you're ready to wash with your favorite, gentle floor cleaner. Don't have a favorite wood floor cleaner? Try tea! The tannic acid gives the floor a wonderful shine. Use several tea bags to brew a quart or two. You can have a cup if you like, but let the rest cool to room temperature before using. Wring a soft cloth out in the tea. Make sure the cloth is damp, not wet. Overwetting the floor could warp it or damage the finish. Just in case I haven't been clear on this: *Yes, I am suggesting that you get down on your hands and knees.* Sorry, but anything else is just a shortcut, and if you want to clean your floors thoroughly, this is the only way to go.

- Start at the edges and move your hand across the floor, using a small circular motion.

- Keep the cloth well rinsed and continue until the entire floor is done.

- For vinyl or tile floors use the same cleaning method, substituting 1 gallon of warm water combined with 2 tablespoons of 20 Mule Team® Borax for the tea.

- For marble floors try the ACT Natural™ Microfiber

Mop. It uses nothing but water and thousands of little scrubbing fingers that pick up the dirt without scratching. It won't leave a film, either.

AND DON'T FORGET . . .

• Give the inside of kitchen cupboards a wash with a simple solution of warm, soapy water. Anything sticky can be removed with a little baking soda.

• Grind some lemon rinds and ice cubes in the disposal to keep it clean and sharpen the blades, too.

• Vacuum your mattress with the upholstery attachment, then flip it for even wear. A plastic bag, such as a dry cleaner's bag, placed between the box spring and mattress will help ease the strain of this task. (Best not to take any chances, so if you have young children leave out the bag and let your muscles do the work.)

• Since you're flipping your mattress, don't forget to wash your mattress pad, blankets and pillows before putting the bed back together.

• Yes, even that self-cleaning oven needs to be cleaned.

• Draperies should be cleaned once a year. Please read the care label carefully and don't try to wash curtains that should be dry-cleaned.

You can extend the life of your window coverings by vacuuming them frequently.

• Not every room requires the same effort or attention, so decide before you begin what clean means to you.

• If you use the space under your bed for storage, remove the storage containers, vacuum the carpet and clean the containers before you put them back.

• If the woodwork on your walls is dirty, you should carefully wash it even though you do not wash the walls.

• Take down the globes from the overhead light fixtures, wash them and put them back up. While you're at it, when the lightbulbs are cool, dust them, too.

• If hinges are squeaking every time you open a door, lubricate them with a quick spray of silicone.

• Don't overlook door handles—wash and polish them. They get used constantly and seldom get washed.

Wearing of the Green Doesn't Have to Mean Grass Stains

Now that winter white is starting to disappear, just make sure that the greens of spring don't appear on your clothes!

Grass stains can be removed from clothing with the help of a little white, nongel toothpaste. Brush the toothpaste into the stain using an old, soft toothbrush—rinse and then launder. Zout® Stain Remover will also do the trick. Work a liberal amount into the fabric with your thumb and forefinger, then wash as usual.

Grass stains on jeans should be treated with rubbing alcohol. Saturate the stain, let sit for 10 to 15 minutes, then pop the jeans into the wash. Check to see that the stain has come out before you put the jeans into the dryer. Heat will set the stain and make it impossible to remove, so if you need to repeat the procedure, it's best to find out *before* you use the dryer.

For grass on white leather athletic shoes, try molasses. You heard me—*molasses!* Massage the stain with a dollop of molasses and let it sit overnight. Wash the shoes with soap and water the next morning, and the grass stains should come off along with the molasses.

Fabric shoes such as Keds® can be cleaned with baking soda. Dip a wet toothbrush into some baking soda and brush vigorously. Rinse well and dry out of the sun. No baking soda? Use white, nongel toothpaste instead.

If those blue suede shoes have had a meeting with the green, rub the stain with a nylon sponge that has been dipped in glycerin. Rub until the stain has been removed, then blot with a cloth dipped in undiluted white vinegar. Brush the nap to reset in the right direction, and allow the shoes to dry out of the sun.

Grass stains on carpets should be removed with a good quality carpet cleaner such as Spot Shot Instant Carpet Stain Remover®. Just follow the directions on the can. For stubborn stains, apply rubbing alcohol; wait 10 minutes, blot, then treat with your favorite carpet cleaner.

April

Allergy season *and* tax time? If it weren't for Easter, April really would be the cruelest month. Don't fret. You can shorten the sneezin' season by allergy proofing your home. As far as taxes are concerned, well, I can't tell you how to pay less, but I can help with things like pencil marks and sweat stains. So turn your attention to Easter and the beauty of the month—those blue skies that remind us that the best things in life are free.

Spring Fever

The experts say that allergies are reactions to harmless substances that don't bother most people. Huh! If that's the case, why do so many people suffer from them? Seasonal allergies are caused by factors such as trees, grass and pollen. Year-round allergies are reactions to things like dust particles, animal dander, mold and dust mites. Whatever their cause, allergies can make us sneeze, sniff, cough and generally feel miserable—but you don't have to take it lying down.

CAN YOU DO WITHOUT IT?

Many detergents contain petroleum distillates—a major irritant for allergy sufferers. If freshly laundered clothes make you sneeze or itch, consider changing detergents. Be selective. Look for products marked "dye and perfume free," and check the label for colors or perfumes—you'll want to steer clear of them. I like PUREX®, a gentle detergent that does a great job on laundry. People with severe allergies or asthma may benefit from environmentally friendly products, such as those manufactured by Soapworks®. If you or anyone in your family suffers from allergies, you owe it to yourself to shop around.

Dryer fabric softener sheets can exacerbate allergies—best to do without them.

> *Allergy sufferers should use pump dispensers rather than aerosol sprays, which can fill the air with minute particles of irritants.*

• If you must use hair spray, apply it outside the house so that the fumes won't linger.

• Look through your cleaning supplies and eliminate those with a strong scent, those loaded with chemicals, and those you've had for a long time. Products can undergo changes after time, and irritants can increase.

• Don't mix chemicals.

• Look for natural cleaning products such as baking soda, lemon juice, club soda, white vinegar, etc.

• Furniture polish can attract dust and dust mites. Best not to use it.

• Stuffed animals are huge dust collectors, so if your children have allergies, it's best to limit their exposure. Any cloth or fuzzy toy can be a potential allergy problem. If your child is having difficulties with allergies, remove toys one by one to determine those that can be tolerated—and those that can't.

Stuffed fabric toys that can't be washed can still be cleaned. Just place in a plastic bag with some baking soda and salt and shake vigorously a few times a day for several days. This should remove dust, dirt and odor.

FILTERS: NOT JUST FOR COFFEEMAKERS

• If there's a filter, clean it! This means vacuums, fans, air purifiers, etc.

• Change the furnace filter at least once a month or invest in one that can be washed. Make sure to wash it frequently.

• If your allergies are severe, consider wearing a filtration mask while vacuuming and dusting.

DON'T GET HAULED ON THE CARPET

• Dust and dander cling to carpets, so if you have severe allergies you may want to consider hard floors such as wood, laminate, and ceramics. These floors can be washed frequently and will do a lot to keep allergy symptoms at bay.

• If you have severe allergies but are unable to remove carpets, apply benzyl benzoate dry foam or 3 percent tannic acid, then vacuum using a cleaner with an effective filter system. Tannic acid breaks down mite allergens, and benzyl benzoate dry foam actually kills mites and helps remove them—and their waste products—from carpet.

Avoid placing houseplants directly on carpets and rugs. Moisture in the plant can cause condensation, and that in turn can cause mildew—a powerful irritant to allergy sufferers.

• Vacuuming can stir up dust mites and their droppings, so don't vacuum too frequently. Once a week is fine.

• Vacuum hard floors prior to mopping so that you don't stir up dust.

• Wash all hard floors with a quality cleaner created with allergy sufferers in mind. Try At Home All-Purpose Cleaner from Soapworks®.

• Damp-mop hard floors with a good quality mop that can be washed in the washing machine. Try the ACT Natural™ Microfiber Mop.

• Change the bag in your vacuum frequently. If you have a vacuum with a collection canister rather than a bag, empty it each time you vacuum.

SOFA, SO GOOD

• Stay away from fuzzy or flocked fabrics that are difficult to clean. Buy only upholstered pieces that can be cleaned with water.

• Vacuum upholstered pieces weekly.

• Stay clear of furniture with ruffles or fringes. They're notorious dust-catchers and notoriously difficult to clean.

• When shopping for upholstered furniture, look for pieces without loose pillows. Buy tailored pieces in tightly woven fabrics.

AND SO TO BED

• Sealing your bedroom door with weather-stripping will give you more control over your sleeping environment.

• Keep pets out of your bedroom.

• Something as innocent as wallpaper can cause mildew, so keep walls—especially bedroom walls—clear of papers and fabrics.

• Use an air purifier in your bedroom.

• Vacuum your mattress frequently. Invest in a good mattress cover—one that forms a protective cover but still allows the mattress to breathe.

• Wash all bedding in 130-degree water at least every 10 days. That includes blankets, pillows, comforters and mattress pads.

• If you can't wash pillows and comforters as frequently as you'd like, try placing them in the dryer on air fluff. That will help.

• Keep bedspreads, dust ruffles, decorator pillows, etc., dust free. Better yet, get rid of that dust ruffle.

• Stay away from down and feather pillows. They can aggravate allergies, even if you're *not* allergic to them. Use foam pillows encased in hypoallergenic covers that can be zipped shut.

AND DON'T FORGET ...

• Wash windows and screens frequently.

• Keep the house closed up as much as possible, especially on windy days.

• Plant flowers and trees that produce as little pollen as possible, such as ivy, African violets, and leafy plants such as philodendrons, piggyback plants, creeping pileas, and prayer plants.

• Install an air cleaner on the furnace or invest in a stand-alone air purifier.

• Don't keep fresh flowers indoors, no matter how beautiful.

• Keep your fireplace clean and make sure the damper is closed.

• Use natural lambs wool dusters. The lanolin traps the dust and keeps it from spreading.

• If you don't like to use lambs wool dusters, use a clean, damp cloth.

• Insects love stagnant water, so don't allow water to stand in fountains and plant bases.

• Remove dried flower arrangements. These dust catchers are very hard to keep clean.

• Invest in a dehumidifier and maintain it well. Empty it weekly and clean it, too. Wash it with a solution of 1 quart warm water and 2 teaspoons of chlorine bleach. Make sure you wipe down the coils, and pay special attention to the container that catches the water.

• Make sure your curtains are made of synthetic fiber. Natural fibers contain more lint and may aggravate allergies.

• Dust mites survive in dampness, so do everything in your power to keep the air dry—except moving to my house in Arizona!

• Keep cooking pots covered to eliminate steam.

• Use an exhaust fan over the stove when you cook.

• Don't hang clothes in the house to dry.

🧶 The Cat's Meow

• Brush your pet outside and often. Try to wash him weekly—if he'll let you!

• Allergy sufferers should avoid cleaning litter boxes. If that's not possible, use a filtration mask and dispose of waste outside, never in a trash can.

• If your pet hates a bath, wipe his coat with a damp ACT Natural™ Microfiber Cloth. This will remove loose hair, dander and dry saliva—all of which contribute to allergy problems.

• Don't take your dog for a run in the woods, through fields or in tall grass where he can pick up allergy-causing mold spores, dried grass, leaves and pollen. Hmph. . . . Dogs!

 Zack

Taxing Times

Now that we've dealt with allergies, it's time to deal with those other seasonal irritants—taxes! Read on to find out how to deal with those stains and other little annoyances that come up at this time. Just think of me as your own personal support group!

No, I'm not going to tell you how to launder your money.

First, stock up on aspirin. You can use it to treat underarm stains, as well as that tax-season headache! (What do you mean you're not sweating?) For underarm stains on tee shirts and other cottons, dissolve 8 to 10 aspirin tablets to 1 cup of warm water, then saturate the underarm area of the garment. Allow to sit for 30 minutes and then launder as usual. If you're wearing the same tee night after night (hey, no judgments), rub the underarms with a bar of Fels-Naptha® Laundry Soap—then go change your shirt!

Pencil marks? Just take a nice, clean, soft eraser and gently rub the mark away.

If you're one of those confident types who prepares her taxes in pen, treat ink stains by soaking the garment in milk for several hours before laundering. You can also blot with rubbing alcohol or Ink Away®, available at office supply stores.

Paper cut? After disinfecting, secure it with a piece of Scotch® tape. The tape will protect the cut from the air and will also help to ensure that it doesn't get pulled farther apart. And if it doesn't get pulled farther apart, it won't hurt!

If you don't have any tape on hand, even a dab of super glue will help. Really—it's a great little healer. A little dab on the paper cut and no more pain! Is it dangerous? No, just don't use it on deep cuts, and please, don't glue your fingers together. Uncle Sam will not accept that as an excuse for late filing! You did glue your fingers together? A little acetone polish remover will un-stick you—fast!

Okay, you're almost done. You've prepared your return, made out your check, sealed the envelope and are just about to leave the house for the post office when you realize you've forgotten to enclose the check. Dang! Don't despair. Reach for Un-Du™. It will open the envelope right up. No tears, no muss, and you'll be able to re-seal it safely. Un-Du™ is available in home centers, drugstores, hardware stores and discount stores. It has such a wide range of uses. Use it to remove kids' stickers from walls, price stickers from any-thing but fabric and bumper stickers when you change party affiliations. No home should be without it.

If you don't have any Un-Du™, try putting the envelope in the freezer for an hour or so, then roll a pencil under the envelope flaps. With a little bit of care that envelope will open right up faster than you can say "Mata Hari!"

You don't owe? You're my hero! You say you're getting a refund? Give me a call . . .

It's Easter

Now it's time to turn our attention to something more cuddly than the taxman! I have such fond memories of gathering around the table to dye Easter eggs with Dad and the Queen Mother. It's something the King and I love to do, too, and we love to include as many friends and family members as possible. The Queen Mum always insisted on covering the kitchen table with an old plastic tablecloth to prevent those stains from spills (where did you think I got it from?) so that our creations wouldn't harm the table. Here's what else you can do:

Place a clean washcloth or potholder in the bottom of the pan and add cool water. Gently place the eggs in the pan, being careful not to overcrowd them. The cushion on the bottom of the pan will help prevent cracks, but if you add a tablespoon of white vinegar you'll be sure to avoid them altogether. (Vinegar will seal any cracks and help the egg to congeal.) Turn the heat on to medium and bring the eggs to a gentle boil. Continue to boil gently until they are done—about 20 minutes.

Check your eggs for freshness by placing them in a bowl filled with cold water. Eggs that float to the top are old and should be discarded.

• Keep raw eggs fresh in the refrigerator by applying a light coat of solid vegetable shortening. The shortening seals the egg, which keeps the air out and helps the egg last longer.

- If you drop a fresh egg during any of this process, just sprinkle it with a heavy layer of salt, wait several minutes then wipe up with a dry paper towel. The salt will "cook" the egg so that it is easy to remove. A turkey baster also works well.

- Prepare for coloring by putting out several glasses of hot water (plastic will stain). Add 1 tablespoon of vinegar to each cup. The acid in the vinegar will help the dye adhere to the eggs.

- You can use natural things to make great Easter egg dyes. Mustard and turmeric create a wonderful yellow shade, coffee and tea turn eggs tan to brown, red onion skins soaked in water create a purple dye, hot cranberry and cherry juice make vivid reds, and heated orange pop gives you orange! Use your imagination and create additional colors or mixtures.

- Remember: If you plunge hard-boiled eggs into cold water as soon as they are cooked, you won't be bothered with that gray ring on the inside of the egg white.

- Need to know which eggs are boiled and which are raw? Just give them a spin on the counter. A hard-boiled egg will spin easily, whereas a raw egg will wobble.

- One last important piece of information. If you are going to allow your colored Easter eggs to sit out in baskets, don't eat them. Eggs spoil rapidly at room temperature and can cause anyone who eats them to become very sick.

# May

May is one of my favorite months. The uncertain weather of early spring is a thing of the past, and the whole summer seems to stretch out before us. What better time to get reacquainted with the garden? I came by my love of gardening naturally: I inherited it from my mom! The Queen Mother taught me to garden the natural way, with minimum fuss and *no* chemicals. I'm going to pass that along to you! I'm also going to share some recipes for homemade personal care products because there's nothing nicer than pampering yourself after a warm afternoon in the garden. And because May is the month of Mother's Day, why not treat her, too?

A Garden of Ideas

BEFORE YOU GET STARTED

Get a head start on summer! Plant seeds in an egg carton to which you have added a small amount of soil—don't pack it too hard, and don't let it spill out over the sides. Keep the soil moist, taking care not to overwater. When you've seen the last frost, it's time to pop the seedlings out of the egg container and plant them in the ground. Still impatient? Speed up germination by laying a piece of plastic wrap over the seedlings to keep them moist and warm. Leave the plastic in place until the plants start to poke their heads through the soil.

• Try latex gloves in the garden instead of cloth. They're easier to clean—you can just rinse them under the hose and let them air-dry—and they don't stiffen up like canvas gloves do.

Tie a used fabric softener sheet around your belt to keep mosquitoes away while you garden.

• For a moisturizing treat while gardening, rub your hands with hand cream or petroleum jelly before donning your gloves.

• Don't like to wear gloves? Scraping your fingernails over a bar of soap before you get started will prevent dirt from penetrating under your nails and will protect them from breaking.

• Use a little wagon to haul your supplies around the garden. Check garage sales for good deals.

• Carry a quart spray bottle filled with water and a squirt of liquid dish soap. If you see bugs attacking your flowers, just give them a squirt and they'll vamoose!

• Need a kneeling pad? Take a 2- or 3-inch piece of foam, wrap it in plastic or put it in a large resealaable bag and you're all ready to go.

FERTILIZERS

• Crushed eggshells worked well into the soil make a wonderful fertilizer. Terrific for gardens and houseplants, they aerate the soil, too.

• Bury some used coffee grounds in your garden to provide much-needed acid to soil that has a high alkaline content. You'll notice much greener greens!

• Fish tank water is loaded with nutrients. Use it for gardens and houseplants.

• Plants love starch, so save the water each time you boil noodles or other pasta. Just make sure to let the water cool down first.

• Dampened newspapers placed on the ground around plants will help keep the soil moist and hold weeds at bay. Wet the newspapers well—you need the weight of the water to hold them down—then sprinkle lightly with soil. The papers are biodegradable, so they will eventually dissolve.

PEST CONTROL

• Keep pests such as aphids, mites, and whiteflies off roses, geraniums, hibiscus, and other plants by spraying them with a combination of 1 quart of water and ½ teaspoon of liquid dish soap. Reapply the solution every two weeks.

Planting garlic, parsley or basil among your flowers will deter bugs. Marigolds also work well. Just plant them as an edging around the garden.

• Dissolve 1 to 1½ teaspoons of baking soda in 1 quart of water to kill bugs on flowering plants. Spray every 7 to 10 days.

• Powdered milk can kill aphids on roses. Mix ⅓ cup of powdered milk in one quart of warm water, and spray. The aphids will get stuck in the milk and die. Hose the roses down occasionally and re-apply as needed.

• Here's a great natural way to control black spots on roses. Add 1 tablespoon each of baking soda and vegetable oil to 1 gallon of water. Then add 1 drop of liquid detergent and shake well. Spray directly on the foliage, and spray every 5 to 7 days during humid weather. Make sure to wet both sides of the leaves.

• Chase away pests that feed on your tender plants by mixing 1 tablespoon of hot mustard or red pepper with 1 quart of water. Spray directly on the foliage. One hot taste and the pests will be gone!

WHO KNEW?

• Old panty hose make great ties for plants and tomatoes. They're strong and flexible, but soft enough so that they won't cut into the plant.

Cutting roses and trimming bushes can be a prickly job, but if you grip thorny stems with barbecue tongs or clothespins . . . no more pierced fingers!

• Tuck a bar of soap inside a mesh bag and tie it around the outside faucet. After gardening cleanups will be a breeze.

• Hands that are very dirty can be cleaned with a thick paste of oatmeal and water. Rub well into hands before rinsing and washing as usual.

• Kill weeds with a natural toddy of 1 ounce of white vinegar, 1 ounce of inexpensive gin, and 8 ounces of water. Pour on the weeds and say good-bye.

Keep on the Grass

Morning is the best time to water your lawn. Grass that's damp with dew will absorb water better than grass that's fully dry. Parched grass can be resistant to moisture, so don't wait till your lawn is dehydrated before you bring out the sprinkler. And try not to water your lawn at night if you can avoid it. Night watering can encourage fungus.

You can cut grass that's still damp with morning dew by spraying the blades with vegetable oil. The wet grass won't stick, and you can get on with the rest of the day. Car wax works well too, but it's probably best to skip the drive through the car wash!

How do you know when it's time to water the lawn? I like the barefoot test. If you feel comfortable walking across the grass barefoot—if the lawn isn't crackly and springs back up when you walk across it—there's no need to water. But if the grass feels unpleasantly spiky and lays down flat after you've left the area, it's time to water.

A good soaking of water will promote a healthy lawn. That means strong roots and good color. I put a small empty can of Zack's cat food on the grass when I water the lawn.

When the can is full I know I've given the grass about an inch of water, and that's plenty.

Try not to cut grass too often. A closely manicured lawn may be fine for the golf course, but longer grass is actually healthier because it holds moisture longer. Use the high setting on your mower for best results.

The Cat's Meow

Bothered by moles and gophers? Some people swear by castor bean plants, but the leaves and seedpods are poisonous to children and pets—yikes, that's me! Try human hair instead. Hair is an irritant to these small rodents, but it won't harm them or anything else. Ask your hairdresser for a bag of clippings and stuff the hair into the hole. It won't be long before these little critters move on. (If you have any hair left, you could try knitting a toupee for your uncle Jack.)

If dogs, raccoons or other animals are tipping over your garbage cans, tie a couple of rags soaked in ammonia to the handles. All it takes is one sniff and your garbage can will no longer be attractive to critters. *Dogs . . . sheesh!*

Discourage fleas and flies from gathering around your pet's outside eating and sleeping area by planting rue *(Ruta graveolens)* nearby. You can also rub rue on furniture to keep cats . . . like me, from scratching. Just use care that you don't discolor upholstery.

Keep the neighborhood dogs and cats out of your flowers by mixing equal parts of mothballs and crushed dried red pepper (cayenne) in and around the flower beds. No more four-legged visitors! Not that I would ever do such a thing . . .

 Zack

JUST TOOLING AROUND

Take good care of your garden tools and they'll last you a lifetime.

Keep a container of sand in the garage or shed, and push your shovels and trowels into it when you've finished your chores. Sand is a wonderfully natural abrasive. It will clean your tools and stop them from rusting. Not only will this tool-time sandbox prevent dirt from spreading around the garage area, but you'll always know where to find your garden tools!

> *Spray your garden tools with nonstick cooking spray each time you use them. The dirt will be easy to remove when you are done. In fact, it should fall right off.*

Paint the handles of your yard tools a bright color and they will be easier to spot among the green of your yard. Not only that, you'll be able to identify your tools if you loan them out.

If rust has disfigured a metal tool, try rubbing with a stiff wire brush. Scrape a metal file across dull edges and they should come back to life if they're not too dull. Naval jelly sold at hardware stores is also a good alternative for rust on metal. Follow the directions on the container.

You can help protect your tools by applying Clean Shield® Surface Treatment or a thin coat of paste wax to the metal. The wax will form a barrier between the metal and the elements and should retard the growth of rust.

Rough handles mean rough hands, so make sure to take care of your tools. Wood handles that have become jagged and coarse can be made smooth again with a good rubbing of some light-grade sandpaper. Apply a generous coat of linseed oil when you've finished sanding and you'll protect the wood from cracking and splitting.

If you still find the handles too difficult to hold, try wrapping them in tubes of foam insulation, the kind used to insulate water pipes. Slit the foam lengthways, slip it onto the handle, and wrap lightly with heavy-duty tape. Not only will the foam protect your hands from the wood, it will also protect the wood from the elements.

Don't forget to store your tools out of the elements.

A Mom for All Seasons

When you hear the words "Mother's Day" I'm sure you think of your Queen Mother just as I do mine. Naturally, we all want to do something nice for our mothers . . . and naturally is what it's all about. So read on to find out how you can make your own collection of personal care products that are easy to make, and natural too. Give these to your own Queen Mum and every day can be Mother's Day!

LET'S FACE IT

An oatmeal scrub will treat dry skin and draw impurities from your complexion. Mix ¼ cup of oatmeal, 1 teaspoon of honey and enough milk, buttermilk or plain yogurt to make a paste. Apply liberally to your face—making sure to avoid the delicate eye areas—then gently massage in small circular motions. Allow the mask to dry before you rinse with warm water. Once the mask has been removed, give your face an invigorating finish by splashing with cool, clear water. Apply your favorite moisturizer, or for a more thorough facial, follow with the tightening oatmeal mask.

Grandma loved this tightening oatmeal mask, and you will too. Mix 1 tablespoon of oatmeal with the white of 1 egg. Apply to your face and allow to dry. Rinse off using cool water.

Very dry skin? A little mayonnaise added to the tightening oatmeal mask will give you a smooth finish.

> *Prone to breakouts? Apply a thin mask of milk of magnesia once a week. Allow to dry and rinse with cool water.*

Need a four o'clock revival? Try witch hazel. Keep a small bottle in your desk at the office, along with some cotton balls. Dampen the cotton balls with the witch hazel, then blot your face and neck . . . prepare to be revived! It's that easy. Keep the witch hazel in the refrigerator if you can. And for an extra treat, pour some in a spray bottle for an after-workout spritz!

THE EYES HAVE IT

These remedies aren't new, but they're worth repeating.

• A slice of chilled cucumber on each eyelid will relieve tired eyes. And that 15-minute rest won't do you any harm, either!

• Cold tea bags are great for puffy eyes, so keep some on hand in the refrigerator.

• A little bit of Preparation H® helps keep puffy eyes at bay. Just make sure to avoid tear ducts and the eye itself.

• Dab some castor oil on the skin around your eyes before going to bed at night. Stay well away from the eye area, and make sure not to use too much oil.

YOUR CROWNING GLORY

Restore luster to dry hair with a light, natural oil such as corn oil or sunflower oil. Those of you with very dry hair may like to use olive oil, but make sure to use a light touch. Olive oil can be extremely difficult to wash out. Another warning: Oil heats up very quickly and can cause severe burns, so avoid the microwave. The best and safest way to warm oil for a scalp treatment is to place the oil in an egg cup, then put the egg cup inside a mug or small bowl that you have filled with hot or boiling water. Heat the oil to lukewarm—about 1 teaspoon should do—and apply to dry hair with the palm of your hands. Make sure that the shaft and ends are well coated (not saturated, though), but avoid getting oil on your roots, which will weigh hair down. Cover your hair with a plastic bag and try to leave it on as long as you can—overnight is best. Finish with a thorough shampoo, lathering twice. Skip the conditioner and get ready for the compliments!

I hate it when that happens . . .

Static electricity causing your hair to stand on end? Rub your brush and comb with a fabric softener sheet before brushing your hair. No more annoying static!

Mayonnaise also works well—it's a combination of egg *and* oil. Don't heat the mayonnaise or it will separate. Just remove a quantity from the jar—a couple of tablespoons should be fine, unless you have very long hair—and let stand at room temperature for a few hours. Rub on just enough mayonnaise to soak the hair thoroughly (remembering to avoid the roots), and comb through. Leave on for 30 minutes, shampoo well and rinse with water and lemon before that final rinse of cool, clear water.

LET'S SEE A SHOW OF HANDS

Make your own hand cream by mixing 2 parts glycerin to 1 part lemon juice. Massage a little into your hands after washing and at bedtime. This absorbent cream works well and smells lovely!

Soften hardworking hands and feet by rubbing with equal proportions of cooking oil and granulated sugar.

Cuticles may be softened by soaking in a bowl of warm olive oil. Push them gently back with a cotton swab. If cuticles are really dry, coat them with olive oil at bedtime.

Lemon juice is great for removing stains and whitening hands. Bottled or fresh-squeezed, just massage it into hands before washing with good old soap and water.

Your nail polish will last longer if you apply a little white vinegar to each nail. Just coat each nail with a cotton swab prior to applying your nail polish. The acid in the vinegar encourages the polish to stick to the nail so you get better coverage and longer-lasting wear.

Speed up the time it takes to dry nail polish by plunging freshly polished nails into cold water. Shake hands to dry. And to prevent nicks and chipping, brush baby oil on just-polished nails!

Let's Dish!

Of course, nothing says "Mother's Day" like breakfast in bed!

Orange Blossom French Toast

12 slices bread

6 egg yolks

½ cup half-and-half or whole milk

⅓ cup orange juice

1 tablespoon grated orange peel

¼ teaspoon salt

¼ cup butter

Leave bread out to dry overnight.

Next morning, in a medium bowl, slightly beat egg yolks, then mix in half-and-half, orange juice, orange peel, and salt. Dip bread in batter, turning to coat both sides.

Heat butter in skillet and cook bread on both sides until golden.

Serve with syrup and love. Makes 6 servings.

June

Summer—it's finally here. The kids are out of school and it's time to hit the road on the family vacation. Frightened of an endless chorus of *Are we there yet?* It doesn't have to be that way. The kids don't have to be bored and neither do you. There are many things you can do to make that trip a good one—enjoyable *and* safe. So let's put our imaginations to work and have some fun.

Hit the Road, Jack

You're going on a family trip . . . in the car. You may be in there for hours. If that strikes fear in your heart, you're not alone. Hit these pages before hitting the road.

BEFORE YOU LEAVE

It's fun to take a little time away from home. And if you take some time to prep the house before you leave, your homecoming will be that much sweeter.

• Lock the doors and windows, but leave the shades up and curtains open. Put the lights on automatic timer.

• Clean out the refrigerator and remove any perishables.

• Want to know if your freezer has shut off while you've been away? Take a child's ice pop—the ones that come in the clear plastic push-up wrapper—lay it flat to freeze, then prop it against the freezer door. If the freezer goes off while you're away the pop will be hanging over the inside of the door instead of standing straight up. You'll know then that freezer food *isn't* safe to eat.

• Store your valuables in a safe place. The freezer, jewelry box and lingerie drawer are not secure choices.

If you've read about it in a book or newspaper column, chances are it's not a safe place to store your valuables. Burglars read, too. Use your imagination and your discretion.

• Turn off small electrical appliances. Unplug decorative lights and fountains.

• Smokers will want to make sure that ashtrays are empty. Odor from cigarette butts can linger long after the cigarette has been extinguished, and there's nothing worse than coming home to a house that smells like a stale ashtray!

• Suspend delivery of the newspaper and the mail.

• To keep plants watered when you're not at home, gather them up and sit them in the bathtub in about an inch of water. The plants will absorb the water gradually, enough to last a week or two. For those plant pots that don't have a hole in the bottom, fill a glass with water, insert one end of a coarse piece of string in the glass, and bury the other in the plant. Believe it or not, this homemade water wick will keep most plants moist while you're away!

• Leave a key and contact number with a trusted neighbor who will keep an eye on things during your absence.

WHAT TO PACK

No two vacations are alike, so consider what you want from your trip *before* you start to pack. If your weekday routine dictates that you wake at 6:30 to head off for work each morning, then chances are the last thing you want to hear is the ringing of your alarm. If, however, you want to be first in line at Disneyland, you're going to need that clock.

Here's a sample list to get you started:

• Small sewing kit
• Travel hair dryer
• Umbrella or raincoat
• Hunting or fishing license
• Alarm clock
• Swiss army knife
• Small fold-up tote for all those extras you'll buy
• Small amount of laundry detergent for those "oops!"
• Exercise gear
• Camera and film

Take along an almost empty liquid soap container filled with water. It makes a handy cleaner for all those little emergencies.

- Batteries
- A few plastic garbage bags for holding dirty laundry
- Bathing suits
- Plenty of tee shirts
- Tweezers—they come in very handy
- Gallon-size, Ziploc™ bags for damp swimsuits, etc.
- A few clothespins and some safety pins

AND DON'T FORGET THESE NECESSITIES

- Personal medicines and spare eyeglasses
- Children's aspirin and remedies for upset tummies
- Sunglasses, suntan lotion, insect repellant
- A first-aid kit, some paper towels and tissues
- Proof of insurance—auto *and* health
- A duplicate set of car keys
- A spare tire, car jack, flashlight, windshield scraper and emergency repair kit

Spray the front of the car with nonstick cooking spray before you hit the road. Bugs and grime will wash right off.

- A few gallons of fresh water—for you and your radiator
- Maps
- A 1-800 number for credit card companies
- A small notebook and pen
- Picture ID

Backseat Drivers

Traveling with children requires special care and preparation, not to mention a good dose of imagination and patience. So plan ahead. Keep children occupied and try to avoid mishaps *before* they happen. You'll be glad you did.

DOS AND DON'TS FOR A SAFE TRIP

- Do lock all doors and teach your children not to play with the door handles.
- Don't permit children to ride with their heads, arms or hands outside of the car through open windows.
- Do set a good example for your children by buckling up each time you enter the car.
- Don't leave children or pets in the car alone—even for a short time.
- Do make sure that children sit in the backseat.
- Do make sure to make frequent stops so that children can stretch their legs.
- Don't allow children to suck on suckers while riding. A sudden stop could be disastrous.
- Do make sure to take plenty of cold water.

WE'RE NOT FINISHED YET

Children are resilient, but their little bodies can be especially sensitive to the environment. Keep a close eye on small passengers, and be on the lookout for any signs of car sickness and upset tummies. Sometimes a quick stop for some fresh air is all it takes to avoid a problem.

Keep sugared snacks to a minimum. Children high on sugar are not going to be good travelers.

• Keep a new toothbrush in the glove box, along with a small tube of minty toothpaste. If a little one does get carsick and vomit, brushing his teeth afterward will make him feel much better. Just make sure to stay away from sweet or flavored toothpastes, which may aggravate nausea.

• When preparing snack foods for a car journey, make sure to avoid small foods on which a child can choke, like hard candy and peanuts.

• Baby wipes are great for wiping sticky hands and faces—for you *and* your children. They're terrific for cleaning hands after pumping gas at the self-serve, too.

• Little ones will need a change of clothes. Everybody will benefit from having a spare, fresh tee shirt. And don't forget the diapers!

NOW FOR THE FUN STUFF

• Children love to play with office supplies such as Scotch® tape, paper and Post-it® notes—and they can't hurt themselves, either. Don't give children pens or pencils, though, and don't give them scissors.

• Play money is great fun. Your child can set up her own mall in the backseat! Just make sure to avoid giving coins to small children.

• Squares of aluminum foil are great for making sculptures and jewelry, and they can be used again and again. (Don't give foil to young children who may be tempted to put it in their mouths.)

• High-tech kids can still enjoy singing songs and reciting rhymes. Encourage children to make up their own verses. Don't be afraid to get creative!

• Paint books—the kind that already have the paint on the page—are very popular with young children. All you need is a little brush and an inch or so of water in a cup. No fuss and no paint to spill.

• Don't forget the classics. Hangman, tic-tac-toe and "I Spy" are great, as are crossword puzzles.

• Don't forget the bubbles!

• Have your child make some paper bag puppets before you leave. They'll be distracted with their craft, and that will give *you* some uninterrupted time to prepare for the trip. And of course, children will be pleased to take their new creations with them in the car.

• Children love to use binoculars.

• Tattoos, the kind that press on with a wet cloth, are lots of fun.

• Go Fish card games are great. Even children too young to know the game will enjoy playing with the cards. Fifty-two pickup, anyone?

• Everyone knows that books on tape are great for long trips, but small children can get bored just listening. So why not let them record their own book? Many inexpensive cassette players have record buttons, so why not pick up a few tapes at the dollar store and let your child try his on-air talents? He can describe the scenery, make up stories and songs, record a letter to Grandma—he could even interview you!

- Kids love disposable cameras. Consider giving one to each child.

- Toddlers can use licorice laces and Cheerios® or Fruit Loops® to make necklaces and bracelets. When they get bored, they can eat their creations!

The Cat's Meow

Please make sure that I'm well cared for when you're away. I need food and water of course, but I need some company, too. I get awfully lonely when you're gone. And please make sure to put a note on the door or window that lets people know that I'm inside. Pets can get lost in all the commotion of a fire. I shudder to think of what can happen ...

If you're taking me with you, please make sure that I have a place of my own in the car, with food and water. Bring my bed if at all possible—just keep me out of the sun.

Give dogs frequent potty breaks and some exercise. Always keep them on a leash, you know how dogs are about running away.

Don't forget my litter tray. A disposable one will be fine. Just don't expect me to go potty at 70 miles per hour with trucks speeding by. I need my privacy.

Make sure that we're wearing our tags, just in case we become lost or disoriented.

 Zack

• Buy some small inexpensive toys at the dollar store—things like plastic dinosaurs and little trolls. Wrap them up with brightly colored paper and dole them out as after-snack goodies. Children love unwrapping the toy almost as much as the toy itself. Keep small toys away from little ones who may put them in their mouths.

• Cookie sheets and breakfast-in-bed trays make great portable work spaces for children. Just make sure not to give little ones sharp and potentially dangerous objects such as pens and pencils. The slightest bump can mean disaster when these items are at hand. Crayons and jumbo markers are best.

• Yahtzee® is still a great traveling game.

At the Car Wash

A long trip can take its toll on your car. Here's what to do to get it looking good again—fast!

• Use a paste of baking soda and water to clean the outside windshield so that it shines.

Rust spots can be removed from car bumpers quite easily—just rub with a ball of tinfoil! If the rust is stubborn, try dipping the foil in a glass of cola! (Don't ask . . .)

• Put some baking soda in your car's ashtray. It may not discourage smokers, but it will help neutralize the odor.

• Keep some used fabric softener sheets in your glove box. Use them to wipe the dashboard, clean the air vents, and polish the rearview mirror. Store them in a Ziploc™ bag and you'll still have room for all those maps and fast-food coupons!

• If birds leave you an unwanted gift on the car, simply take some waterless hand cream, working it in well with an old rag. Let sit for several minutes and it should rub right off.

• Remove road tar by saturating it with linseed oil. Apply the oil liberally to the tarred area, let soak for a while and then wipe with an old rag that has been dampened with more linseed oil. Be sure you dispose of the rag outside in the trash.

• Make your own windshield washer fluid by mixing 2 quarts of rubbing alcohol, 1 cup of water, and 1 teaspoon of liquid dish soap. This will not freeze at 30 degrees below. In summer, add 1 pint of rubbing alcohol and 1 teaspoon of liquid dish soap to the car washer container and fill with water. This will keep the windows clean in rain and warm weather.

• Baking soda on a soft, wet cloth is great for cleaning chrome, headlights and enamel.

• Wipe down windshield wiper blades from time to time to remove road film.

• Wash the car in the shade to prevent streaking.

• Use a couple of squirts of liquid dish soap in a bucket of warm water to wash the car. Start at the roof and wash and rinse in sections so that the soap doesn't dry on the car.

• Dry the car with an old bath towel, then for a super shine, rub down with a good-quality chamois.

Father's Day

You don't think we'd let the month go by without celebrating Father's Day, do you? I always think that the best gift is a gift of time. So why not give your father the day off and let him wander the links for a lovely game of golf. And when he comes home, treat his clubs to some tender, loving care . . .

FORE!

Clean golf clubs by lightly rubbing the head and shaft with dry, fine-grade (0000) steel wool. Don't wet the steel wool. Dust with a dry cloth, then use a damp cloth to give the club a final wipe before buffing dry with another clean, soft cloth.

Cleaning the grips is as easy as using soap and water—but the kind of soap you use makes a big difference. Dampen a soft cloth with warm water, then work up a lather with a moisturizing bath bar, such as Dove® or Caress®. Don't use a deodorizing soap, as that will dry out the leather. Rub well to remove the dirt, rinsing the cloth each time it becomes grimy. Repeat until the grip is clean, then reapply the soap and water one last time. Don't rinse—buff with a soft cloth instead. This will keep the grip moist and prevent it from drying out and cracking. For really stubborn dirt or older clubs, work in a little GOJO™ Waterless Hand Cleaner and wipe until clean. Wash with the soap formula and dry well.

Keep the golf glove in a self-closing plastic bag to maintain softness between games. If you need to clean your glove, use the bar soap method prescribed for grips, keeping the glove on your hand to preserve its shape during the process. Work only with a damp cloth, and make sure not to saturate the glove. Finish by buffing with a soft cloth that's clean and dry, and then allow the glove to dry naturally, out of direct light. To restore a dried-out glove, try rubbing a little hand cream into it—while you're wearing it!

Golf shoes need attention, too. Brush the bottoms of the shoes with a firm brush to remove any dirt and debris. If you have been playing on a wet course, don't do this until the shoes are dry. Wash leather shoes as needed with Dove® moisturizing bath soap, removing scuff marks with a little nongel toothpaste or rubbing with a little cuticle remover. For fabric-type shoes, brush well and spot with a damp microfiber cloth. Always keep the shoes treated with a good quality water repellent for those rainy days and dewy mornings. Got a little odor problem? Put some ODORZOUT™ in the toe of an old nylon or sock and keep it in the shoes when you store them to eliminate odor.

Clean golf balls by soaking them in a solution of 1 cup warm water and ¼ cup ammonia. Rub lightly, rinse and lay out to dry. Store extra golf balls in an egg carton. The compartments are the perfect size!

Having trouble identifying your golf and tennis balls? A tiny drop of colored nail polish is just as good as any monogram.

July

Even the most devoted couch potato ventures out of the house in July. So haul out the baseball equipment, hop on that bike, put on the skates, go for a dip in the pool to cure those summertime blues. Sound too energetic for you? Then how about becoming a chaise lounge or hammock potato at a beautiful campsite for a week or so. That can be a wonderfully relaxing way to recharge your body, let the kids run off some steam, and have some quality family time, too.

Let the Games Begin!

Take me out to the ball game . . . just make sure the equipment is clean and in good working order before you do. Otherwise, it's one, two, three strikes you're out!

Wash your baseball glove with a damp cloth and Dove® Moisturizing Bath Bar. Buff with a soft cloth—no rinsing necessary. Keep the leather soft and supple by rubbing with a little petroleum jelly from time to time. Store your ball in the palm of your glove to help keep its shape.

Want to know the best way to clean your bike? Treat it

like a car! Wash the frame with some hot water and a little dishwashing liquid. Rinse well, dry, then apply a coat of car wax to prevent rust. Wash the seat with a little bit of bar soap on a soft cloth and buff dry.

Dented Ping-Pong balls? Just drop them into a bowl of hot water and let them float for a few minutes. Dings should pop right out. Sorry—balls that are cracked or have large dents can't be repaired.

Give your skateboard an occasional wash with good old soap and water. Pay special attention to the wheels by scrubbing with a brush to remove any embedded soil and stones that may slow you down.

Wearing petroleum jelly under your socks can prevent blisters. Apply a thin layer on tender parts before you exercise. And never wear sports socks more than one day running.

Odor can be a problem with skates—both inline and ice. I recommend sprinkling with ODORZOUT™, a first-rate odor eliminator. Shake some into the boot, leave overnight, then gently shake out the following morning. ODORZOUT™ is an odor eliminator, not a perfumed cover-up, so your skates will stay fresher longer. Don't have any? Try baking soda instead.

To clean skate boots, try using a microfiber cloth such as ACT Natural™. The ACT Natural™ cloth can be used on its own—no harmful chemicals to damage those expensive skates.

Before you exchange that hockey equipment for baseball gear, make sure to store your pucks in the freezer. They'll stay harder and more resilient that way!

Who Says There Ain't No Cure?

Summer isn't all fun and games. There are hot nights and insect bites, sunburns to soothe and lawn furniture to clean—what we in the trade commonly refer to as the *summertime blues.* Read on for some handy cures.

• Remove dirt and mildew from a child's wading pool by flushing with warm water and baking soda.

• Sprinkle baby powder on sandy beach bodies and the sand will fall right off.

• A hot night and no a/c? Baby powder on your sheets will absorb moisture and give you a more comfortable night's sleep. What, no baby powder? Use cornstarch instead!

• Wipe exposed skin with undiluted white vinegar to discourage biting insects.

• Apply a compress of warm salt water if you're bitten by a mosquito or chigger. For long-lasting itch relief, mix a little salt and solid shortening, such as Crisco®, and dab it directly on the bite.

That frosty film on the carton of ice cream is not a protective coating, and it can be prevented. Just cover the top of the ice cream with wax paper and press firmly. No more "protective crystals"!

• Deodorant that contains aluminum (and most do) can be put on a bite to control the itch.

• Sliding doors get a lot of use in the summer, so be sure to keep tracks clean and well lubricated. The easiest way? Spritz tracks with furniture polish, then wipe with a dry cloth or paper towel. The polish will pick up grime, and will keep the tracks better lubricated than a cleanser would. If you want to add some glide between cleanings, just wipe the tracks with a square of waxed paper. Works every time!

• A plastic shower liner makes a great tablecloth. It's washable and inexpensive.

• Sheets make better beach blankets than blankets. They don't hold sand and they're easier to launder when you get home. Pick up some spares at a thrift store.

• Black pepper will deter ants. Just sprinkle under rugs or cupboard liners. Silverfish can be kept at bay with Epsom salts: Just shake some in cupboards and under lining paper in drawers.

• Put sunburned kids in a cool (not cold) baking soda bath for half an hour. This also works well for chickenpox and mosquito bites.

I hate it when that happens . . .

Tar on bare feet? Remove it by rubbing vigorously with toothpaste.

• No need to use chemicals or expensive products to clean lawn furniture. Just rinse with warm water and baking soda.

Sprinkle dry baking soda directly on stubborn marks—this natural abrasive will take them right off!

Camping

If slow room service is your idea of camping, you may want to skip this section.

THE NECESSITIES

• Campsites can be very dark in the evening, so make sure to bring along a torch, a candle or flashlight. Even better, bring along all three. And don't forget the batteries!

• Remember that Swiss army knife you got for Christmas three years ago? Now's the time to use it. You'll need some good kitchen knives, too, so don't forget to bring those as well.

• Toilet paper in a lidded coffee can to keep it dry. Need I say more?

• Bring a few candles, a votive or tea light.

• Make sure to bring along a little dishwashing liquid, a scouring pad and some absorbent towels.

• A cooked breakfast is one of the joys of camping, but bacon and eggs are *not* finger foods. Don't forget the cutlery, cooking utensils, a pot to boil water in, and a frying pan.

Rubbing two sticks together to make a fire is highly overrated. Don't try to be macho. Bring along matches or a lighter.

• Bring along a length of nylon rope. You can use it for dozens of things, such as drying clothes, elevating food so that animals don't get at it, and knocking up emergency shelter. You can even use it to replace those lost guy ropes. Use your imagination . . . just don't tie up the kids!

• Bandannas are wonderfully versatile. They make good napkins, facecloths, bandages and slings. Tuck one under the back of your baseball cap to keep the sun off your neck, foreign-legion style!

• A first-aid kit is a must. Make sure yours is stocked with bandages, antiseptic, tweezers, a thin needle for splinters, Imodium® for those tummy troubles, aspirin or aspirin-substitute, sunscreen and sunburn relief, insect repellent and a whistle to call for help in an emergency.

Cell phones are great, but the batteries on whistles never run down.

• Bring soap. You can find the water when you get there.

• Dental floss and a darning needle will come in handy for quick repairs to holes in clothes and tents.

• Duct tape is indispensable.

FIRE STARTERS

There's an easy way to dry out wet kindling. Construct a small tepee out of your kindling, making sure to leave an opening into which you can insert a tea light or votive candle. Insert the lighted candle, then watch as the kindling crackles and dries. You should have a fire under way by the time the candle has burned down.

Pinecones make great kindling. They heat up fast and burn for a long time.

Bring along a few cardboard tubes from paper towels or toilet paper. Twist a few sheets of newspaper to fit inside the tube (I find the business section works best), making sure to leave some paper hanging out the ends. Toss a few of these in with twigs and wood and you'll have a roaring fire in no time!

My dad and I learned—quite accidentally—that grease from cooking pans makes a great fire starter! Use paper towels to wipe up the grease from pots and pans, then store them in self-closing plastic bags. The next time you need to start a campfire, wrap some twigs in the paper and set them alight!

Keeping matches dry can be a challenge, but if you dip the match head and part of the matchstick into some candle wax, it will resist water. Light as usual—the act of striking the match will remove the wax. (This only works on wooden matches, not cardboard.)

Rub the outside of pots and pans with a bar of soap before you use them. Do this to both the bottom and sides of the pan, and soot will wipe right off, along with the soap.

LOITERING WITHIN YOUR TENT

• Rocks, twigs and other sharp objects may damage your tent, so make sure the ground is clear before you set up camp.

- Avoid wearing heavy shoes inside the tent.

- Use extreme caution around open flames. Nylon tents melt easily.

- Pack tent poles carefully to avoid punctures.

- Prolonged exposure to direct sunlight can weaken tent fibers, so wherever possible, set up the tent in a shaded area.

- A strip of glow-in-the-dark tape wrapped around tent stakes will ensure that you never trip over them again!

- Drive tent stakes twelve inches into the ground to provide adequate stability, even in the wind. The stakes should be at a 45-degree angle, slanting *away* from the tent. Paint each stake at the 12-inch mark and you'll never have to guess again!

CLEANING YOUR TENT

Make sure to store your tent correctly—that means cleaning it first. With proper care your tent can last for years.

Shake off all loose debris before packing and storing the tent. Clean any spots with a wet brush rubbed over a bar of Fels-Naptha Soap®, then rinse. Air-dry thoroughly. A damp tent is a breeding ground for mildew.

Stakes should be stored alongside the tent, but make sure to put them in a canvas bag or even a few old pillowcases—something to ensure that the stakes will not tear or puncture the tent itself.

Take action at the first sign of mildew—an organic rotting odor, black spots or a powdery white smudge. Sponge the tent with a solution of ½ cup of Lysol® and 1 gallon of warm water. Allow to dry on the tent (think *leave-in conditioner*) and air-dry thoroughly prior to storing. For advanced mildew use a combination of 1 cup of lemon juice (real or bottled) and 1 gallon of warm water. Rub onto visible mildew and allow to dry facing the sun.

Spray zippers with a silicone lubricant to ensure smooth action and prevent freezing. Rubbing with paraffin or candle wax works well, too.

REPAIRING YOUR TENT

Stakes and tent poles cause the majority of tears in canvas tents. Either the pole slips and tears the fabric next to the eyelet, or the canvas itself is tied too tightly to the ground stakes. Bear this in mind when setting up your tent.

Canvas is too heavy for most home sewing machines, so if your tent is generally in good condition, you may want to consider getting it repaired by a tent or sail maker.

For a cheaper alternative, glue an appropriate-sized square of canvas to the tent. Make sure you overlap the tear by about one to two inches. Putting a patch on both sides of the tent will reinforce the repair. Use fabric glue or even a hot glue gun and remember to waterproof the repair once the glue is dry.

Duct tape is great for making emergency repairs. Just make sure to tape both sides of the tear. And remember: This is just an interim measure. Have your tent properly repaired once you get back home.

Nylon or cotton hiking-type tents can be repaired on a home sewing machine. Look for patch kits, available where tents are sold.

*Never underestimate the power of a large
darning needle and dental floss.*

IT'S IN THE BAG

Keep your sleeping bag clean and mildew free by washing it
in a large capacity machine. Add ½ cup of 20 Mule Team®
Borax to the water along with your detergent, and ½ cup of
white vinegar in the rinse instead of fabric softener.

Make sure that the sleeping bag is totally dry before storing to prevent mildew. When ready to store, place about a
quarter cup of ODORZOUT™ in a nylon stocking and tuck
inside the sleeping bag to prevent odors. A good sprinkling
of baking soda will help to keep it fresh, too. Store your
sleeping bag inside a king-size pillowcase to keep it clean.

August

Where did the summer go? Seems like only yesterday we were preparing the garden for spring, and now we're thinking about how to make the most of this final summer month. I hate to be a drag, but it's time to give your house the once-over before autumn starts. That means paying attention to those tasks that everybody seems to ignore—cleaning the driveway *and* the gutters. It's not all chores, though. We still have some time for that last summer picnic!

Driveway Dilemmas

Driveways take quite a beating, but we never seem to pay much attention to them—until they're covered with oil spills and weeds. Put off caring for your driveway, and like most jobs, it will become more difficult and time-consuming when you finally do get around to it. So sweep your driveway regularly—say, once a month in the summer—and wash it thoroughly once a year. You'll be glad you did.

Give your driveway a good sweep. Use a stiff push broom or long-handle brush, and make short brisk strokes to direct debris away from the center of the driveway.

• Wash concrete driveways with a simple solution of water and washing soda. Dissolve 1 cup of Arm and Hammer Washing Soda™ in a bucket of warm water and apply to the driveway with a long-handle brush or stiff push broom. Scrub well, then rinse with clear water.

• Oven cleaner works well for those really tough stains. Spray it on, let sit for a few hours, and then rinse well. Just make sure to keep the kids and pets a good distance away.

• For old marks and blotches, apply a heavy layer of a good laundry stain remover, such as Zout®, and allow it to sit for five minutes before sprinkling with powdered laundry detergent. Apply a small amount of water to get a good lather going, then scrub with a stiff broom and rinse well.

• Kitty Litter™ is good at absorbing oil. Just make sure to grind it into the stain with your feet.

• Patio blocks can be cleaned with washing soda or laundry stain remover. Don't use the oven cleaner method, though. It can remove color and damage the blocks.

• Kill weeds that grow through the cracks in driveways and patios by saturating them with 1 gallon of warm water to which you have added ¼ cup of salt.

• Prevent weeds from growing in these cracks by sprinkling salt directly into the crevices. That's all there is to it—just let nature do the rest.

Get Your Mind *into* the Gutter!

Gutters are designed to carry rainwater and melting snow off your roof and away from your house. They are not storage places for leaves, Frisbees™, and tennis balls. Keep them clean.

Check your gutters to see if they're in good working order by spraying a hose directly into the trough. If the water runs through the trough and out the spout, you're in good shape. If, however, the water flows over the sides, it's time to give those gutters a good cleaning.

Use a ladder to clean gutters. Never approach them from the roof. That's asking for trouble. If the ground beneath your ladder is soft, sit the legs of the ladder into a couple of small cans, such as those from tuna fish. The cans will help distribute the weight, and the ladder won't slope or sink into the ground at uneven levels.

Once you're confident that the ladder is secure, climb to the height of the gutters and, wearing rubber gloves, scoop out the debris that's collected there. Hang a couple of shopping bags onto your ladder and use them to hold the debris. When one is full, just toss it to the ground and start filling the next. (Just don't forget to shout, "Look out below!")

Once you've removed the debris, flush the spout with water to make sure it flows freely. Usually, a forceful stream of water directed down the spout will be strong enough to push out anything that's blocking it. If that doesn't work, try inserting the hose *up* the spout. That should loosen the debris. One final blast of water from the top down should then be enough to dislodge whatever is blocking it.

You can avoid a lot of this hassle next year by placing a screen or netting over the gutters, which will prevent leaves and other debris from settling.

Time for a Picnic

A sunny day, a brightly colored checkered tablecloth, something good to eat . . . sounds like heaven to me! There's nothing quite like a picnic to round off an afternoon of outdoor fun, but insects and food poisoning can ruin the day. Read on to find out how to ward off those uninvited guests, as well as for advice on how to relieve that burn from the last of the summer sun. Oh, and let's not forget how to care for and clean that barbecue grill!

DON'T BUG ME

• Insects are attracted to intense colors—bright *and* dark. Bear this in mind when selecting tablecloths and paper plates, as well as your clothes for the day. This is not the time to be bold!

• Citronella candles are great standbys. No picnic should be without them.

• Insects love grapes, melon, and sweet fruit drinks, as well as strongly scented foods, such as tuna, strong cheeses, and meats. Think about this as you prepare your picnic.

• Choose a picnic site that's away from rivers, lakes, and streams. Insects tend to gather around water.

Flies ruining your picnic? Keep them away by wiping the table with some undiluted white vinegar or laying some citrus peels on the tablecloth.

• Odors can broadcast mealtimes to insects, so keep foods sealed in plastic containers until you're ready to eat.

• Make sure to cover serving plates so insects can't touch down on your meal—even for a moment. Domed food covers are great, as are pieces of inexpensive nylon netting. Don't have either? Try turning a large bowl upside down over platters.

• Don't let a bug surprise you in your soda or juice. Cover the glass with a piece of aluminum foil and then push a straw through it.

• Ants can't make it through water, so the best way to deter them is by sitting the legs of your picnic table in tin cans filled with water. Disposable pie tins or old Frisbees™ work well for tables with thicker legs.

• Entice insects away from your picnic by giving them a picnic of their own. Put a pie plate filled with water and sugar several yards away from your eating area. The bugs will rush to their meal, leaving you alone to enjoy yours! (Don't forget to pick up the pie plate before you leave.)

Cuts and scrapes may come with outdoor fun, but the ouch that comes with bandage removal doesn't have to. Just rub some baby oil around the bandage before pulling it off.

FOOD FOR THOUGHT

Picnics may be the ultimate in casual eating, but that doesn't mean you should be casual about the way you prepare and store the food. Bacteria thrive in hot weather; that's why it's

easy to become sick from food poisoning. So take a few precautions and have a lovely, stress-free day.

• Keep hot foods hot and cold foods cold. That means
making sure you have one cooler set aside for cold foods,
and one for hot.

*A tear or hole in a picnic cooler
can be repaired with candle wax. Gently warm the
bottom of a candle over a flame, then rub it on the tear until
the seam can no longer be noticed. A wax scar will form,
and that should prevent further splitting.*

• Insulate foods by wrapping them in layers of newspaper or brown paper grocery bags.

• Large blocks of ice keep food colder and last longer
than their smaller counterparts, so use your imagination
when choosing containers for ice. Milk cartons, for example, do a great job! Rinse out the carton (no need to use
soap), fill it with water about two inches from the top, then
pop it into the freezer until you're ready to go. Don't cut
the top off, and don't tear it open, either. Resealing the
spout once you're ready to go will ensure that this ice block
stays cold a long time.

• Think of that foam cooler as your "hot chest." Put all
of your hot foods together, wrap them well in layers of
paper, and the combined heat will create a thermos to keep
everything hot for a few hours.

• Add mayonnaise to foods when you're ready to eat

them, not before. It's not the mayonnaise that's the problem; it's usually the foods you mix with it that carry bacteria. Mayonnaise deteriorates quickly in warm conditions, and can act as a host for bacteria-growing food.

I hate it when that happens . . .

Ketchup too slow for your liking? Tap firmly on the side of the bottle, and the ketchup will come right out.

• Ketchup and mustard deteriorate in hot weather, so leave the big bottles at home. Now's the time to use up all those extra packets of ketchup and mustard you picked up at fast-food restaurants.

• Don't eat picnic leftovers or food left out for more than two hours.

• If it smells or looks bad, throw it out. Don't take chances.

THE GRILL DRILL

Never use gasoline or kerosene to start a fire. These substances are extremely flammable and very difficult to control—and they're not safe to use around food, either.

Don't try to revive a smoldering fire with a squirt of charcoal lighter fluid. The fire could flare up and you could be engulfed in flames. Revive a fire by dampening a few fresh pieces of charcoal with lighter fluid and carefully placing them—one at a time—in with the old coals.

Dispose of ashes with care. Douse them with water, stirring them with a metal fork, then douse with yet more water. You can also dispose of ashes by dumping them into a metal can. Wait at least 24 hours before putting in with other garbage.

Clean the exterior of gas and charcoal grills with GOJO Crème Waterless Hand Cleaner™. Dip a paper towel into the GOJO™, work it into the outside of the grill, and watch the dirt, grease and barbecue sauce come right off! Buff with a clean paper towel and the grill will sparkle like new—with the added benefit of a nice protective coating.

The easiest way to clean a grill rack? Lay the cool rack upside down on the grass and leave it overnight. The dew will work to soften any burned-on food and the next morning you can simply wipe it off!

Grilling at the beach? Clean the grill rack by rubbing it with sand!

Place a layer of sand in the bottom of a charcoal grill to prevent the charcoal from burning through the bottom.

Remove burned-on foods with black coffee. Just pour the coffee over a hot grill rack and wipe with aluminum foil.

The Hot News on Sunburn

Ouch! You forgot the sunscreen and now the damage has been done. It happens to the best of us. Sunburns hurt. Bad.

But there are some steps you can take to cool the heat and soothe the pain. Read on.

• A cool bath helps. Shake in some baking soda, or about ½ cup of salt. Soak for about 30 minutes or so, then apply aloe gel to still-damp skin to keep the temperature down. (Works on mosquito bites and chickenpox, too!)

• A thin layer of Preparation H® is soothing to hot, itchy skin and is especially good on delicate facial areas. Yes, I am serious.

• Make up compresses of 1 part milk to 3 parts water, then lay on burned areas for soothing relief. The protein in the milk will draw out the heat.

• Moist tea bags can offer much-needed relief to eyelids that are burned and swollen. Lay the cold bags over closed eyes, then relax for 30 minutes or so.

• Heavy lotions can trap heat rather than soothe it, so try gels instead, particularly those containing aloe.

• Your grandmother may remember this old-fashioned remedy: Whip 1 egg white with 1 teaspoon of castor oil, then apply to affected areas. Let dry. Rinse off with cool water.

• Spraying on a 50/50 solution of cider vinegar and tepid water will cool the burn on contact.

• Vitamin E is a wonderful moisturizer for burned skin.

Don't you hate it when pet food gets dry and sticks to the bowl? I know I do—and I'm not the one who has to clean it out! There is a solution, though: Give the bowl a quick spritz of nonstick cooking spray before dishing out the food. No more stuck-on food. No more difficult cleaning jobs.

A little bit of oil in my food will also help with that bowl cleanup. And it's also good for my coat!

A lot of people like to use Dustbusters® to clean up scatterings of cat litter (apparently not all kitties are as fastidious as I am), but not many of them know that a used dryer fabric sheet makes a great addition to the filter. Easy to clean and fresh smelling, too!

 Zack

September

Children are grumbling. Parents are rejoicing. It must be September—back to school! Doesn't matter if you're dealing with a first grader or a high school senior (or whether you yourself are heading back to college), going back to school can be exhilarating—and stressful. So get organized. Plan ahead. Establish rules. Consider your schedule and your family's needs, and with a little bit of imagination, you can get the school year off to a good start.

School Daze

FIRST THINGS FIRST

Try not to buy any new clothes for your kids without taking stock of what you have on hand. Go through their closets first, *then* hit the back-to-school sales.

Take an afternoon—a rainy one if you can—and sift through your children's closets. If they're at an age when they're interested in what they wear, enlist their help and consider it a joint project. This is a terrific opportunity to show them the benefits of being organized. Come armed with a few large plastic bags and some silly jokes. Let them pick the music to play and let them decide (with your help) what stays and what goes. The more you involve your children in the process, the more likely they are to cooperate. And if there are any squabbles down the road; well, remind them that the choices were made by both of you!

The first step to an organized closet? Get rid of anything that's too small or that you know won't be worn anymore. If repairs are needed, now's the time to do them. Hem hems, fix zips, sew on buttons and tend to any mending that you can. Then make use of those large plastic bags and get rid of whatever can't be used. Can't find a mate to that sock? Get rid of it. Elastic gone on those underpants? Use them as cleaning rags. Be ruthless. If an item of clothing is not up to the task, throw it out. Those torn jeans may be old favorites, but if they're ripped beyond repair, let your son say farewell to them and put them in the trash. That pink blouse may have been your daughter's favorite, but if it didn't fit her last year, it's not going to fit her now. Donate the blouse to a thrift shop and move on to the next item. This is no time to be sentimental. You've got a closet to organize.

Now look into that pared-down closet and see what you've got left. At this point, I like to remove everything so I can organize it anew. Take all the clothes out of the closet and put them on the bed. You might find it easier to make separate piles—one for shirts or blouses, one for pants, one for skirts, sweaters, and so on. Your child's style will dictate how many different mounds of clothes you have. You don't have to be precise with your categories, just separate clothes into logical groups so they're easier to put back.

Now comes the fun part. There's only one rule when it

comes to organizing: It has to work for you, and you have to be consistent. (Well, I guess that's two, but who's counting?) So, if your daughter wants to organize her closet by colors, let her. If your son wants to organize his clothes by day of the week, let him. Just make sure your child knows that he or she will be responsible for the upkeep of the system, *every single day.* Take the time to talk to your child. Offer her some choices. Blouses here, tee shirts there, skirts over here and pants down there. If your daughter rarely wears those two blue dresses and is keeping them for special occasions, you may want to suggest that she keep them near the back of her closet and bring more frequently worn items to the front. If your son wears mostly tees and sweatshirts, ask him if he'd rather keep these items in baskets. (Do you know a child who *likes* to hang up his clothes?) Talk about the best ways of organizing and you may come up with some nifty ideas that will suit your child well. Be imaginative and flexible. The more realistic you are in planning the closet, the more likely your child is to keep it tidy. And isn't that what it's all about?

A few suggestions:

• Make it easy for your child to put his clothes away by installing hooks at easy-to-reach levels.

• Install low bars so that little ones can hang up their own clothes.

• Baskets and buckets are great for holding children's socks and underwear.

• Let your child select some bright hangers in her favorite colors. Clothes are less likely to end up on the floor that way.

- A baseball-cap holder is great for that Little-League enthusiast.

- Everyone knows that an over-the-door shoe rack is great for shoes. It's also great for tee shirts, gym clothes, swimsuits and dance gear.

- Use plastic storage bins to hold clothes that aren't used daily. And make sure to label them well. If your child is too young to read, let him draw pictures so he knows what's inside.

- Encourage children to make use of all of the racks and shelves in their closets—the ones they can reach, anyway.

- Give each child a colorful laundry hamper, and let older children know that they're responsible for bringing their laundry down to the laundry room.

One last thing: Now that your children know the work that goes into organizing a closet, you might want to remind them of that old adage *Work saved is work done.* Encourage your children to keep their closets organized and their clothes clean. Remind them to put away their school clothes when they remove them, not several hours later when the wrinkles have had time to set. Who knows . . . they might even listen!

CLOTHES CALLS

- When hitting those back-to-school sales, remember to save some money for those new fads that show up the first few weeks of school—those things the kids *just can't* do without.

• Read the care labels on new clothes. Make sure you know whether an item has to be handwashed or dry-cleaned *before* you buy it.

• If your child is having problems with a zipper, try rubbing a pencil over it a few times. The graphite will help the zipper to glide as smooth as ice!

New school shoes causing your child to slip?
Score the soles with the tines of a fork.

• If new school clothes are too stiff—a problem with jeans especially—break them in by throwing ½ a cup of table salt in with the wash. They'll come out nice and soft!

JUST FIVE MORE MINUTES

I wish I could give you more time in the morning, but I'm a Queen, not a magician. There are, however, some things you can do to make your mornings less hectic.

The school bus leaves in ten minutes and all across the country kids are screaming, "I can't find it!" Don't let this happen to you. Help each child select a designated spot for books, homework and sports equipment—plus anything else they need to take to school in the morning. Baskets are great, as are bright plastic buckets. Canvas bags hanging on coatracks are good, too.

Designate another safe place for report cards (did I just shiver?), notes from teachers, and permission slips that need to be signed. And let your children know, firmly, that the morning of is *not* the time for signatures.

An over-the-door shoe rack in see-through plastic can be great for holding those small items that kids never seem to be without—and never seem willing to leave the house without. Label a few pockets for each child and tell them it's their own little holding bay. These pouches can be used to hold skipping ropes, GameBoys™, caps and small toys, not to mention hats, scarves and mittens. Give top pockets to older kids and save the easy-to-reach pouches at the bottom for the little ones.

Television is a great distraction. Keep the TV off in the morning and you'll all save time.

If kids want to agonize over what goes with what (not to mention who's *wearing* what), that's fine. Just remind them that 8:00 in the morning is not the time to be doing it. Save yourself a headache and let the kids select what they want to wear to school, but get them into the habit of setting out their clothes *the night before.*

WHO'S ON FIRST?

A large family calendar is a must. Keep it displayed in a location that's prominent *and* convenient. Older children can be taught to log in their own events; just make sure they tell you first. Use the calendar for school functions, sports events, doctor's appointments and birthday parties. Keep a bulletin board nearby. You can use that to hold any relevant papers, like invitations, cards and notes.

A daily visit to your family calendar is not a bad idea. It just takes a minute or so to prevent overlaps that may lead to conflicts.

Get your children in the habit of looking at the calendar, too. Show them how their week is shaping up *before* they enter into it. Let your children know that four busy days in a row might not be such a good idea, and encourage them to use their calendar to make choices. Everybody needs to be reminded that they don't have to say *yes* to everything.

If nothing's scheduled on a particular day, why not use the calendar for other things? Jot down a knock-knock joke or an encouraging word about a child's performance. An organized life doesn't have to be boring!

Accept the fact that things don't always run smoothly. Some days *are* better than others. Take a deep breath and don't sweat it. Tomorrow offers another chance to get it right.

GET IT OFF YOUR CHEST

Now that you're in the mood to get organized, why not extend the project for just a few more minutes and tidy up your medicine chest? This small but important project could mean a lot to your family's safety.

Remove everything from the cabinet and place the contents onto a large flat surface, such as a table. Again, organize the contents into logical groups. Medicines here, bandages there, and so on. Now:

- Toss out anything that doesn't have a label.

- Get rid of any medicines that have passed their expiration dates.

- Take note of any duplicates you may have but don't, for heaven's sake, combine them. You may have two half-empty bottles of aspirin, but putting them together in the same bottle to save space is a bad idea, especially if they have different expiration dates.

- Blister-pack pills are often separated from their boxes. If you aren't certain of the medication or if you don't know the date of expiration, get rid of them. This is no time to be frugal.

- Chances are, you have at least one tensor bandage that's lost its elasticity. Get rid of it.

Cleaning out a medicine chest is similar to cleaning out a closet, except you don't have to sew on any buttons!

Unwanted medications can still be dangerous, so make sure to dispose of them safely. Flushing them down the toilet may be satisfying in a dramatic sort of way, but that can be bad for the environment. Don't just toss pills in the garbage, either. They can be deadly to children and animals. The best way to get rid of medication is to put it in a child-proof container, then in another jar (which you seal), and then safely in the garbage. Don't take chances.

Despite its name, the medicine chest is probably the worst place to store medicines. Not only does it suffer fluctuations in temperature, but it's damp and steamy, too!

Take this time to clean out the shelves of your medicine chest. Metal shelves can be cleaned with a little bit of baking soda and water. Glass shelves can be cleaned with vinegar. Make sure that surfaces are dry before restocking, and take this opportunity to be a rebel and store anything *but* your medicines in your medicine chest. That's right!

Store your medication in a place that is clean, dry and safe from curious youngsters. Save the medicine chest for the cotton balls.

The Last Word, and a Very Important One at That!

Carbon monoxide is a tasteless, odorless killer. It can be released by wood-burning stoves, fireplaces, furnaces, kerosene lamps and gas-fired heaters, and it occurs when these items burn without enough oxygen. When fresh air is restricted, carbon monoxide can build up in your home and cause an irregular heartbeat, headaches and fatigue. In very high amounts, it can cause death.

Please, take the following precautions against this silent killer:

- Ensure that adequate air is available in any room that contains a gas-burning appliance.

- Have your furnace, chimneys and flues checked regularly for cracks and leaks.

- Make certain that door and stovepipe connections fit tightly on all old wood-burning stoves.

- Use a range hood and fan with a gas stove.

- Keep a window slightly open when using a space heater that operates on oil, gas or kerosene.

- Never barbecue in a house or closed garage.

- Always make sure the garage door is open when running the car.

The most important thing to do to protect yourself and your family is to purchase a carbon monoxide detector. It's not expensive, but it may turn out to be priceless.

October

The days are getting shorter. The nights are getting longer. And that nip in the air tells us without a doubt that the seasons are changing. I hate to be the one to mention this, but it's time to get ready for the colder months. So, let's store our summer clothes and soon-to-be out-of-season sports and gardening equipment. Then let's move inside and turn our thoughts to brighter things, like lighting fixtures. Once we've done that, we can get dressed up in costumes and scare the living daylights out of the neighbors. What else is Halloween for?

Storing Summer Clothes

Summer is finally over and now it's time to store your warm weather clothes. Try to avoid the temptation to just push them to one side of your closet. You'll feel better organized all year long if you make the effort to adjust your closet to the seasons. You won't have so many items to sift through when looking for something to wear, and your clothes are less likely to become wrinkled in the crush.

Clothes should be washed before storage; otherwise, stains will have a nice long time to set, and you'll never get them out. It's best to have everything laundered (or dry-cleaned, as the case may be), even if they seem to be clean. Some stains are hard to detect and only materialize over time, like a rash. Best to tackle them right away.

Another good reason to launder clothes before storing them? Moths are attracted to your scent.

Try to avoid using fabric softener on clothes you're about to store. Fabric softener can leave grease spots, which can attract undesirables and weaken fibers. Best to forego the softener, or use a vinegar rinse

For surprise spots on washable clothes, try using ½ cup of hydrogen peroxide and 1 teaspoon of ammonia. Saturate the stain and allow to sit for 30 minutes. Then launder. Zout® Stain Remover is also great on old stains; use as directed.

Make sure that swimsuits are washed before storing them. Chlorine residue can damage fibers and may give you a nasty shock when you head to the beach next year. It's best to wash swimsuits using your machine's gentle cycle and cold water along with your favorite laundry detergent. (If you have been swimming in salt water, soak the suit in cold water for 15 minutes *before* washing.) If you handwash your suit, make sure to rinse well to get rid of all detergent. Air-dry your suit out of the sun. Don't put it in the dryer. Heat can break down the elastic and spandex that keeps the shape of your swimsuit.

Don't forget to protect your natural fibers from those natural predators: moths. Mothballs work well, although some people find the odor offensive. Cedar chips are also reliable. Just insert a handful into the container with your clothes. Perhaps the best deterrent, though, is this lovely homemade citrus remedy: Take some oranges, grapefruit, lemons or limes, remove the peels and cut them into thin strips. Place the strips on a cookie sheet (making sure it's clean) and leave in a warm place to dry. You can also speed the drying process by placing the tray in a 300-degree oven. Preheat the oven, then turn it off before putting in your citrus tray. Prolonged heat will burn the peels. Once the peels are dry and cool, put them into clothes pockets, storage drawers or boxes. No nasty smells, and no damage from moths, either.

Suitcases come in handy for storing seasonal clothes, but I like under-the-bed storage boxes best. Choose between cardboard or plastic, whichever suits your space and budget. I like the transparent plastic boxes because they allow me to see at a glance what's inside. Nevertheless, I also tape a list of the contents to the top of the box so I can get to things in a hurry, if need be. (I *am* an organized Queen!)

Don't store clothes in plastic dry cleaner bags. They can cause yellowing.

Be creative as to *where* you store your boxes. Under-the-bed storage boxes don't have to go under the bed. Look at the unused space in children's closets, for example. And who says that the linen closet it strictly for linens? Just be careful of storing clothes in the basement, attic, or other places where mold and mildew can damage clothes.

Give some thought as to how you want to pack the boxes *before* you start the process. Use separate storage receptacles for each person, try not to overstuff boxes, and be sure to group types of clothes together. You'll be glad you did when, next summer, you find how easy it is to unpack boxes that have already been organized with care.

Bring the Outdoors In

Now that summer is drawing to a close, it's time to take a few steps to make sure that your tools and summer gear are safe and dry for the winter ahead. A word of caution: If you store your seasonal equipment in the garage (and most of us do), don't forget to leave room for your car!

• Lawn chairs and summer gear can be suspended from the ceiling of your garage with sturdy hooks.

• Open rafters make great storage space, too. Secure items there with bungee cords.

• Don't overlook the simple solutions. A shopping bag hung on a nail can be great for storing small and medium-sized balls.

• An inexpensive string hammock, the type you might use to display a child's collection of stuffed animals, makes a great home for soccer balls and other large items.

• Pegboards are endlessly versatile. Use them to hold hand tools and other small equipment. There's a reason they've stood the test of time!

• Sand doesn't freeze, so store your small gardening tools in the same container of sand that you've been using all summer.

• Garden hoses can crack and split in severely cold weather, so store them inside. Just make sure they're empty first. Pockets of water can collect and freeze in cold weather, and that can result in a tear.

• Take steps to ensure that your lawn mower will start in the spring. Old, unleaded fuel can solidify over winter and that will clog up the workings on your mower. Empty the gas tank and then run the mower till it stops. Only then should you store it for the winter.

Let There Be Light

Now that it's too cold for outdoor lanterns and citronella candles, let's turn our attention to indoor lighting, namely, the main light in your dining area. It may not be the chandelier from *The Phantom of the Opera,* but the light over your dining room table is still important. Keep it clean and sparkling—it will reflect well on you.

Use a premoistened alcohol wipe to quickly shine chandelier crystals for no drips and lots of sparkle!

Chandeliers have a reputation of being difficult to clean, but it doesn't have to be that way. First, turn off the light and give the bulbs a chance to cool down—don't start until they're cool to the touch. Place a small, plastic snack bag over each bulb and secure with a twist tie to prevent moisture from seeping into the socket. Next, position a table directly under the chandelier, covering it with a sturdy plastic table cover and a good layer of old rags (towels work well). This will give you a work base and will also catch the cleaning solution as it drips off the chandelier.

Now for the cleaning solution: Make a mixture of 2 cups of warm water, ½ cup of rubbing alcohol and 2 tablespoons of an automatic dishwasher spot stopper, such as Jet Dry™. Pour the solution into a spray bottle—you can pick them up quite cheaply at the dollar store—then spray the chandelier liberally. Allow it to drip-dry. Pour the leftover solution in a cup and you can use it to hand-dip the crystal teardrops or other decorative hanging pieces. No need to remove them from the chandelier; just dip them and let them drip-dry. The chandelier will be sparkling.

I hate it when that happens . . .

If a lightbulb breaks off in the socket, just grab a bar of soap and push it into the jagged edges. Turn the soap counterclockwise and presto! You've safely removed the broken bulb!

But wait: You're not finished—not until you clean the bulbs themselves. Lightbulbs collect dust and that prevents the beauty of the light from shining through. Make sure that the bulbs have had a chance to cool down, then wipe them with a soft, dry cloth. Don't apply much pressure to the bulb—it may break.

Of course not all overhead lights are chandeliers. You may have traditional fixtures with a flat base attached to the ceiling. You may have track lighting or lights connected to a fan. The glass may be clear, frosted or colored. No matter, it still needs to be cleaned. Remove fixtures carefully. If the light is hard to reach, make sure you use a step stool or ladder to remove it—easier on you, and easier on the light. Keep one hand firmly on or under the fixture while you undo the screws or brackets that hold the fixture to the ceiling, and remove with great care. You don't want to chip the edges.

Now, place an old towel in the bottom of your sink. That should prevent the fixture from hitting the hard bottom and breaking or cracking. Fill the sink with warm water and a little bit of dishwashing liquid. Wash the fixture gently, then remove it from the water and sit it safely to one side on another towel. Empty the sink, then fill it up again with warm water, this time adding ¼ cup of white vinegar. You'll need to put another towel in the water, too. Place the fixture in the sink one last time and leave it there for a minute or so before removing. Gently remove excess moisture with a soft, lint-free cloth, then allow to air-dry thoroughly. Use this dry-time to gently wipe down any metal components with a damp cloth. Buff well with a dry one, and wipe down the lightbulb(s) with a soft cloth. Be sure the fixture is shut off and the bulb and metal are cool. Now you can put the fixture back in place and let the light shine through!

Trick or Treat

Okay, the chores are done and now it's time for fun. And because it's October, that can mean only one thing—Halloween!

THE TREAT

• Makeup is much safer for children than masks, which can obscure their vision.

• Remove glitter makeup and heavy dark makeup from kids' faces with petroleum jelly. Gently work in the jelly (use care with glitter makeup not to get it into the eye area), then tissue away the makeup. Wash face well when done.

• Make sure to leave plenty of room for your child's clothes under the costume. And make sure the costume isn't trailing on the ground. You don't want your child to trip!

• Make sure to check your children's candy before you let them eat it. If little ones are impatient, give them a piece of the candy you bought until you've had time to check the bounty.

• Put some reflective tape on costumes and shoes so that your child will be visible. Consider making a cute flashlight part of the costume.

• Did you color your hair green for Halloween only to discover that the color won't come out? Don't give up hope. Reach for the baking soda, liquid dish soap and shampoo. Make a paste the consistency of thick shampoo, work it well into your hair—concentrate on your hair, not your scalp—then rinse thoroughly. No more green!

THE TRICK

Sometimes those little pirates and princesses come home with a lot more than candy. Here's how to treat those muddy problems.

• When mud gets tracked onto your carpet, don't try to clean it up right away. Cover the wet mud with baking soda; that will absorb the moisture from the mud. Once the mess is dry, vacuum, using only the hose. A beater bar will grind the mud into the carpet, but a hose will concentrate the suction on the muddy area. Finish off with your favorite carpet cleaner.

• Wet mud on your clothes can be treated by flushing the wrong side of the fabric with lots of cool water. Hold the garment under a faucet and direct a forceful stream of water at the clean side of the garment. (Flushing the dirty side with water will only grind the mud into the fabric.) Once the water runs clear, work some Fels-Naptha Heavy Duty Laundry Bar Soap® into the area and launder as usual.

• Muddy shoes should be allowed to dry, then vigorously brushed with a shoe brush. Use fast, downward strokes rather than circular motions, which could grind the mud into the shoes. If mud remains on leather shoes, clean with a bar of soap (Dove® Moisturizing Bath Bar works well) and a soft cloth. Canvas or athletic shoes should be cleaned using Fels-Naptha Soap® and a nailbrush.

• Mud on car upholstery, whether fabric or leather, should be allowed to dry before treating. Use the attachment hose on your vacuum to remove all the mud you can. For fabric upholstery, use your favorite carpet and upholstery cleaner (I like Spot Shot Instant Carpet Stain Remover®), following the directions on the container. On leather, wash the area using a moisturizing bar soap, such as Dove® and wipe with a clean soft cloth.

The Pumpkin Patch

Pumpkins decay and mold quickly, so make sure to put something under your pumpkin, such as a couple of paper plates or a plastic tablecloth. You don't want to have a black stain as a reminder of the holiday.

If you already have a black stain you may be able to remove it with one of the following remedies.

For pumpkin mold on a porch or concrete, try cleaning the area with oven cleaner. Spray the area with the cleaner and allow to sit 10 minutes, then agitate with a brush and rinse well. Do this on a cool day, and make sure to keep kids and pets away.

For wooden tabletops, use a little nongel toothpaste on a damp cloth and rub in a circular motion. You can also try some 0000 steel wool dipped into turpentine. Do this in a very small inconspicuous spot first. Apply some lemon oil to the area when you are done, let it soak in and buff with a soft cloth. You can avoid that stain altogether by making pumpkin pie out of that pumpkin.

Let's Dish!

Dad's Favorite Pumpkin Pie

2 cups canned pumpkin

1 can evaporated milk and ⅓ cup regular milk to equal 2 cups

1 cup granulated sugar

2 eggs, well beaten

½ teaspoon ginger

1 teaspoon cinnamon

½ to ¾ teaspoon nutmeg

½ teaspoon salt

1 deep 8- or 9-inch pie shell

Using a mixer, combine all ingredients thoroughly.

Pour into pie shell. Bake for 15 minutes at 425 degrees, then turn down temperature to 350 degrees and bake until a knife pushed into the center of the pie filling comes out clean, approximately 30 minutes. Serve with whipped cream or nondairy topping.

November

It's November, and the year is almost over! Where did it go? Thank heavens for Thanksgiving and the time to pause, to give thanks for what we have. Thanksgiving is a time of tradition—a big turkey dinner with all the trimmings, Grandmother's silverware, Aunt Jean's china, and Uncle Jim's bad jokes. Nobody wants to keep Jim's bad jokes, but the silverware and china, well that's something we hope to have for a good long time. That's why proper cleaning and maintenance is a must. Take the time to care for these precious heirlooms, and not only will you enjoy them for years to come, but you'll be able to pass them along to your children, your grandchildren, and perhaps even your great-grandchildren! Oh, and when you're finished with the china and silverware, take a moment to get ready for the snow. November is the gateway to winter after all.

Traditions at the Table

THE CHINA SYNDROME

First things first. You'll need to evaluate what you have, so remove everything from the cabinet and place it on the dining table. Don't put the china on a bare table (you could scratch the finish), and don't put it on the floor where you might break something—those *I Love Lucy* situations are best avoided!

Now's the time to get tough. If you're *really* going to repair that teacup—you know, the one that's been broken since the Carter administration—now's the time to do it. If it can't be repaired, and if it doesn't really have any sentimental value, throw it out. Bear in mind that cracked dishes can be unsafe to eat off of because food and debris can settle in the cracks and not come out during washing. If in doubt, throw it out.

If you have a piece of china that has great sentimental value but is broken beyond repair, consider putting it in a sturdy paper bag and giving it a good whack. Collect the pieces (there won't be a million—trust me) and glue them around a picture frame or on a trinket box. Add some jewels, pearls, or artificial flowers, letting your imagination run wild. You'll end up with a lovely keepsake.

Never use the dishwasher for antique china, china with metal trim or hand-painted china.

Dishes that don't get regular use should be cleaned before use. Soap and water will generally do the trick. Just make sure to rinse well. For special challenges, like black cutlery marks on china plates, use nongel toothpaste on a soft cloth to rub the marks away. If you have fine, hairline cracks in old china, soak it in warm milk for 30 to 60 minutes. The cracks should disappear when you remove the plate from the milk. Wash as usual and dry well. If food has left any stains on the china, make a paste of lemon juice and cream of tartar, and rub gently. Rinse the piece well when you're done.

The next step is to dust the cabinet shelves with a soft cloth. Then wash them with a cloth that has been immersed in a mild, soapy solution (1 teaspoon of liquid dish soap to 1 gallon of warm water) and then wrung out until just damp. Wash well and dry thoroughly with a soft, lint-free cloth. You may prefer to wash the shelves with a solution of brewed tea (1 quart of warm water and 1 tea bag). Allow the solution to cool to room temperature and wash the shelves using a soft cloth. Then dry thoroughly. A damp microfiber cloth can also be used.

Glass doors should be cleaned with a solution of 2 parts warm water to 1 part rubbing alcohol. Apply the solution directly to the cloth, then wipe gently in small circular motions. Make sure to clean the corners of the glass, too. Buff with a dry, lint-free cloth.

Never spray glass cleaner directly onto glass doors, picture frames or mirrors. The solution can seep into the wood and can cause damage to the surrounding areas.

Sliding doors have tracks that need to be cleaned from time to time. The crevice attachment on your vacuum cleaner is perfect for this. After you've vacuumed, wash the track with a damp, soapy toothbrush and dry with a soft cloth.

Keep the track and doors running smoothly by rubbing them with a little lemon oil or spraying with some furniture polish.

Okay. You've cleaned your cabinet and evaluated its contents. Now's the time to put everything back. Take stock of what you have before returning items to the shelves. What are your favorite pieces? What do you want to display, and what would you rather conceal? Bear this in mind as you arrange your cabinet. Put larger pieces at the back of the cabinet, smaller items in front. Create groupings. Keep one set of china together, silver together, and crystal together, and so on. Put the things you seldom use in the back or on the shelf that's most difficult to reach, and keep them clean by covering with plastic wrap. Always empty sugar from the china sugar bowl.

Stack dinner plates, dessert plates, saucers and other flat items together, and insert a napkin or paper towel between each one to avoid scratches. Sit groups of these flat items on each other to make the most of your space. Cups are more delicate and easily broken, though, so don't stack them more than two deep. Be creative with your groupings. Try putting some of your old and new pieces together. You may just see things in a whole new light!

If you plan to wash your china in the automatic dishwasher, take one piece (say, a cup) and wash it over the course of a month to determine if it's dishwasher safe. Just leave the cup in the dishwasher and let it run through the wash with your everyday dishes. Take a look at the piece every few days or so. If it appears that the trim is changing color, the pattern is fading or small cracks are occurring, you'll want to stop the experiment. If the piece remains unharmed, you can follow with the rest of your set. For best results, use the "china" or "short" cycle, as well as the "energy saver" or "no heat" drying cycle. (You'll save energy and money, too!) I wish I could tell you another easy test you could try, but there isn't one. If you are buying a large set of china, you might want to consider buying one extra, inexpensive piece to try this dishwasher experiment.

Crystal that stands up securely in the rack can be washed in the dishwasher. It should not lean, lay sideways or hook over the prongs on the dishwasher rack. Don't allow crystal pieces to bump against each other during washing—they'll chip. Avoid water spots on crystal by adding 1 teaspoon of 20 Mule Team™ Borax to your automatic dishwashing detergent.

Place a towel in the bottom of the sink when handwashing crystal. The towel will cushion the crystal and prevent breakage.

When handwashing crystal, wash only a few pieces at a time and make sure not to overload the sink. Crystal should be cleaned in hot water, but not too hot. As a general rule, if the water is too hot for your hands, it's too hot for the crystal. Sudden changes of temperature can cause crystal to crack, so place it sideways into the water instead of bottom first. For a squeaky clean finish, add 1 tablespoon of white vinegar to the water, along with your liquid dish soap.

Crystal should be stored upright, as you would drink from it. A lot of people like to store glasses upside down to prevent dust from accumulating in the goblet or flute, but it's not a good idea. Moisture can be trapped inside the glass, causing damage to the crystal and the shelf on which it's stored.

Cranberry stains on that tablecloth? Remove them with a little Wine Away Red Stain Remover™. Works like a charm.

HI HO SILVER

Acidic foods and their residue can tarnish silver and may even cause it to pit. Salt, egg yolk, fish, broccoli, mayonnaise and mustard are the biggest offenders. Get into the habit of rinsing your silver right after you clear the table. You may not be able to wash the dishes right away—I know it's not *my* idea of an after-dinner treat—but a thorough rinsing will go a long way to prevent permanent damage.

Wash silverware in hot water and mild dishwashing liquid. Rinse well, and dry with a soft, lint-free cloth. Don't allow silver to air-dry, as this can result in water spotting. Silver *must* be dry before storing, so make sure to dry well.

Did you know?

Rubber causes silver to tarnish, so don't dry pieces on a rubber mat or store it wrapped in rubber bands.

• Silverware washed in a dishwasher should never be mixed with stainless steel cutlery. Pitting may occur.

- Never store silver in plastic bags or plastic wrap. That traps condensation and can encourage tarnish.

- Store silver in a tarnish-proof bag or wrap it in acid-free tissue paper. If you wear clean, soft gloves when doing this task, you won't leave finger marks—that's where tarnish can begin.

- For quick silver cleaning, put strips of aluminum foil in a large bowl, place the silver on top of the foil, pour boiling water over the silver and add 3 tablespoons of baking soda. Soak for a few minutes, then rinse and dry. Don't use this method on hollow or glued pieces.

- Rubbing silver with a damp cloth dipped in baking soda will also remove tarnish. Or try a little nongel toothpaste on a soft, damp cloth. Rinse and dry thoroughly before using.

Just boiled some potatoes? Let the water cool and then pour over silver. Allow it to soak for 30 minutes. Wash, rinse and rub with a soft cloth. The starch in the potato water will clean the silver.

- Never store salt in silver saltshakers. This could lead to tarnish.

- Remove tarnish and other stains from the inside of silver coffeepots by rubbing with a fine piece of steel wool dipped in white vinegar and salt. Use grade 0000.

- Place several sugar cubes in a silver coffeepot before storing, and you'll never have an old, musty smell. The Queen Mum taught me that one!

• Store silver teapots and coffeepots with the lid open or off so that moisture is never trapped inside.

• Clean the inside of silver teapots by filling with water to which you have added a small handful of Arm and Hammer Washing Soda™. Let soak overnight, rinse and dry well.

• Clean silver-plated items as you would real silver, but be gentle—silver plating can rub off.

• Cleaning silver is important, but be careful not to rub too hard on the hallmark. If you wear it off or distort it, the value of the set will be reduced.

Silver takes on a beautiful patina with age and with use—rather like a Queen!—so don't just keep it stored away in a drawer. A beautifully set table is an important part of a holiday meal, and your silverware is a meaningful part of that setting. So use your silverware, treat it well, and each time you set the table you'll have beautiful memories to enjoy.

If someone spills gravy on your tablecloth during dinner, sprinkle the spill with baking soda or salt to absorb it and enjoy the rest of the meal. After dinner, treat with Zout® Stain Remover and launder as usual.

There's No Business Like Snow Business

So you're thinking *What does a woman in Arizona know about snow?* Well, I lived in Michigan for more than forty years (we don't have to go into details here), so believe me, I know what I'm talking about when I talk snow!

GIVE SNOW AND SALT THE BOOT

• Keep boots looking their best by applying a good coat of quality paste polish and following up with a spray of water protectant.

• Damp or wet boots should be dried standing up. A roll of cardboard or a bent wire hanger will help them keep their shape. Never allow boots to dry on a heat register—the leather could crack.

• Remove salt stains by wiping with a mixture of 1 part water and 1 part white vinegar.

Buttons on heavy winter coats have to do double duty, what with that heavy fabric and the constant on-and-off as you go from indoors to out. Try sewing them on with dental floss instead. It's stronger and longer-lasting than most thread, so you'll never be bothered with missing buttons again. If your coat is dark, just finish off with a few loops of dark thread to avoid an ugly contrast.

CAR DETAIL

• Don't wait until it's too late. Schedule a tune-up and winterizing appointment for your car.

• Give your car a thorough cleaning before the winter sets in. Don't forget to vacuum the carpet and upholstery, and treat it with a good-quality fabric protector.

• Make sure the dashboard and defroster are clear from obstructions.

• Rubber mats with deep, diagonal grooves really help to capture melting snow. They're a good investment.

• Locks frozen in your car? If your car is in the garage near an electrical outlet, use a blow-dryer on the low setting to direct the warm air into the lock, from a distance of about six inches. That should do the trick. If your car is outside, heat your key with a match or lighter and insert it into the lock. Leave it there for a few minutes, and then gently turn the key. You may have to do this a few times, but it should work. *Don't try this method if your lock has an electronic device.* You could damage the chip.

• Rub Vaseline™ on the gaskets so doors don't freeze.

Prevent frozen locks in your car by covering the lock with a couple layers of masking tape. The tape will keep the lock free from moisture, and that's what causes the ice to form.

• Getting stuck in the snow can be a real pain in the radials, so keep a bag of Kitty Litter™ in your trunk for some much-needed traction. A few layers of newspaper work well, too.

• Don't run out of windshield washer fluid. One part rubbing alcohol to 1 part water, and a few drops of liquid dish soap, work well on winter windshields. And if you treat them first with Clean Shield® protectant, they'll be that much easier to clean. Snow and grime will wipe right off.

• You can shave a few minutes off your morning snow detail if you place an old beach towel on the windshield the night before a forecasted snowfall. Tuck the towel beneath the windshield wipers before the snowfall, pull it off afterward, and you won't have to scrape your windows. Just give the towel a good shake and dream of sunnier days. A mitten placed on your sideview mirror will save you time, too!

• It's always a good idea to keep an emergency kit in your car during winter. Nobody leaves the house saying, "I think I'll get stuck in the snow today," so be prepared. Take along the following:

> Blanket
> Flashlight and some extra batteries
> Two bottles of water
> Chocolate bar (for emergencies only!)
> Piece of red cloth to tie to the car

SHOVEL IT

Every year hundreds of people suffer heart attacks from shoveling snow. Follow these simple rules to minimize the hazards.

- Never shovel snow after a heavy meal.
- Dress in layers and always wear a hat.
- Don't shovel snow after you've been drinking.
- Don't overload your shovel—snow can be very heavy.
- Always bend from the knees.
- Make sure someone knows where you are.
- Pace yourself. Take frequent breaks.

Give your snow shovel a coat of nonstick cooking spray before you start to tackle the driveway. You won't be bothered with those annoying clumps that stick to the shovel!

December

Christmas comes but once a year, which is a good thing if you're the one who has to do all the work. Try to make Christmas as stress-free as possible by planning ahead and enlisting what help you can. Don't be a holiday hero. Involve even the youngest members of your family, and don't decline those offers of help. Make lists. Plan ahead and try not to abandon your family's routine. The closer you follow yours—regular mealtimes and bedtimes, for example—the more you'll be able to enjoy the excitement of Christmas without the chaos. So go ahead and deck those halls . . . just don't forget to dust them first.

Holiday Hints

TEN TIME SAVERS

1. Tell your children that Santa only comes to a clean house. Don't laugh—it worked on me for years!

2. Take the time to clean your house *before* you bring in the tree and all the decorations. Sure, you'll probably need a quick vacuum once you have the tree in place, but it's easier to clean a house when you don't have to

maneuver all those holiday adornments around. Trust me on this one.

3. Make lists and stick to them. It's amazing how much time and effort you'll save.

4. Never say no to those offers of "Can I bring something?" or "Can I help?"

5. Shop early in the morning or late at night when stores aren't as crowded. Make use of the Internet and catalogs whenever possible.

6. Consider these quick gifts: a phone card, a wine club membership, a framed photo of a special time, this book, a gift certificate for a favorite coffeehouse, and pretty stationery with stamps.

7. Use gift bags instead of wrapping paper.

8. Make your own frozen dinners by preparing extra portions when you're cooking a big meal. Great for dinner when you're rushed, and great for the kids when you're on your way out to a party.

9. Get your holiday clothes cleaned and ready in advance. Hang the clothes and accessories together and you will have time for a leisurely bath, too!

10. Remove the word "perfection" from your vocabulary.

IT'S A FAMILY AFFAIR

• Enlist the whole family in a quick cleanup. Small children can dust, older ones can vacuum, your spouse can do the dishes, and you can tidy up and put things away. It's amazing what you can accomplish in thirty short minutes.

• Involve children in sending out Christmas cards. Older

ones can address the envelopes, and little ones can lick the stamps!

• Let your children bake some Christmas cookies. They're easy to prepare and require little supervision—just make sure to keep small hands away from the oven. You can make things easier by giving cookie cutters a quick spritz of non-stick cooking spray to prevent dough from clinging. And for those stubborn cookies that won't come away from the baking sheet? Slide a length of dental floss under each cookie and they'll glide right off.

• Children love to make pictures with artificial snow, but it can be difficult to wash off. Prevent snow from sticking by preparing the surface with a light misting of nonstick cooking spray. If you forget this step you can still remove it easily: Just rub with a little bit of white, nongel toothpaste.

• Let the kids wrap some gifts. The outcome may not be just as you'd like, but the kids will have fun and they'll be proud of their accomplishment.

O' CHRISTMAS TREE

• Know the height of your living room before you select your tree. Make sure to allow for the stand (about a foot) and the treetop. Size does matter!

• Older trees are dry and will drop needles when shaken, so make sure to shake the tree before you buy it. Choose one that has sturdy, flexible needles and a strong, fresh scent.

• The first thing to do when you bring your tree home is to cut off a small diagonal section at the base of the trunk. Trees need a lot of water, and this small act will help them to absorb it.

• Pine tree needles will last longer if spritzed first with fabric sizing or spray starch. Just make sure to do this *before* you put the lights on.

• Put a plastic tablecloth under the base of your tree to help protect your carpet from spills.

• If you do have a spill from your Christmas tree, clean it up as soon as possible or you'll have mold on the carpet. Slide the tree carefully to one side, and blot up all of the water by standing on some heavy towels placed on the carpet. Absorb all you can. Clean the area with your favorite carpet cleaner, and let a fan blow across the area until it is thoroughly dry, at least 24 hours.

Nourish your Christmas tree with a mixture of 1 quart of water, 2 tablespoons of lemon juice, 1 tablespoon of sugar and ½ teaspoon of liquid bleach. If you want a simpler solution, try 2 ounces of Listerine® or 1 tablespoon of maple syrup.

• Add water to the reservoir of a Christmas tree with a turkey baster, and you'll keep spills to a minimum.

• Make sure to water your tree daily.

• Rub a little petroleum jelly on the trunk of your artificial tree before inserting the branches. They'll be easier to remove in the new year.

• Put lights on your tree before adding any other decorations. And when choosing your lights, remember that white bulbs give off more light than colored ones.

• Ran out of hooks and hangers? Use paper clips, bobby pins, twist ties, pipe cleaners or dental floss. These makeshift hooks work well, but they're not very attractive, so try putting these ornaments deeper in the tree, where you're less likely to see the fastener.

Protect your door by securing a piece of weather stripping under your wreath.

AT THE TABLE

• Finding your good napkins wrinkled from storage can be frustrating. Don't despair. Just throw them in the dryer, along with a damp towel. After 10 minutes or so the creases will relax and you won't have to iron them.

• Don't throw away those empty rolls of wrapping paper. If you make a slit down the side of the roll and slide it over a coat hanger, you can use it to hang tablecloths without worrying about creases.

Put a few layers of foil in the basket before you add the napkin and rolls. Your bread and buns will stay warmer longer. Just about everybody likes warm buns!

• Clean your dining table the natural way, with tea! Make a pot of tea. Sit down, have a cup yourself, and wait until the tea is cool to the touch. Pour the liquid into a small container, saturate a clean, lint-free cloth, and wring it out till barely damp. Then wipe the table and leaves in the direction of the wood grain. Buff dry with a soft, dry cloth.

The Cat's Meow

Christmas may be an exciting time for people, but it can be a little nerve-racking for those of us with four legs. Here are a few things to watch out for:

- Holiday plants such as holly, poinsettia and mistletoe can be toxic. Please keep them away from us—and from small children, too.

- Cats love to play with tinsel, but we also like to eat it. This can wreak havoc on our intestinal tract. Please keep the tinsel and other stringy decorations out of our reach. If you want to put tinsel on the tree, avoid the lower branches.

- We may like to eat rich foods, but they're not good for us and can make us sick, especially chocolate. If you can't resist our soulful faces staring up at you while you're eating dinner, give us some carrots and a small piece of turkey without gravy. Of course, it's best not to feed us from the table at all, but don't ever say I told you that!

- Bear in mind that I may not be the party animal you think I am. If you're having lots of company, please put me in a room by myself, with my food, water and litter box. Better include a chew toy for the dog—you know how they get . . .

Zack

• Remove white marks from your table with a little bit of mayonnaise. Just make sure it's regular mayonnaise— low-fat won't do the trick. Mix the mayonnaise with table salt or cigarette ash. Massage the mixture into the mark for about 45 minutes. Yes, 45 minutes! It's a long time, but it's the massaging that gently buffs the mark away. Allow the mixture to sit for several hours, preferably overnight. Linseed oil and rottenstone (both available in hardware stores) work well, too.

• Use wax sticks or crayons to cover scratches. Make sure you get these from the hardware or furniture store (your child's crayons won't work here), and take care to match the shade of the stick to the table. Once you've applied the crayon according to the manufacturer's instructions, heat the area with a blow-dryer and buff firmly with an old rag for an almost invisible repair.

IT'S A WRAP

• Keep rolls of wrapping paper handy by standing them up in a wastebasket or in a small, clean garbage can.

• Empty wrapping paper rolls can also be used as kindling. Slide small twigs, dried leaves and broken bits of pine-cones in the tubes to make the foundation of a wonderful, crackling fire.

Be creative when wrapping packages. Fabric,
wallpaper, maps, tee shirts and sheet music
all make great gift coverings.

- Run out of wrapping paper? Recycle some old gift wrap by spraying the back with spray starch. Press with a warm iron and you're ready to go!

- Keep the end of the tape from disappearing by folding it over a paper clip. You'll never have to pick at bits of tape again.

- Don't burn foil wrapping or magazines in a fireplace— they emit noxious, dangerous gases.

- Recycled Christmas cards make great gift tags.

That Oh-So Common Cold

Christmas may be a time of giving, but nobody wants a cold. Here are some things to minimize your chances of getting this seasonal nuisance. If you do get a cold, look here for some comforting remedies . . . and some solutions for the stains those remedies can cause on your soft flannel sheets!

AN OUNCE OF PREVENTION

- Contrary to the old wives' tale, you can't catch cold from being out in the cold weather. Colds are caused by viruses. Avoid the virus, avoid the cold.

Help prevent colds by washing your hands for as long as it takes to sing "Happy Birthday" . . . twice! That's the amount of time you'll need to wash your hands properly.

• Wash your hands frequently and wash them well. Use water that is comfortably hot. *Always* use soap.

• Avoid touching your eyes, nose and mouth.

• Use tissues instead of handkerchiefs, if at all possible. Tissues are more easily disposed of, along with their germs!

• Don't leave tissues in an open trash can. Dispose of them in a plastic bag kept just for that purpose. You don't want anyone else picking up your germs!

• Try not to share things with someone who is ill. That includes towels, glasses and cooking utensils.

Be particularly vigilant about sharing phones. Use a soft cloth dipped in Listerine® Mouthwash or rubbing alcohol to swab down phone mouthpieces, door handles and computer keyboards. Alcohol wipes work well, too.

• Continue to share kisses—there's nothing like a little love when you're sick. Just confine it to the cheeks.

COLD CARE

• Keep your feet warm. Believe it or not, cold feet can cause your nostrils to become cold and dry, and that can aggravate your cold.

• Wash bedding and pajamas in the hottest possible water.

• The fragrance of fabric softener can irritate delicate noses, so soften flannel sheets and cotton towels with ¼ cup of white vinegar when you have a cold.

> *Make sure you check the date on those cold medicines before you take them.*

• Rubbing some Vicks Vapor Rub® on the outside of your throat and chest will soothe that congestion, no matter how old you are.

• Put a dash of wintergreen oil in a basin of hot water, lower your face to the water (no closer than twelve inches, though), and put a towel over your head to create a tent. Breathe deeply for some much-needed relief.

> *Prone to cold sores? Dab on some Pepto Bismol® when you feel that first tingle, and chances are the sore won't make an appearance!*

HUMIDIFIER HEAVEN

Moist air is heaven to dry throats and nasal passages, but if you don't keep your humidifier clean and free from mold, you may find your cold aggravated by airborne pollutants.

Remove mineral deposits from detachable parts, such as the plastic rotor tube and locking ring, by submerging them in a pot of hot white vinegar. Bring a pot of vinegar to boil, remove it from the stove, and then immerse the tube and ring in the vinegar for about five minutes. Rinse well in clear water and make sure that all parts are dry before returning them to the unit.

Clean a humidifier by swishing around a solution of 1 cup of bleach in 1 gallon of water in the container that holds the water, allowing it to soak for a few minutes, if necessary. Scrub any mineral deposits with a brush and then rinse. Make sure the humidifier is cool and empty before you start.

WHAT TO DO FOR THOSE COLD MEDICATION STAINS

Rubs, liniments, eardrops and ointments are oil-based stains, so you should treat these as soon as you can. Rubbing the stain with a good waterless hand cleaner such as GOJO Crème Waterless Hand Cleaner™ is your best bet. Apply directly to the stain, and rub it in well with your thumb and forefinger. Wait 10 minutes, then apply a good stain remover, such as Zout®, before laundering in the hottest possible water.

Baby wipes are great for removing stains caused by medicated ointments. Rub the stained fabric firmly with the baby wipe, then pretreat and launder as usual.

Cough syrups and other red-based stains can be removed quite effectively with Wine Away Red Wine Stain Remover™ or Red Erase™. Apply liberally, as directed on the container, then launder as usual. Alternatively, soak the stained area in 1 cup of warm water and 1 tablespoon of salt.

Fabric stained from hot toddies and medicated drinks should be flushed under cool, running water as soon as possible. Be sure to direct the water to the *wrong* side of the fabric. Next, make a paste with 20 Mule Team® Borax and cool water. Use about 2 parts borax to 1 part water, adding more water as needed to create a pastelike consistency. Apply to the fabric, then have a cup of tea and watch your favorite sitcom. Once 30 minutes have passed, it's time to loosen the mixture by applying more cool water. Work the loosened mixture between your thumb and forefinger, then launder as usual in the hottest possible water for the fabric type.

Americans suffer from more than one billion colds a year. That's nothing to sneeze at!

Let's Dish!

Mom made these cookies every year for as long as I can remember. When I got old enough I got to "help"—I loved the decorating part best and I admit to sneaking a bite of the dough, not a healthy thing to do.

The Queen Mother's Christmas Cookies

2 cups flour

1 teaspoon baking powder

½ teaspoon baking soda

½ teaspoon salt

½ cup shortening

1 cup sugar

¼ teaspoon nutmeg

¼ teaspoon lemon extract or grated rind

2 eggs

Mix together the dry ingredients in a bowl.

Using a mixer, cream together the shortening, sugar, nutmeg and lemon extract until well blended and light in color. Beat in the eggs and add the dry ingredients a little at a time, beating between additions.

Chill the mixture in the refrigerator for an hour or so, and then bake in one of the following ways:

Roll out the dough and cut with cookie cutters and place on a greased cookie sheet.

Drop by rounded tablespoons onto a greased cookie sheet and flatten with the bottom of a drinking glass dipped in flour.

Decorate the cookies by placing a raisin or nut in the center. Sprinkle with granulated sugar—colored granulated sugar is nice for Christmas.

Bake in a 375-degree oven for 10 to 12 minutes. Do not overbake. Makes about 3 dozen cookies.

Think I'll go call my mom . . .

Resource Guide

ACT NATURAL™ CLOTHS: See Euronet USA.

AT HOME ALL-PURPOSE CLEANER®: See Soapworks®.

BORAX: Better known as 20 Mule Team® Borax, this laundry additive can be found in the detergent aisle.

BRILLIANT BLEACH®: See Soapworks®.

CALGON WATER SOFTENER®: Look for it with the laundry additives at the grocery store.

CHAMOIS: Found in hardware stores and home centers.

CHARCOAL: This is the type made for fish tanks and is available at pet supply stores.

CLEAN SHIELD® SURFACE TREATMENT (formerly Invisible Shield®): This is such a wonderful product—just the name gives me goose bumps! It turns all of those hard-to-clean surfaces in your home (tub, shower, shower doors, sinks, counters, stovetops, windows, any surface that is not wood or painted) into nonstick surfaces that can be cleaned with water and a soft cloth. No more soap scum or hard-water deposits! It never builds up on surfaces so it won't make them slippery, and it's nontoxic, so you can use it on dishes and food surfaces, too. Call 1-800-528-3149 to find a supplier near you.

CLEAR AMMONIA: There are two types of ammonia, clear and sudsy (sometimes called "cloudy"). Clear contains no soap and should be used where suggested for that reason.

CUTICLE REMOVER: The gel you apply to your cuticles to soften them. Let's be clear, it is cuticle remover, NOT nail polish remover.

DENATURED ALCOHOL: This is an industrial alcohol reserved for heavy-duty cleaning. Don't use it near an open flame, and dispose of any rags that were used to apply it outside the home. Launder or clean anything that you treat with it as soon as possible. Look for this in cans at hardware stores and home centers. Remember the Queen's rule: always test in an inconspicuous place before treating a large area with this product.

ENERGINE CLEANING FLUID®: A great spotter. Look for this at the hardware store, the home center and even in some grocery stores (usually on the top shelf with the laundry additives).

EPSOM SALTS: Usually used for medicinal purposes, but handy for household uses, too. Look for it in drugstores.

EURONET USA: Makers of the ACT Natural™ Microfiber Cloths and Mops. They clean and disinfect without chemicals, using only water. They have been scientifically proven to kill germs and bacteria and even come with a warranty. They are easy to use, great for people with allergies, and can be cleaned and sanitized in the washer (this is particularly important with the mop). Use them in the kitchen, bathroom, to spot carpet, on windows, mirrors, hard furniture, in the car, virtually anywhere you clean. Call 1-888-638-2882 or visit www.euronetusa.com. They are a wonderful investment. My mop is almost two years old and is still doing the job.

FELS-NAPTHA SOAP®: What a wonderful laundry spotter and

cleaner this is. You'll find it in the bar soap section of the grocery store. It's usually on the bottom shelf in a small stack and always has dust on it, because nobody knows what to use it for. Call 1-800-45PUREX.

FINE STEEL WOOL: Look for the symbol "0000" and the word "fine." And don't try soap-filled steel wool pads. They are not acceptable substitutes.

FRESH BREEZE LAUNDRY SOAP®: See Soapworks®.

GLYCERIN: Look for glycerin in drugstores in the hand cream section. Always purchase plain glycerin, not the type containing rose water.

GOJO CRÈME WATERLESS HAND CLEANER™: People with greasy hands have used this product for years. It's a hand cleaner and so much more. Look for it at home centers and hardware stores.

HYDROGEN PEROXIDE: Choose the type that you use on cuts and to gargle with—not the type used to bleach hair. That will remove color from carpet or fabric.

LINSEED OIL: You'll find this at the hardware store, usually in the paint and staining section. It is combustible, so use care in disposing of rags or paper towels used to apply it. Keep it in the garage or basement away from open flame.

MEAT TENDERIZER: Use the unseasoned variety please, or you will have a whole new stain to deal with. Store brands work fine.

NAIL POLISH REMOVER: I caution you to use nonacetone polish remover, which is much less aggressive than acetone polish remover. (Straight acetone is exceedingly strong.) Use only where recommended and with great care. Look for this product at beauty supply stores.

NATURAL SPONGE: A natural sponge is the best sponge you will ever use. It has hundreds of natural "scrubbing fingers" that make any wall-washing job speed by. Look for these at home centers and hardware stores and choose a nice size to fit your hand. Wash them in lukewarm water with gentle suds. You can put them in the washing machine if you avoid combining them with fabrics that have lint.

NONGEL TOOTHPASTE: This is just a fancy name for old-fashioned plain white toothpaste. Gels just don't work, so don't even try.

ODORZOUT™: A fabulous, dry, 100 percent natural deodorizer. It's nontoxic, so you can use it anyplace you have a smell or a stink. It is especially effective on pet urine odors, and since it is used dry it is simple to apply. Call 1-800-88STINK, or visit their website at www.88stink.com.

PREPARATION H®: Sold in drugstores. An ointment intended for hemorrhoids.

PUREX® LAUNDRY DETERGENT: Available wherever detergents are sold or call 1-800-45PUREX for a location near you.

RED ERASE®: Made by the same people who make Wine Away Red Wine Stain Remover™, Red Erase™ is for red stains such as red pop, grape juice, grape jelly, etc. Look for it at Linens 'n Things, or call 1-888-WINEAWAY for a store location near you.

RUST REMOVER: These are serious products, so follow the directions carefully. Look for products like Whink® and Rust Magic® at hardware stores and home centers.

SHAVING CREAM: The cheaper brands work fine, and shaving cream works better than gel.

SOAPWORKS®: Manufacturer of wonderful nontoxic, user- and earth-friendly cleaning, laundry, and personal care products. Try their At Home All-Purpose Cleaner®, originally designed for allergy and asthma sufferers. Soapworks® products are very effective, and they are economical, so everyone can use them. Call 1-800-699-9917 or visit their website at www.soapworks.com.

SOOT AND DIRT REMOVAL SPONGE: These are used to clean walls, wallpaper, lampshades and even soot. They also remove pet hair from upholstery. These big brick erasers are available at home centers and hardware stores, usually near the wallpaper supplies. Clean them by washing in a pail of warm water and liquid dish soap, rinse well and allow to dry before using again.

SPOT SHOT INSTANT CARPET STAIN REMOVER®: My all-time favorite carpet spotter and I have tried them all! Try SPOT SHOT UPHOLSTERY STAIN REMOVER® too. Available most everywhere, or call 1-800-848-4389.

SQUEEGEE: When buying a squeegee for washing windows, look for a good quality one with a replaceable rubber blade. Always be sure that the rubber blade is soft and flexible for best results. Look for these at hardware stores, home centers and janitorial supply companies. They come in different widths, so be sure to think about the size windows, etc., that you are going to use it for. A 12-inch blade is a good starting point.

TANG™ BREAKFAST DRINK: Yes, this is the product that the astronauts took to the moon! It is also a great cleaner. (Store brands work just as well.)

TRISODIUM PHOSPHATE (TSP): Cleaning professionals have used this product for years. It is wonderful for washing walls, garage floors and any tough cleaning job. Look for it at hardware stores, home centers and janitorial supply stores. Wear rubber gloves when using it.

TYPEWRITER ERASER: A thing of the past, but still available at office supply stores. Shaped like a pencil with a little brush where the pencil eraser would be, they can be sharpened like a pencil and will last for years.

UN-DU™: Removes sticky residue from fabric and hard surfaces. Look for it at office supply stores, home center stores and hardware stores.

WASHING SODA: I like Arm and Hammer® Washing Soda, which can be found in the detergent aisle at the grocery store along with other laundry additives. No, you cannot substitute baking soda, it is a different product!

WAX CRAYONS: These are sold in hardware stores and home centers and come in various wood colors for concealing scratches in wood surfaces. Don't be fooled by the color name; try to take along a sample of what you need to patch to get the best possible match.

WD-40® LUBRICANT: I bet you will find a can in your garage or basement. Fine spray oil for lubricating all kinds of things, it's a wonderful product for regenerating grease so that it can be removed from clothes. Look for WD-40® at the hardware store, home center and even the grocery store.

WINE AWAY RED WINE STAIN REMOVER™: This unbelievable product can remove red stains, such as red wine, red pop, cranberry juice, red food coloring, grape juice, etc., from carpet and fabric. It is totally nontoxic and made from fruit and vegetable extracts. I just can't believe how well it works! Look for it where liquor is sold or call 1-888-WINEAWAY for a store location near you.

WITCH HAZEL: An astringent/toning product sold at drugstores.

ZOUT® STAIN REMOVER: A very versatile laundry prespotter, Zout® is thicker than most laundry spotters, so you can target the spot. It really works! Look for it in grocery stores and places like Kmart, etc.

The Queen of Clean®
of
Conquers Clutter

This book is dedicated to my friends and fans in
Arizona, where it all started.
You made me the Queen of Clean.
Because of all of you, it's good to be Queen.

Acknowledgments

Special thanks to everyone at KTVK-TV's *Good Morning Arizona,* where it all began.

Beth McDonald, and Bill Austin, hosts of *Beth and Bill in the Morning,* KESZ Radio, Phoenix, AZ. You have been with me every step of the way and I have learned so much from you about radio, integrity, and kindness.

Louise Burke, Publisher at Pocket Books. Thank you for your tireless dedication to quality.

Brenda Copeland, editor and friend. Thank you for ridding my manuscript of clutter.

Jaime Putorti, Carole Schwindeller, Cathy Gruhn, Marisa Stella, Barry Porter, and everyone at Pocket Books. Your efforts make me look so good.

Duane Dooling. Your friendship is a treasure.

Claire Bush, for your invaluable help in putting this book together.

Special friends Brian Gilbert, Norman Clark, Jim Ranaldo, Lisa and Bobby Aguilar, Betty Archambeau, Peggy

Barker, Alan Centofante, Catherine Holland, and all our neighbors who put up with camera crews and satellite trucks at all hours of the day and night.

Dr. Kevin Mueller and staff. Thanks for the smile!

Win and Carolyn Holden, partners, but more important, friends.

Last, but most important, I thank my family. The Queen Mother, who is also my best friend; husband John, The King, who is with me each step of the way; and our combined family: David and Janette; Victoria; Pat and Laura, John, Justin, April and Desmond; Nanette, David and Patrick; Nancy, Doug, Drew, Ashley and Lilly Ann. Cousin, Charlene Staub. The Pussycat Princess, Zoey, for providing research material. Without the love and support of all of you, there would be no joy in the palace.

To all of you who are reading this, I thank you for Conquering Clutter with the Queen of Clean®.

Contents

Introduction

A place for everything and everything in its place. Who hasn't heard that phrase? And who hasn't thought of it as a fantasy? No one has clutter in their fantasy, but in reality, everyone does. Let's face it: No matter how big your home or how much storage space you have, clutter always seems to have a life of its own, abiding by that law of physics that says matter expands to fill the space available. If you have to stop to clear a work area every time you start to carry out a task like cleaning, cooking, or laundry; if you're constantly losing your keys and you have to wade through eighteen months of unread *Reader's Digests* to get to the *TV Guide;* then you have a clutter problem. But in case you think clutter is just an aggravation, consider this: Clutter is costly! Have you ever:

- Paid late fees on a bill because you misplaced it until it was too late? Those credit card bills are high enough without tacking on late fees.

- Bought duplicates of the same item without knowing it? Okay, it's nice to stock up on lightbulbs, but twelve boxes?

- Forked over unnecessary fines at the library or video store? Sure, *Caddyshack* may have given you a lot of laughs, but forget to return the tape on time and that $8 fine will do a lot to wipe the smile off your face.

Mistakes happen, but habitual disorganization can lead to more than your fair share of unhappy consequences. Consider a good friend of mine who carefully arranged every detail of her wedding—but forgot to bring the key to the reception hall for the caterers. While the food and supplies were being unloaded on the sidewalk, the frantic bride had to dispatch a friend to her home for the missing key. The unlucky caterers had to hastily set up the wedding feast while the ceremony was taking place. Not an auspicious beginning to a lifetime union. Then there was the mother who baked and iced two dozen cupcakes for her son's class birthday party—and left them on the kitchen counter in a last-minute dash to get out the door on time. And what about the health care executive whose closet was so hopelessly disorganized that he once attended an important meeting wearing one black and one brown shoe! Do any of these stories sound familiar? Situations like these are upsetting and stressful, but you'll be happy to know they're also unnecessary—a little less clutter and a little more organization is all it takes.

You know, the reasons for holding on to clutter are as many and varied as clutter itself. Often we are loath to get rid of a particular item because we think it might come in handy "sometime" or "somewhere." We hold on to broken goods, thinking that the day will come when we'll have the time or the know-how to repair them or scavenge the parts to repair something else. We keep possessions because they have sentimental value, or because they hold promises that we aren't willing to part with. I have a friend whose shelves are full of good intentions: Tae Bo™ tapes that were going to transform her into a feisty size 6, a French language course for a trip that never materialized, a basket full of wool that one day hopes to become a sweater. Is that you? It doesn't have to be.

We all have our favorite things that we don't want to part with. That's fine. Nobody but the most strident organizational fiend would suggest that you get rid of all your sentimental favorites in your clutter clear out. And yet, what happens when everything is a sentimental favorite, when you're so crowded by things from the past that you don't have room for the present? Memories are great—until you have to dust them.

I'm going to let you in on a trade secret. You *can* get out from all that clutter. You can live a life that's more organized and, consequently, less stressful. And you don't have to spend money to do it. The key to getting out from under all that clutter and getting organized is not a matter of adding anything: it's the thoughtful elimination of time- and space-wasting things. In most cases, you don't need to buy a single new product to get yourself organized; you can use what you've already got to control the clutter monster in your life—and keep it tamed.

You already have what it takes to conquer clutter and get organized. So let's work together to get it done. It's easier than you think!

CHAPTER I

Twenty
Questions

*E*nquiring minds want to know, right? I'm a Queen with a mission—to help you find out what will work best to keep your life clutter-free and organized. Just go down this list and answer these twenty questions. And be honest. We don't give out demerits. This isn't about *right* and *wrong*. It's about identifying your strong points—knowing what you're good at, what you have a knack for—as well as finding out where you need to improve your clutter-containing skills. Just remember: No matter how big your home, the biggest room is usually room for improvement!

1. Are you constantly running late?
   ❏ Never   ❏ Sometimes   ❏ Often

2. Do you have trouble letting go of objects that have long outlived their use?
   ❏ Never   ❏ Sometimes   ❏ Often

3. Are you using eyeliner and lipstick to write down messages because you can't seem to find a pencil or pen in your drawers?
   ❑ Never   ❑ Sometimes   ❑ Often

4. During the last six months, have you had to search for your car keys ...
   ❑ Never   ❑ Sometimes   ❑ Often

5. Do you organize and reorganize, but always end up with the same amount of stuff?
   ❑ Never   ❑ Sometimes   ❑ Often

6. Have you ever run the baby's formula through the automatic coffee maker because the microwave is used for storage and you couldn't find a pan?
   ❑ Never   ❑ Sometimes   ❑ Often

7. Have you ever missed a doctor appointment or social engagement because you just plain "forgot" all about it?
   ❑ Never   ❑ Sometimes   ❑ Often

8. Is your closet filled to the rafters with clothing and shoes? Does it contain clothes of all sizes?
   ❑ Never   ❑ Sometimes   ❑ Often

9. How many times during the past year have you given unneeded items to charity?
   ❑ Never   ❑ Sometimes   ❑ Often

10. Have you ever tucked in a pile of clothes because there is so much stuff on the bed you can't tell if your child is in there or not?
    ❑ Never   ❑ Sometimes   ❑ Often

11. Have you ever found an item you needed—after you'd purchased its replacement?
❑ Never ❑ Sometimes ❑ Often

12. Do the kids think that everybody turns their underwear inside out on Tuesday, Thursday, and Saturday to get an extra day's wear out of it?
❑ Never ❑ Sometimes ❑ Often

13. Are there papers on your desk that you haven't looked through for over a month?
❑ Never ❑ Sometimes ❑ Often

14. Do your neighbors come to your house first every time there is a scavenger hunt?
❑ Never ❑ Sometimes ❑ Often

15. When you start cleaning and organizing your house, do you tend to get sidetracked and start another project?
❑ Never ❑ Sometimes ❑ Often

16. Do you generally know what time it is, or do you usually need to consult your watch?
❑ Never ❑ Sometimes ❑ Often

17. Is your idea of clearing off the countertop sliding everything off it into the wastebasket or drawer?
❑ Never ❑ Sometimes ❑ Often

18. Does your car sit outside because you need your garage for storage?
❑ Never ❑ Sometimes ❑ Often

19. Are you able to shut all of your dresser drawers without clothes hanging out the sides?
   ❑ Never   ❑ Sometimes   ❑ Often

20. Do you have to remove dirty pots and pans from your oven before you can use it?
   ❑ Never   ❑ Sometimes   ❑ Often

Now it's time to check your responses. For each time you answered NEVER, give yourself 1 point. For each SOMETIMES answer, give yourself 2 points, and give yourself 3 points for each time you answered OFTEN. Now add up your score and let's see how you did.

If you scored 20 to 35 points, you are indeed a royal organizer. Good for you! Use this book to help you hone your best organizing instincts and make yourself the Queen of your own castle. You probably have a lot of the basics in use, so now's the time to pay attention to the small organizing details you may previously have overlooked. Fine-tune your storage systems and banish clutter once and for all, and make sure you are spending enough time on evaluating and eliminating.

If you scored 36 to 45 points, you fit into the largest group of clutter conquerors. Constantly trying to improve, you nevertheless feel like you are running on a treadmill as the clutter continues to grow ... and grow. ... You're not part of the remedial organizing group (see the next paragraph), but you still have a ways to go to get your palace organized and clutter-free. Why don't you start with the chapters that pertain to your biggest problems? You'll make great strides if you really question and take stock of the areas you want to conquer—find out what's not working before you come up with solutions. Take it in small stages and work through your clutter crisis area by area.

If you scored 46 to 60 points, then, yes, let's just say it—*you have a clutter problem. A BIG ONE!* But we're not going to lock you in the dungeon and throw away the key (there probably wouldn't be room for you, anyway). Chances are you look at the clutter accumulating around you and feel defeated before you begin, and so haven't begun. Until now. Let me walk you through this book. Select a small area to start your clutter busting so that you can step back and appreciate your efforts almost immediately. Once you begin and get a feel for conquering clutter (even in the smallest way), you'll begin to believe in order again. Remember, it took time to collect all of that clutter, so it will take time to remove it. Read on to elevate your royal status in your home and eliminate some of the stress that you deal with every day. And don't get discouraged. Rome wasn't organized in a day!

CHAPTER 2

Getting Started

*A*re you a Harried Harriet? Harriet unlocks the front door with a heavy heart. It's past dinnertime already. An unexpected phone call and a long line at the supermarket have made her late—again. Dodging a lone sock in the hallway (how did that get there?), she can hear the answering machine go off: "Mom! Pick up! I'm waiting for a ride at soccer practice!" Harriet slides her bags full of groceries onto the kitchen counter, where the movie the family watched last night still sits patiently waiting. Darn, she meant to return that to the video store. That's another $3 in fines. The dog has chewed a slipper again. His leash has been missing since yesterday, and no one has been able to take him for a much needed walk. Harriet is—well, harried! She's tired, hungry, and frustrated. Dinner's not made, and the house is a mess. Does this sound like the end of your average workday?

Life is becoming increasingly complex. Spending time at home should be a relaxing, fun experience, not an exercise in frustration. There is an easier way to live than Harriet's daily routine. Wouldn't it be much nicer to come home like Peaceful Pauline? Pauline opens the front door, placing her keys in the basket on the hall table and her handbag on a handy wall hook nearby—right next to the dog's leash! Tonight's dinner is already cooked and ready to be popped into the oven. Last week, Pauline cooked a double batch of spaghetti and froze the second half for another day. That leaves half an hour to change clothes and read and sort the mail before it's time to eat. After dinner, the kids can take the dog for a walk. This evening, the family will watch a video together, and Pauline might even have time to call her mother for a chat. No wonder Pauline is peaceful!

What's the difference between feeling like a Harried Harriet and a Peaceful Pauline? It comes down to this: clutter control and organization. Controlling clutter and organizing your life may seem like an impossible task, but just think of all the impossible tasks that you do every day. And think how much easier they would be if you weren't surrounded by clutter and chaos! Conquering clutter really does pay off—in fact, conquering clutter has such terrific benefits that once you begin, you'll soon become hooked. If you've gotten used to living in clutter and chaos, you'll be pleasantly surprised to find how enjoyable conquering clutter and getting organized can be. You can relax in your own home, find things when you need them, enjoy your day-to-day activities, and feel in control of your life. And, if you're like most of us in these days of instant gratification, take heart: conquering clutter pays off immediately!

I once had a fortune cookie that read: "Every journey, no matter how long, begins with a single step." What is the first step in getting organized? Having a system, of course. A workable solution for daily life that really gets results. And that's where I come in! I've worked up a little system so that you can take me with you from room to room, so you can let me—the *QUEEN*—be your guide! It's a little reminder to help you follow through with your clutter-busting intentions, to keep you from getting distracted or feeling defeated before you begin. Give it (me!) a try.

*Q*uestion

*U*npack

*E*valuate

*E*liminate

*N*eaten up!

*Q*uestion. What is the purpose of this room, cupboard, drawer? What do I see that doesn't work here? How can I make better use of this space? Why am I keeping this article of clothing? What am I happy with? What works here and what doesn't? If the twins are teenagers, why do we still have two shelves of Dr. Seuss books on display? If the summer sun is shining, why do we have four mismatched mittens on the table in the hall?

*U*npack. Get it all out in the open, one thing at a time. For example, if you're working in a closet, do only the shoes first. Sort through one shelf in the linen closet. Remove the contents of one drawer in the kitchen. Remember, only by taking things out will you really have a sense of what you have and what you need to do with it. You can't conquer clutter if you can't see it.

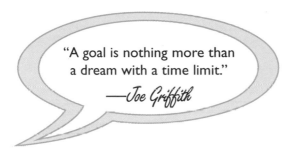

"A goal is nothing more than a dream with a time limit."

—*Joe Griffith*

*E*valuate. It's judgment day. Ask some questions: When was the last time I used this? Do I really need this? If so, is this where the item should be? Then prepare to stash it or trash it. Okay, I know, this is the hard part. If your heart is saying you need it and your mind says it hasn't been used since Nixon was president, sometimes it's hard to be impartial. Look at things as if you were helping a friend. If the things weren't your possessions, what would you do? Then do it.

*E*liminate. One bag is for the neighbor, a charity, or the school fund-raiser. The other bag is headed straight for the trash. Every item that isn't destined to go back into that drawer, closet, or shelf belongs to one of these two bags. Get rid of the excuses for keeping things while you're at it. I've heard them all: *I might need that someday. Aunt Margaret gave me that. Somebody might be able to make use of that, so I'll hang on to it.* Eliminate your excuses as you eliminate your excess stuff. They're both clutter, and you'll live better without them.

*N*eaten Up. This is the fun part. Oh, how clever you'll feel as you admire your rows of neatly organized shoes, freshly straightened spices, or tidy stacks of towels. This is the time you get to put things where you want them and stand back and admire your work. Don't be afraid to be unconventional. If you like storing your underwear rolled in clear hanging racks on the back of the bedroom door, that's fine, as long as it works for you. Try things out, and change them if they don't work the way you hoped they would.

So, now that you have a system, what's the best way to use it? Start small. I'd like to suggest that you devote just 15 minutes at a time to this process—that's all it takes to really get results. If you like, you can even use your kitchen timer to remind you—or release you, if you're really resisting the idea. So often we feel discouraged because a task seems overwhelming. This simple 15-minute rule lets you off the hook. You don't have to eliminate your clutter all in one day. You can chip at it over time. Believe me, I've tried many ways to manage my day-to-day life, and this is the only one that works consistently. Don't be surprised if your 15 minutes slip away before you realize it! Then, if you like, you can reset the timer for another 15 minutes and tackle another drawer, shelf, closet, or box. It's up to you! You never realized organizing could actually be fun, did you? C'mon. Let's get started!

CHAPTER 3

You Can Take It with You

Making Cents of Your Wallet

I told you we were going to start small! Let's begin by tackling that wallet—you know, the one that still holds your high school library card and the ticket stubs from your senior prom... (Not to mention the shoe rental receipt from your bowling league that ended in 1994, and the unlucky lottery ticket from last year's big draw.) Don't fret. Ten minutes is all it takes—if you take the  with you, that is.

*N*ot only will organizing your walle get you started on your clutter bust ing—and make you feel more orga nized almost instantly—it may eve improve your health! Men can actuall develop back and hip problems fron sitting on that bulging wallet; wome may find their wallet is the heavies thing in their purse next to the cos metic bag. And heavy purses can mea sore shoulders.

*Q*uestion: *What do I want from this space? A streamlined wallet in which I can find things when I need them, a wallet that doesn't bulge or pop open unexpectedly.*

*U*npack: Pull out your wallet, take a seat at a table or desk, and get ready to de-clutter. Empty your wallet. Remove everything—yes, money too!

*E*valuate: Now put the contents of your wallet into three piles. One pile should contain discards, the things you are *really* going to throw out this time, such as the photo that "made you look skinny" in 1992. One stack will hold items to be put away or stored somewhere else. These are things like your original social security card, original birth certificate, and the directions for your personal organizer. (If you don't know how it works now, you never will.) The last grouping will contain the things you *really* need and will return to your wallet. These are items such as your driver's license, credit cards, organ donor card, emergency medical information, and the all-important money!

*E*liminate: Once you have finished sorting, go through the items you'll be discarding one last time, to be sure you aren't throwing out anything you should keep. Don't discard receipts from items you may still want to return, or might need for warranty information, for instance. These items need to be filed. Phone numbers you've jotted down should be transferred to your address book, and business cards should be put away in a Rolodex® or other appropriate place. Now is the time to get the scissors and cut up expired or unwanted credit cards too. Cut them or shred them so that the number is not readable. You might even want to mix the pieces up in separate trash baskets. Remember, even though your old card is expired, the number on the new one is the same with a new expiration date.

*N*eaten Up: Now take some time to reorganize your wallet. Think about how you use the things in your wallet and what you have to search for each time you want it. If you have a frequent-coffee-drinker card, and you use it each morning, put it where you can find it the minute you open your wallet. Organize your paper money by denomination and you will never give away a ten-dollar bill thinking it's a single. Tuck the seldom used items in the out-of-the-way pockets. Keep frequently used credit cards up front and make sure they are always tucked in well. If you carry emergency medical information, keep it in a prominent spot, perhaps a window area in the wallet.

A Word to the Wise

Don't keep valuable original papers such as social security cards or birth certificates in your wallet. The Social Security Administration recommends that you keep these documents with your valuable papers and bring them out only when required, such as when you get a new job or open a bank account. A lost or stolen social security card could create huge problems, so take a moment now to remove it and your birth certificate from your wallet. Take the time also to jot down the numbers of your credit cards, driver's license, and health insurance cards from your wallet or, better still, photocopy them on both sides. File this information in a safe place. Should your wallet get stolen, having this information at your fingertips will save you time and maybe even money.

If you've had the unfortunate experience of losing a wallet, then you already know the importance of canceling your credit cards, but there's more: call the three national credit-reporting organizations to place an immediate fraud alert on your name and social security number. A fraud alert means that you must be contacted by phone before any new charges can be made on your credit cards. No contact, no charges—simple! In addition, a call to the Social Security Fraud Line ensures that your social security number cannot be used to forge new documents or for any other fraudulent purpose. The numbers you need are:

Equifax® 1–888–766–0008

Experian® (formerly TRW) 1–888–397–3742

Trans Union™ 1–800–680–7289

Social Security Administration Fraud Line
1–800–269–0271

Loosen Those Purse Strings

Any man who has ever heard the words "Can you hold my purse for a minute, dear?" knows how heavy a woman's handbag can be. Many women use shoulder bags that are so heavy that carrying around these "mini-suitcases" leads to neck and shoulder pain. Keeping purses as light and clutter-free as possible can eliminate many aches and pains! Ladies, now it's time to organize those purses.

Again, empty everything out on a counter, desk, or work-table. Next, unpack, sorting out the obvious junk (used tissues, fuzzy Life Savers, gum without wrappers, and that Christmas card from two years ago), and discard. Now we'll work with what's left. Rescue the necessary items, such as your wallet, keys, cosmetic bag, cell phone, and appointment book, and set aside. It's time to evaluate and eliminate the rest of the items. Think "lighten up"—your neck and shoulders will thank you for this!

You should need only one cosmetic bag. Try using a light-colored one: it will be easier to find inside the dark interior of your purse. Empty out your cosmetic bag, and give the inside a quick wipe-down using a clean cloth or damp paper towel moistened with your favorite dish soap. Wipe dry, and replace only the cosmetics you really use. Be ruthless here: one lipstick, a compact, some eyedrops if you use them, a spare mascara and eyeshadow, should be all you need. Discard any broken or old tubes of makeup, keeping in mind that cosmetics manufacturers recommend replacing your eye makeup at least every six months to lessen the risk of infection to delicate eye tissue.

Turn your purse inside out or hold it upside down, and give it a good shake. Wipe out the interior with a clean, soft cloth. Revitalize your leather handbag by running a damp cloth over a bar of moisturizing facial soap (such as Dove®), then wiping down your purse; no need to rinse. Patent leather bags will shine like new if you rub a little petroleum jelly into the surface and buff with a soft cloth. Vinyl purses can be cleaned with a damp cloth and a little dishwashing soap, then wiped dry. Remove stubborn scuff marks from vinyl with lighter fluid, taking care to dispose of the rag or paper towels outside. Now for the fun part. When your purse is clean and dry, neaten up by returning your wallet, cosmetic bag, keys, and other necessary items. If you have a purse with different compartments, try keeping each item in the same place so you can simply reach for things rather than hunting for them. It helps when you are feeling for something you need. (I always keep my wallet on the left side of my purse and my cosmetic bag on the right.)

Backpack—Or Pack Mule?

If you feel like a pack mule every time you shoulder your backpack, it's time to lighten up. Serious hikers know that the maximum weight to be carried in a backpack is 38 pounds—and that's for a three-day hike, folks! Anything more can cause back and neck injuries. Lest you scoff at this figure, step over to the bathroom scale and weigh your pack. You may be amazed at what you've been toting around. Parents, in particular, should take care that kids empty their backpacks regularly. Those schoolbooks are heavy, and excess weight on the back is not good for growing strong, healthy spines.

Again, you'll want to empty your backpack and examine the contents. Get rid of old papers, leaky pens, that leftover peanut-butter-and-jelly sandwich, and empty water bottles. If you reuse your water bottles, fill them with warm water and add one teaspoon or so of baking soda. Put the lid on and shake well to clean the bottle. Make sure you wipe the neck of the bottle well with a damp cloth and baking soda, and then rinse well, refill, and put in the refrigerator. Water bottles do need to be cleaned regularly, and using baking

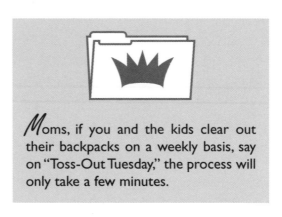

*M*oms, if you and the kids clear out their backpacks on a weekly basis, say on "Toss-Out Tuesday," the process will only take a few minutes.

soda instead of dish soap will eliminate that soapy taste in your water. Arrange books and folders in one stack, personal items like headphones, water bottles, cell phones, and cosmetic bags in another. Wipe down the inside of the backpack with a clean, damp cloth and let dry. Return books, papers and personal items to the pack, and keep like items grouped together: books, folders, papers, and tape in one pocket; headphones, cell phones, and spare batteries in another; lunch bag and water bottle kept separately. You can't always have everything in an exact place, but at least you'll know what's in each pocket without searching through all of them.

Now step back and admire your work. Almost makes you want to go back to school, doesn't it?

A Brief Word About Briefcases

Do you use a briefcase? Then follow these steps for de-cluttering your "office away from the office." Again, start on a flat surface and remove everything. Discard obvious clutter such as sandwich wrappers, junk mail, and last week's newspaper. Place receipts in one pile, files and papers in another, electronic equipment like laptops, headsets, and cell phones in a third. If you need receipts for business purposes, file them. Otherwise, toss them away. You can use ordinary legal-size envelopes for receipts, labeling them by month for easy reference. Use manila folders to organize your papers: they're cheap, neat, easy to label, and don't take up much space. Go through your folders, discarding outdated paperwork; then return everything to the inside of the briefcase. Again, group related items together and arrange the interior of your case the same way each time so that you can find files, pens, or paper clips without searching.

See, that wasn't so hard. A few minutes spent organizing the things you use each and every day is worth the time you'll save trying to find that elusive credit card or the receipts for this month's expense report.

CHAPTER 4

Enter at Your Own Risk

*I*s your entry hall so filled with day-to-day clutter that you can barely get through the room, let alone find anything in it? Do you sometimes feel that your front door should have a sign posted that says Enter at Your Own Risk? When you come home, do you have to wade through a pile of shoes, boots, backpacks, several empty coffee cups, and a week's worth of newspapers to get to the front closet? Whether up front or at the side of the house, entry halls are often very small spaces—and small spaces have a habit of attracting clutter. So let's continue with my "start small" approach and tackle the entry hall before you lose another umbrella—or goodness me, your youngest child.

Approach this task in 15-minute blocks of time. Do what you can in that period and then stop if you want to. Of course, if you are feeling so energized with all you've achieved and want to keep going, that's okay too.

The key to organizing the entryway is to assign a logical space for things that are used every day, then stick to it. This will get you out the door and on your way to school, work, or errands without searching for necessary items.

Welcome

Step outside (careful, don't lock yourself out) and walk up to the door. Is the front walk swept and clear of clutter? Can you see all seven letters on the WELCOME mat? If the entry looks clean and appealing, good for you! If not, grab a broom and give the front porch a good sweeping. While you're at it, pull down any cobwebs you see hanging around. Odds and ends like skateboards, dog dishes, or old newspapers should be picked up and tossed out, or assigned to their proper place. Take a moment now to mix up a bucket of warm water with a squirt of your favorite all-purpose cleaner to wash down the front door if it needs it. If your doormat has seen better days, consider replacing it. You can find inexpensive doormats in a variety of designs at discount stores. (Best not to get one that says "Smith" if your name is "Jones"—even if it is on sale!)

Do Come In!

Now step inside the entryway. Pick up everything that doesn't belong, and ask yourself honestly, "Do I really need this?" It pays to be ruthless. You don't want to just move objects from one area of your home to another. This just spreads clutter; it doesn't eliminate it.

*R*emember you can only stay organized once you accept that *Less is more.* Less clutter equals less cleaning time, less frustration, and more space and enjoyment for you and your family.

Do you have a hall table or stand? Great. Let's start with that. Empty out any drawers, and toss out mystery keys and other clutter. Restock with a working flashlight, a couple of candles and some matches, and a supply of spare change. A decorative basket on top of the stand can hold mail (incoming and outgoing). Don't have a hall stand? Visit a thrift store or yard sale and keep an open mind. Storage options show up in all sorts of unusual places. A friend of mine bought an old piano bench for a song to use as a hall table; the seat lifted up and was great for storage. There are no rules here, just your imagination.

If you live in a rainy area, an umbrella stand in the corner is a nice touch. Coatracks are handy too, not only for jackets and sweaters but for hanging purses and backpacks. Hooks are a great storage option, especially in households with kids and pets. Make sure when you install the hooks that you leave enough space for even heavy coats to hang freely. You'll want to assign each child his or her own hook, perhaps a different color for each child, and be sure they check this area before they leave for school each morning. Use this area to hang the dog's leash too.

Get into the Closet

Make the most of your hall closet. Keep it well lighted by installing a battery operated light, and add a full-length mirror on the inside of the door. This allows a last-minute check before you go out the door. The mirror will also add a feeling of spaciousness when you open the door for guests.

If you have children, design a kid-friendly storage space in the closet. There are several methods you can use for this—just be sure that your child's possessions are within easy reach.

- You can assign a shelf or a portion of a shelf for each child's backpack, library books, and school papers. Use colored tape or masking tape with colored markers to identify each child's shelf or area.

- Plastic storage cubes are another great option for children's things; each child gets his or her own colored cube for easy identification.

- Over-the-door hangers (the kind used for shoes) can also create more space for storage in a closet. Use clear ones so that you can see what's hiding in each pocket. Again, assign pockets for each child to hold papers, books, gym clothes, and sweaters.

- A mesh laundry bag hung on a hook is great for organizing kids' toys and such.

The hall closet is also a logical place to create an area for pets' supplies too. If Fido wears a sweater or has a special outdoor toy, store that close by. If you use a towel to wipe those wet and muddy doggy paws, store it there too. Pick up a cute decorative basket and attach it to the wall near the leash and keep all of the doggie extras in it. Just remember to leave room for guests' coats.

Departure Area

Organize a "departure area" for everyday things that you use each day, such as your purse, briefcase, backpack, keys, cellular phone, laptop computer, and anything else you'll need to attend to, such as videos or library books that need returning. Don't forget your sports bag for a pre- or post-office workout.

Another handy time-saver in the entryway is a family bulletin board. Create an area for this by using a corkboard for reminder notes such as, "Honey, pick up Patrick from soccer at 5:00" or "Brittany and Stephen, here's the money for your

I like to keep an empty laundry basket in my car trunk for those days when I have lots of things to transport; I load the car the night before, lock the trunk, and in the morning I'm ready to go!

field trip." (Of course, this will only work if you have children named Patrick, Brittany, and Stephen.) Consider dividing the board into a section for each family member with colored tape or ribbon. Don't use a chalk or white board for this purpose; the pens and chalk seem to disappear like magic, and it's frustrating to spend your time searching for something to write on the board with.

Toss-Out Tuesday

Once everything is organized, allow a few quick minutes once a week to sort out anything that doesn't belong. I've had success using a method I call Toss-Out Tuesday. This is the day of the week I spend an extra minute or two sorting through my jewelry box, makeup bag, car glove box—whatever I use on that day—for unneeded items. Staying organized this way doesn't seem like extra work, since I'm doing it as I go along, and if I feel overwhelmed during the week (who doesn't?), I can always do Toss-Out Tuesday even if it's Friday or Monday. Try it and see if Toss-Out Tuesday works for you!

CHAPTER 5

Room for Living

These days, houses can have family rooms, living rooms, and "great rooms." You may have one of these rooms, or (lucky you!) all three. Still, it doesn't really matter whether your main family living space is the size of a spare bedroom or as spacious as a garage; it doesn't really matter what you call this room; and it doesn't really matter how big it is either—clutter accumulates in large rooms just as easily as in small. And the same clutter-conquering principles apply.

It's All in the Family (Room)

Family rooms are just that—spaces for the whole clan to hang out. What these areas all have in common is that they're the one room (next to the kitchen) that's a magnet for the clutter that seems to collect on a day-to-day basis. You know, the newspapers, magazines, mail, books, videos, crafts, hobbies, toys, items clipped from the newspaper, even office work and homework. If there ever was a room that needed organization with a capital O, it's this one!

Make sure that the family room doesn't become a drop-off spot for what everyone carries home at the end of the day. Backpacks, briefcases, and purses need to make it to the family entry/exit staging area for the next day, while sporting goods should go back to their proper storage area after use. A friend who has a house full of children and a husband who is a sports fan finally hit on a sneaky way to keep her family room from being declared a hazardous area. She has a rule that the television doesn't get turned on until skateboards, soccer balls, empty food dishes, and other clutter are cleared out of the room and returned to their proper place. Now it's amazing how quickly the place gets picked up—especially before a big football game on TV!

The best way to reorganize your family room is to step into the room on an especially cluttered day, like the Tuesday after a holiday weekend. With paper and pencil in hand, first see what needs to be removed, what needs storage, and what needs to be relocated. Do you have a pile of toys in one corner? Are there videos strewn all over the top of the television set? Is there a ball of knitting tucked into a corner of the sofa, with one needle missing? Do empty ice-cream bowls and snack wrappers congregate on the coffee table? Determining where your clutter comes from will help you hone in on the source of the problem. Often by making some changes in other nearby rooms, you will gain some control of the family room.

What's on TV

Let's consider the television area, since this is often the focal point of the family room. Where is your VCR or DVD player stored? Enclosed storage spaces are great for hiding electrical equipment as well as keeping videos out of sight. Video players that are stored in an open area such as a TV stand should have the videos stacked on a shelf or bin nearby. While we're talking about videos, are they in labeled boxes so you know what is on each tape? Or will you pop in "George's Birthday Party" only to be greeted by a rerun of *Star Wars*? Preview and label the videos clearly, and group together the videos that can be reused to tape programs. Then, alphabetize your purchased videos for quick reference.

Are you constantly looking for the remote control or *TV Guide*? Use Velcro® to park the remote on a lamp base or the TV. Create a little arm cover with a pocket to hang over your chair arm and keep the *TV Guide* and remote in it. Whoever shuts off the TV is responsible for putting the remote in its assigned spot.

Use Velcro® to attach game controllers to the top of the game console, and

*F*amilies with camcorders often find that their tapes become scattered and disorganized. Why not round up all the homemade videos for a family evening? Pop a bowl of popcorn, and settle in to watch videos you've taped of the family over the years; then vote on the ones that stay and the ones that can be used for retaping.

label them so that you can easily identify what they go with. Keep the games in their cases near the TV on a shelf or in a cabinet. Keeping the game CDs, DVDs, and cartridges in a box or plastic container makes it easier to put everything away and find it again. Label the end of the container so that you know at a glance what's in it.

Magazines—Don't Subscribe to Clutter

Be open-minded about the types of storage you can use in your family and living room areas. For instance, wicker wastebaskets are great for storing magazines. When my son was younger and into hot-rod magazines, our magazines were always combined in one basket and while he searched for his, mine ended up on the floor. To solve the problem, I purchased several square wicker wastebaskets from the dime store (that would be the dollar store these days), and stacked the baskets on top of each other on their sides, snuggly between the wall and the TV—they looked like cute little wicker cubbyholes! In one basket we kept his magazines and books, and in the other I separated my books and magazines and papers. Each of us was responsible for sorting out the baskets every month or so. He clipped articles he wanted to save from the magazine and stored them in a binder in his room. That solved a major clutter problem and kept our family room organized. Over the years, those baskets got used for lots of things, including towels in the guest bath (rolled up and tucked inside), craft supplies, and more. To this day, I still have a couple of baskets lurking in my storage closet to hold umbrellas, scarves, and earmuffs.

By the Book(case!)

Bookcases and wall units are great, but as so often happens, the unit is filled up on the day it is delivered, and five years later it's still holding the same books and now, outdated catalogs. Go through your books from time to time.

Unpack the bookcase shelf by shelf and look at each book. If you have already read it five times or didn't find it to your taste the first three times you tried to read it, then donate it to a senior center or some other worthy cause. If the kids are teenagers, perhaps it's time to either box up for sentimental reasons or pass on those preschool books. And what about that accounting textbook from the course you took four years ago? These books change annually, and frankly, that 1998 textbook isn't likely to be worth the paper it's printed on. Time to recycle.

Make sure you take a look at your CD collection too. Our taste in music changes. If you have CDs that you haven't listened to in years, give them a try. If they appeal to you, fine; if not, it's time to donate them or put them in the garage-sale collection. If the kids—who are now thirty with homes of their own—have a heavy metal collection taking up space, box it and give it back to them. And if you have a couple of boxes filled with cassettes, but no cassette player, now's the time to get rid of them too.

Putting It All Together

To get you started with your own unique storage needs, why not consider some of these ideas?

- Look around your own home first. Is there a seldom-used bookcase in one of the kids' rooms? Perhaps there's a nightstand collecting dust in the guest bedroom. Either one of these items is a great storage solution. The bookcase can be used as is, if the finish complements the family room furniture, or a quick coat of paint can transform it into a decor piece for storage. Work with the nightstand by adding a coat of paint, or even covering it with a few leftover scraps of wallpaper that match the room.

- Storage boxes from the discount store can be covered in paper to match your decor or in leftover wallpaper to match the room. These can be stored in view and still look nice. Sturdy boxes last the longest and work best, so before you toss out boxes from beverages or laundry detergent, take a second look at them.

- Store craft supplies such as crochet hooks, knitting yarn and needles, and needlepoint projects in an attractive basket near your favorite chair. Purchase a wicker basket in the right size at a discount store or

When selecting furniture for the family room, remember to look for hidden storage options. Hinged ottomans that open up for storage inside, tables with lots of drawers, and shelving that is open on top and has doors on the bottom to keep things out of sight but still handy, are all good options.

garage sale, and don't worry if the color doesn't match. Just zap it with a coat of spray paint (available in a dizzying array of colors for about $1 per can) to match your room. Even a briefcase can be used. It's easy to store and pick up and carry with you.

- Consider a sturdy plastic basket on wheels or with handles to hold kids' toys. This can be easily moved around the room and holds plenty of blocks, dolls, and toys. A square bin turned on its side is wonderful for storing board games too.

- Use empty oatmeal boxes to store Legos and other toys that come in small pieces. Again, cover the boxes in colored fabric, wallpaper, or adhesive backed paper to match your decor. These boxes are great because they're sturdy and come with a lid that is easy for kids to remove and put back. Don't overlook those potato chip canisters with plastic lids either.

- Wicker hampers are perfect for storing afghans and throws, for those chilly evenings, and also favorite "TV watching" pillows.

Of course, these great storage ideas aren't handy unless the family learns to use them. Every evening, just before leaving the room, each person should remove things that don't belong, such as slippers, socks, food dishes, homework, and school or craft projects. Once family members are in the habit of doing this, it will take only a few minutes to tidy up. Even the smallest child can help by picking up their things too. The important thing is to have handy storage so that the cleanup is not a project, but rather a quick act of tidying up.

Great Scott! It's the Great Room

If your home was built in the last fifteen years or so, you may face a new challenge: the great room. This room combines family living and formal living in one space. Needless to say, it also poses a unique motivation to stay organized, since it is a "family" and "guest" room in one. It can be difficult to combine the casualness of family living and the desire for a more formal, less lived-in and cluttered look. How you arrange the room and the storage options you use will determine your success and your happiness with this room.

The interesting thing about a great room is that the very openness that you love can create storage chaos. These rooms tend to attract clutter from other rooms such as the kitchen and the entry. Concealed storage and shelving storage is best for this room. Built-ins are ideal, but freestanding units with doors can also work well. If you have the space, consider turning one wall into a combination of bookcases and cabinets. It will look great, and the storage options are endless. You can find inexpensive bookcases at home centers or even at garage sales. Bring them home and finish with stain or paint

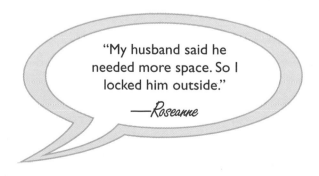

"My husband said he needed more space. So I locked him outside."

—Roseanne

to complement the room's decor. When buying used furniture, keep in mind the size and style you need. Sometimes what looks good sitting in the driveway can be all wrong once it is in your room. I always carry my room measurements with me when I shop. That way when I stumble on a great "find," I can measure to see if it will fit the room.

In the great room you definitely want to do away with what I call the doodad ditties. Make your decorating statement with larger pieces, and assign the small collections and knickknacks to another area of your home. If this is the room where you want to store your collectibles, consider a glass-fronted cabinet to keep things out of the way and eliminate weekly dusting and the chance of breakage.

If you are storing lots of small items in closed cupboards, consider these storage options:

- Small plastic boxes from the dollar store (or raid your daughter's cosmetics box) work well.
- Shoe boxes are another old favorite.
- TV dinner trays have handy little compartments (wash them out first, of course!).
- Fishing tackle boxes are ideal for teeny-tiny items.
- Styrofoam® egg cartons work well for miniature objects. Label the tops of the cartons with a marker and you won't even have to guess at the contents!
- Plastic ice cube trays are also great storage containers for small items.
- Tool boxes are great and come in a wide range of sizes.

- Remember, storage containers do not have to come from expensive stores. Think "recycle"—gift boxes, coffee cans, plastic bowls from the kitchen . . . you get the idea.

One last reminder: Even though you have wonderful cabinets with doors, don't use that as a license to fill up every inch of space and store items you haven't looked at or used in years. If you allow yourself to collect, and stuff your cabinets, you'll soon outgrow them.

Formally Yours—The Living Room

Are you fortunate enough to have a separate room apart from family living quarters that houses a piano, a well-loved book collection, or a crackling fireplace? Then you have what we used to call a formal living room. Today, these rooms are often taking on a new life as a music room or library, as well as a seating area.

Bear in mind that pianos should be placed near an inside wall for easier climate control. These delicate instruments are very sensitive to changes in temperature, even just overnight, and deviations in temperature can require more frequent tuning. Adequate humidity is also important for your piano; if the air in your home is dry, consider adding a humidifier. Your piano is an heirloom that can be passed down from generation to generation, so you'll want to take good care of it. Don't forget to add a hinged piano bench. They're handy for storage of sheet music and odds and ends too.

This is also a good room in which to house collections of beautiful objects. Whether you collect seashells or figurines, a display of them in a corner cabinet would complement the decor nicely. However, keep in mind that these items aren't called dust-catchers for nothing. Along with a weekly vacuuming, you'll need to dust in here once a week, so be sure the items you store here have meaning to you.

In this room your storage needs will be minimal, since it is more of a "sit and visit" room. Incorporate storage ideas from the family room and great room as you need them. Think in terms of closed cabinets and using drawer space in tables for such things as coasters and small napkins, anything that you might need when you entertain guests in this room.

Keeping it tidy and clutter-free means you, your family, and your guests get to enjoy the finer things in life comfortably.

CHAPTER 6

Kitchen Duty

*T*hings in your home may become scattered far and wide, but chances are your kitchen is like the mother ship in a Star Wars movie—everything eventually comes back here to roost! The kitchen is the hub of most family activities, and it's also the place where conquering clutter and becoming organized really pays off. Your kitchen can be a joy to use when things are easy to find and there is logic guiding the tasks you need to do. The proper use of your storage space is the factor that will determine how user friendly your kitchen is.

Counter Attack

Since the countertop space is always at a premium in the kitchen—*location, location, location*—the idea here is to eliminate as much as possible. The rule of thumb for kitchen appliances is that if you don't use an item at least every other day, then it can be stored in a cupboard or pantry just as conveniently. So unplug your bread maker, espresso machine, or Crock-Pot™ and store it on the bottom shelf of your kitchen pantry, in the cupboard above your refrigerator, or in the back of the pots-and-pans cupboard.

Now, survey what remains and begin by grouping related items together.

- Keep the coffee, measuring spoons, and filters in a cupboard close by the coffeemaker. A small plastic basket with rubber suction cups that adhere to your fridge is great for storing coffee filters.

- If you have a bread box, put it and the toaster together, so that making toast is convenient.

- Group your canisters near the cupboard that contains your baking supplies.

- Keep your vegetable basket near the sink where you prepare the vegetables, and keep it out of the sun, so that your onions and potatoes don't spoil quickly.

- Keep your dish soap and other supplies in the cabinet under the sink, so that you don't take up precious counter space. Or, if you prefer, put the big container of dish soap under the sink, and keep a small liquid-soap hand pump filled with detergent next to the tap.

- Cutting boards can be hung on the wall.

- Use a magnetic strip to hold often-used tools such as bottle and can openers—or, in some houses, pizza cutters!

Take a good look around and do what you need to in order to have an uncluttered work surface. Remember: The less counter clutter you have to deal with, the less time you'll take to get the job done—whatever the job may be!

Inspector Gadget

Are you a "gadget-holic"? Then your counters are probably lined with intriguing but seldom-used items that were very appealing when demonstrated at the home show. Here you must be ruthless. Do you really use it? That wok you got in 1991 probably won't be useful if your Chinese cooking skills haven't advanced beyond heating up a package of frozen egg rolls. Ditto the fondue pot if you're lactose intolerant. Say good-bye and donate it or pass it on to a relative or friend. It now becomes their storage problem.

Away with Cupboard Clutter!

It's frustrating to open a cupboard and have a jumble of pots, pans, electrical cords, and lids spill out, isn't it? Let's conquer that cupboard clutter with a few simple steps. And for this task, let's use your *QUEEN*.

*Q*uestion: *What's not working in my cupboards? Do I have to sort through twenty spices to find the cinnamon? Does the flour always end up all over the shelf every time I take it out? Do I have pots, pans, pie plates, and cake pans all stored in a jumble? What do I need to* *do to make things in my cupboards more accessible, easier to take out and put away?*

*U*npack: I know it's tempting to shift things around in the cupboards and try to sort things out without unpacking, but that's like that old shell game—you're just moving things about that will soon show up elsewhere. So empty your cupboards first, one shelf at a time.

Once you've got everything out, fill a bucket with warm water and a squirt of your favorite dishwashing liquid or all-purpose cleaner, and give the insides of the cupboards a good cleaning. Rinse with clear water and wipe dry. Get rid of all that sticky stuff that attracts bugs.

This suggestion may sound like a throwback to many of you, but consider lining your shelves with paper. Not only does it look pretty—shelf paper comes in a lot of lovely colors and patterns—it makes cleaning even easier. If you've used vinyl wallpaper on your

*W*hen arranging your cupboards, sometimes it is a good idea to draw up a plan. Determine what you will store where on paper. Group by logic and common sense.

kitchen walls, you might like to try that. Stay away from paper that sticks to the shelves, though; it's hard to put down and even harder to remove. A better alternative is to use a small roll of no-wax vinyl flooring, which can easily be cut to fit with a utility knife.

*E*valuate: I bet you can guess the next step: Now that you've removed everything, group like objects together. If you haven't baked a pie in three years, you probably don't need a pie tin. Do you still use the blender, the bread machine, and the fancy waffle maker? If the answer is no, then put them in the discard pile.

If you're clearing the cupboards in your pantry, have a good look at the canned goods. If there's a can of pumpkin pie filling that has been there since the Pilgrims landed, best get rid of it. Ever bought something in a three for $2 special, only to find out after the first can was opened that you didn't like it? Then why not donate the other two cans to a food bank?

While canned foods have a long shelf life, it's best not to keep them for more than a year, as the color, flavor, texture, and nutritive value can deteriorate. Canned goods should be stored at a temperature of 70 degrees and no higher than 95 degrees. Don't store them next to or over the stove area.

Pay close attention to the condition of canned goods. Discard bulging cans, because the food inside may be spoiled. Similarly, avoid buying cans with dents on the side seams or around the top and bottom rim seams. If a can is leaky, throw it away. Toss out rusty cans just to be on the safe side. Rust can penetrate the can and ruin the food inside.

*E*liminate: This is sometimes the tough one. Look through your discard pile. Box and bag things up for donation (food banks can always use cooking equipment), garage sale, or trash. Remove the boxes and bags from the room to give yourself working space, and to get rid of temptation.

*N*eaten Up: If you have made a diagram of where you want to store things, pull it out and get started. If you're more of a free thinker (read: someone who doesn't like writing things down), then think the process through before putting things away.

Here are some guidelines to help you get started:

- Nest frying pans and skillets, putting the largest on the bottom.
- Arrange pot lids in a sturdy empty box, or consider installing plastic storage baskets on the inside of your cabinet doors. Even an appropriate size old nightstand drawer with the knobs removed works well.
- Store cookie sheets and baking pans on their sides and slide into cupboards. Use a heavy bookend

or a brick wrapped in fabric to keep them standing. This not only saves space, but provides easy access too.

- Muffin pans, pizza pans, and some pot lids also slide well into those wire racks you get at stationery stores—the ones you use to prop up files.

- It's fine to pile plates and bowls on each other, but don't mix sizes and types.

- Keep the dishes you use most often at the front of the cupboard and the others at back.

- Save the storefront real estate for everyday items such as pots, pans, colanders, and lids.

- Keep little-used appliances such as espresso machines, pasta makers, and the like toward the back of the cupboard.

- Cast-iron skillets should be stored with a piece of wax paper inside to protect the finish from moisture and rust.

- A rack installed on the inside of the cupboard under the sink is perfect for holding aluminum foil, plastic wrap, and other similar products. You can find these racks at discount stores and home centers. Take advantage of awkward cupboard or drawer space for keeping them too. This will free up valuable storage space.

- Use cupboards near the stove to hold pots, pans, spatulas, and cooking spoons. It doesn't make sense to cross the room to get a pan every time you want to fry an egg.

*H*ere's a tip that will eliminate storing the same items day after day: Why not set the table for the next meal as you unload the dishwasher? Kids can be taught this task early on, saving Mom a little extra time each day.

Double Your Drawer Duty

Cleaning out the drawers is an important first step. Remove everything from each drawer, evaluate it, and then discard the trash or find new uses for it. Got some bits of string? The birds will love it for nesting—just tuck it outside in a branch of a tree. What about those old abused birthday candles. Use them for your next pity party. If you have leftover cards, use the fronts for gift cards and toss the rest. Now wash out the drawer with some baking soda and water or some all-purpose cleaner. Rinse and dry and you are ready to neaten up. Here are some double-duty drawer *(phew!)* storage tips:

- Store knives near your cutting board and cooking utensils near the stove. To reduce clutter on the counters, opt for a divided storage container in the drawers. To keep knives sharp and safely out of the way, use a knife storage container that holds them like a sheath. Knives slide in to keep your fingers safe and the finish protected too.

- If drawer space is tight, use a block-type countertop knife holder instead and a decorative ceramic pitcher or urn to hold cooking utensils such as spatulas, whisks, and wooden spoons. A clay flower pot makes a nice utensil holder. If you don't like the natural clay color, you can paint it to match the kitchen. Keep in mind that the more you store on the counter, the more you have to clean.

- Purchase under-the-counter drawers and knife holders at kitchen supply stores. These are ideal for small kitchen areas, or for those who love to cook and need additional storage space for their cooking tools.

Shelf Savvy

What your kitchen lacks in counter space can almost always be compensated for with the careful use of shelving. Look around your kitchen and you're sure to find plenty of wall space that can be put to use.

- Consider installing a shelf above the kitchen counter for your cookbooks. This keeps them handy but frees up valuable counter space.

- Everyone has a collection of favorite recipes. Did you know that your local bookstore carries blank cookbooks with divided vinyl sheets that can be used to hold your treasured family favorites? Assembling a family cookbook is a terrific project for summertime, when kids are out of school. When your recipes are all grouped together in one place, there's no more guessing where you wrote down Grandma's favorite bread pudding.

- Think of using shelves and wall hangers to hold other things you use daily too. Small hooks can hold mugs, kitchen towels, pot holders, and utensils.

- Storing Tupperware® and other plastic storage containers can really be frustrating. Of course, you can purchase storage systems for them, but you can also be creative. I like to devote a small upper cupboard, perhaps the one over the stove, to plastic storage. I stack my containers, by size and type, inside each other. Don't get the stacks too high or they will be frustrating to reach for and use. Stack the lids by size, with the largest against the cupboard wall, and use a bookend or a clean brick wrapped in plastic or fabric to hold them up. For smaller containers, use a low rectangular storage container to hold them. You can lift the large container out, select what you need, and then replace it without all of the plastic tumbling out. Weed out the bowls that are old and sticky and ones you never use—after all, you only have so many leftovers. If you run out of bowls, check the back of the refrigerator to see what is lurking unnoticed in a plastic bowl from dinner two months ago!

- Don't forget to use the space around your kitchen window. You can hang shelves here and arrange dishes, mugs, or even plants for a decorative and useful display.

- Store canned goods in a cool, dry cupboard. Group like items together, and for real ease, alphabetize them so that you can find what you are looking for in a hurry.

- Stored boxed items on a separate shelf and try the alphabetizing here too. This will also make quick work of putting the groceries away. If you have open boxes on the shelf, consider storing the contents in clear plastic containers. Keep any cooking directions you may need and tuck into the container.

- Once cookies are open, store them in a cookie jar or clear container on the shelf. This prevents scattering crumbs everywhere, keeps the cookies fresher, and also eliminates temptation for bugs.

- Spices and other flavorings lose their oomph after about six months (and in less time than that if they're stored near or in excessive heat and humidity), so replace yours frequently.

- Consider a tiered platform to hold spices. (You can find them in kitchen stores and catalogs.) The tiered rack allows you to see spices at a glance, making it much easier to get at the cardamom, or whatever spice you seem to use only at holidays.

- Make your own tiered spice racks by affixing three small shelves about the width of your spice jars to the inside of your cupboard or against a wall. Set up your spice center near the stove and baking center.

- Alphabetizing your spices is smart. Starting with anise in the front and tarragon in the back, you'll save yourself the time and trouble of having to look at each jar.

- Use pegboards for instant storage. Hang near the stove for ladles, spoons, and colanders. I have a friend who painted her pegboard to match her decor, then traced on it the outline of each item so that she could easily replace them after use. You can also stencil your pegboard to match a country, contemporary, or even high-tech kitchen.

- Pan holders that hang from the ceiling have been used in professional kitchens for years. Consider these especially if you have a center island in your kitchen (the pot rack can be suspended over the island), if you have a plethora of cooking pans, or if storage space is tight. Look in kitchen stores or catalogs for these racks, or even make your own.

Shopping Smarts

Let's consider how you shop. Do you stop at the grocery store almost daily to purchase a few apples, a half pound of hamburger, and a jar of pickles? Or are you a "stocker," in love with warehouse stores?

Stockers will require more storage than most regular pantries can provide. Here you need to consider alternate storage, and don't hesitate to get creative. Although I wouldn't advocate it, a friend of mine who loved baking stored 50-pound bags of sugar behind her living room couch! Perhaps a hall closet in which you have installed extra shelves or a designated area in the basement where you've installed some shelving or a freestanding unit would hold your purchases. Keep a contents list posted in your "alternate pantry" so that you

*E*veryone has seen those three-tiered hanging fruit baskets. Why not use them to hold boxes of your favorite tea, or granola bars for the kids. These inexpensive space-makers are very handy.

don't continually stock up on the same items (an occupational hazard for professional shoppers). This also allows you to use up what's on the shelves. This extra pantry space is also a boon for those who enjoy canning their own fruits and vegetables.

Those of you lucky enough to have an extra freezer or refrigerator know how handy they can be to store things you won't need every day. Put a sheet of paper on the front listing what is inside and attach with a magnet. Cross off an item when you remove it and you'll always know what you have. This eliminates reaching into the freezer and finding that year-old package of hamburger with freezer burn.

Store meat in the freezer in freezer wrap. Look for this in your grocery store on the aisle with plastic wrap and aluminum foil. This protects meat from freezer burn for up to a year. Make sure you label the outside of the wrap with the contents of the package and date of purchase. A permanent marker or grease pencil works well for this. Remember to store your food in the freezer according to date, with the freshest food in the back.

Let me share something I learned the hard way. Plug a

nightlight that you can easily see into the same plug as the freezer or refrigerator. Use a red Christmas bulb to make it really stand out. In case of a power outage, you will quickly see that the light is out and you'll be able to take steps more quickly to protect your food investment. Not only does this help keep food from spoiling and save you a nasty cleanup job; it can actually save your appliance from dying a nasty death due to an odor that can't be removed.

Pack a Pretty Pantry

Consider turning several cupboards into a pantry if there is not a designated one in your home. Installing a freestanding cupboard in or near the kitchen works too. Think sliding shelves here for maximum storage. There are firms who can turn stationary shelves into ones that slide; they charge a flat rate per shelf. Ask friends for a recommendation or look under "Shelving" in the Yellow Pages.

- Make maximum use of your pantry by grouping items together as you use them. Store rice, pasta, and packaged potatoes together, and canned tomato sauce, mushrooms, and vegetables nearby. At mealtime, you can see at a glance what's available to be prepared.

- Store spice packages such as taco seasoning in an empty berry basket for easy reference.

- Store open containers of flour, sugar, rice, and cereal in clear square containers. Square containers work better than round in terms of the amount of space they take up. Plastic is better than glass, which can break. Buy containers that will stack on top of each other and you'll save even more room.

- Another alternative to containers is to use sturdy resealable plastic bags. I like to make my own colored sugar for baking cookies, for example. I just mix a few drops of food coloring with white sugar and store each color in plastic bags. These are much less expensive than containers of "decorative sugar" and this is a fun project kids always like to help with too.

*S*toring dry foods such as cereal, brown sugar, and flour in plastic containers eliminates the problem of bugs in open packages.

- Leave the lowest or most inconvenient shelf for items like Jell-O mix, cooking oil, extra ketchup, syrup, and other condiments you reach for only occasionally.
- Double-tiered plastic lazy Susan racks are available at most discount stores. Consider this option if you have limited storage space, as each of these racks can hold plenty of canned goods and are easily accessed.
- Arrange taller cans in back and shorter items in front.

- Place the goodies everyone forages for right up front, where they are readily available, so that no one has to dig through the entire pantry for the Ding Dongs®. You'll keep order that way.

- Consider labeling shelves by applying a piece of masking tape and writing with a marker where each item goes. One row for canned soups, another for fruits, one for cereals, and so on. For families with children, this not only makes putting away groceries a breeze, it gives the kids a reading lesson every time!

*W*hen we were children, our basement pantry always held an extra supply of canned soup, with the shelves labeled by color. Yellow was chicken noodle, red was tomato, and blue was bean with bacon. At lunchtime, we were instructed to go to the basement and bring up "two cans of red and one can of blue soup." It worked!

The "Junque" Drawer

Repeat after me: "I give myself permission to have a junk drawer." Yes, even the Queen has one! Mine has a couple of screwdrivers, some pliers, pens, paper, a couple of puzzling screws (if I ever figure out where they go, the puzzle will be solved), a flashlight, some thumbtacks, and even a few new catnip balls, in case the cat ever has a toy emergency. When the drawer gets too jumbled (about every other month), I just haul the wastebasket over to it and remove everything, put things away in their proper places, and then I'm ready to start again. Allowing yourself one junk drawer means you won't get in the habit of using any convenient space to stuff things in.

The Fridge

The refrigerator and freezer take a lot of abuse. There isn't a person alive, I venture, who hasn't peered into the depths of their refrigerator at one time or another and pulled out a "mystery bowl" lurking somewhere in the back. To stop the science experiments, use these tried and true methods.

Clean out the refrigerator and freezer separately, starting with the refrigerator. First remove the entire contents of the refrigerator, examining things as you go to determine what is a keeper and what can be disposed of. Have a sturdy trash bag standing by to receive any "mystery items." Use a cooler to keep perishables cold while you work. (Don't worry, this won't take long!) "Keepers" are condiments such as ketchup, mustard, and salad dressings—if they are still fresh.

A quick word of advice: Even condiments have an expiration date. They last, open in your refrigerator, for about 12 to 18 months. Take a look at them as you replace them in the refrigerator. If they have changed color or look excessively watery, it's time to toss and restock. And remember, when you are using perishable items such as mayonnaise or salad dressing, return them to the refrigerator as soon as possible to keep them fresh longer.

Now's the time to thoroughly clean the interior of the refrigerator. Remove glass shelves or racks one by one to clean them. As you take them out, wash the wall areas of the refrigerator that can be reached. A mild solution of 1 gallon of warm water and a couple of squirts of dishwashing liquid and 1–2 tablespoons of borax will do the job nicely. Mix this up in the sink or a bucket, and use a sponge or soft cloth. You probably found that box of baking soda in the back that has been deodorizing the refrigerator for months. Remove it and sprinkle some of the baking soda on a damp cloth to remove stubborn food spills from the walls and shelves. When you're done, you can place the box with your cleaning supplies, for many other uses around the house. Put a fresh box in the refrigerator. Wash and rinse the shelves and dry with a soft cloth; then replace them in the refrigerator. Here you'll want to put a coat of Clean Shield® on the shelves before putting items back. This wonderful product creates a nonstick finish that is stain- and soil-resistant. You can mop up spills in your refrigerator with just a damp sponge, making cleanup a lot easier.

- Group keepers by type. Store salad dressings, horseradish, and other condiments together in the door. Jams and jellies can stay here too. Check the dates on your perishables and dispose of anything that's past its prime. Consider how you use things in the refrigerator. If the kids are constantly reaching into the back for the jelly, for instance, move it up front and store less frequently used items in the back.

- Dairy products such as cottage cheese, yogurt, and sour cream should be stored in their original containers. Hard cheese will stay freshest if stored wrapped in foil, wax paper, or plastic wrap after opening.

- Group fruits and vegetables separately, each in their own crisper bins. This way you can pull open the drawer and know if you need to pick up a head of lettuce or some more apples. This also keeps your produce fresher longer, as fruits and vegetables emit gases that cause each other to deteriorate; grouping like things together will keep these vapors from mingling. Remember not to wash produce prior to storage, as this speeds up deterioration.

Is your refrigerator the place where you keep the leftovers until it's time to throw them out?

- A separate section of the refrigerator just for leftovers is a good idea. This keeps you from overlooking them. Store them in see-through containers, and hopefully you won't shove them to the back to linger for six months! Remove any leftovers from cans and store in plastic or glass to keep a metallic taste from ruining the food. Leftovers need to be refrigerated no more than two hours after cooking, so be sure to store them as soon as mealtime is over. As you store your leftovers in the refrigerator, make a list of them and tack it to the refrigerator door. You'll be more apt to remember and to use them and you'll never find a mystery bowl next time you clean.

- Perishables such as eggs should be stored on the top shelf of the refrigerator. Remember that the door is often the warmest place in your refrigerator, and that's where the egg container usually is. It's much safer to store your eggs in their original container until they're used. For this reason, you'll want to store your butter, margarine, and cream cheese on the top shelf too. Leave the door area for your sturdier condiments, such as ketchup and mustard.

- Store meats on the bottom shelf if your refrigerator doesn't have a meat tray. This prevents them from dripping on other items, in case the wrapping isn't tight. Thaw a roast or other large cut of meat inside a bowl, so that as it defrosts the juice will run into the bowl, not all over your shelves.

- If your family drinks a lot of canned juices and soft drinks, a can rack will come in handy. Here's where an extra refrigerator is a bonus too, to hold beverages you buy on sale or use frequently. A word of warning: Do not place warm cans of soda in the freezer to quickly cool them off. The carbonation causes the can to burst. Not a pretty sight.

*D*on't overcrowd the refrigerator, as the premise for keeping food cool is that interior air is allowed to circulate. You'll want to set the temperature dial to less than **40** degrees to keep harmful bacteria from growing. Look for a refrigerator thermometer at home stores; leaving one in your refrigerator will help you keep your food fresher longer.

Leftovers? Think Again!

By now you probably have collected partially used bottles and containers with just a little left in them. Here's what you can do with those leftovers.

- That old odor-absorbing box of baking soda—put it down the kitchen drain followed by ½ to 1 cup of white vinegar for a fresh-smelling, clear-flowing drain.

- Lemon juice—clean your brass with lemon juice by adding salt. Rub it on, rinse, and dry well. Clean stains off counters with a paste of lemon juice and cream of tartar. Remove rust from hard surfaces or white fabrics by putting the lemon juice on the rust. For fabric, lay it out in the sun.

- Ketchup—now's the time to shine that copper by rubbing it with ketchup until it shines. Rinse and dry well.

- Clear soda water that's lost its fizz—use to wipe down white appliances for a great shine. Buff with a soft cloth. Clear soda water also adds vigor to plants and cut flowers.

- If that onion is not good enough for the salad, remove rust from your utensils, such as paring knives, by sticking them in the onion and letting them sit until the rust is removed, usually a matter of hours.

- Put citrus peels from citrus fruit past its prime down the garbage disposal to freshen and deodorize.

- If that potato isn't looking great, cut it in half and rub it on white shoes. Let the shoe dry, and then polish for a streak-proof shine. Or, remove mud from clothes by rubbing with the cut side of a potato.

- Add shine to a wood table by polishing with that last bit of mayonnaise in the jar. Rub it in well and buff with a soft cloth.

Store It Safely

Here is a list of the most commonly stored foods. You may be surprised as you look over the list at the storage life of some foods. The manual that comes with your refrigerator and the web site *www.fightbac.org* can provide you with additional information.

Bacon (cooked)
1 week

Bacon (uncooked)
2 weeks

Bread Dough
3 to 4 days

Butter
1 to 3 months

Cheese (hard)
6 months

Cheese (soft, opened)
1 to 2 weeks

Cheese (soft, unopened)
3 to 4 weeks

Chicken (fresh)
1 to 2 days

Eggs (hard-boiled)
1 week

Eggs (fresh in shell)
3 to 5 weeks

Fish (fresh)
1 to 2 days

Fish (cooked)
3 to 4 days

Fruit or Pumpkin Pies (baked)
2 to 3 days

Fruit or Pumpkin Pies (unbaked)
1 to 2 days

Gravy or Meat Broth
1 to 2 days

Mashed Potatoes
3 to 4 days

Meat (cooked)
3 to 4 days

Olives and Pickles
1 month

Poultry (cooked)
3 to 4 days

Soups and Stews
2 to 4 days

Steaks, Roasts, Chops (uncooked)
3 to 5 days

Stuffing (cooked)
3 to 4 days

Turkey (fresh)
1 to 2 days

White Wine (recorked)
1 to 2 days

Here are some other things that you may want to store in the refrigerator:

- Nail polish (lasts much longer)
- Medicines that require cooler temperatures (check labels)
- Face gels and eye masks
- Facial toner for a cool mist on a hot day
- Exposed film

Now that you have the refrigerator organized, keep food-stuffs in the same area, so that when you unpack groceries after a trip to the store, you will store things in the proper place without thinking. Before you shop for food, make sure you look over the refrigerator and wipe up any spills; use warm water with a little baking soda and white vinegar added. Throw out what is past its prime, and you're ready to restock.

Here's a helpful tip: If you have a computer, make up a master list of foods you commonly buy, such as milk, cheese, eggs, lunch meat, apples, ice cream, and so on. I like to set mine up in the order I shop—produce first, then meats, canned goods, and frozen foods. Make up copies of the list, and keep a copy posted on your refrigerator with a magnet. Add a checkmark as each item is depleted. That way you can know just what to shop for; you can also add other items to the bottom of the list as you need them. (If you'd like a head start, just visit my Web site *www.queenofclean.com* and download my grocery list!)

The Deep Freeze

Now it's time to venture into the depths of the freezer. Remove the food from your freezer, check the freshness date, and throw out anything that is no longer good. Place the things you will be putting back in a cooler to keep them cold.

- Wipe out the freezer with warm water and a little white vinegar before restocking. Make sure your meat is labeled and wrapped in freezer paper to prevent freezer burn. Sometimes standing meat on its edge instead of stacking makes it easier to see what you have and takes up less room. Keep all meat together.

- Now group frozen vegetables. You might consider an expandable freezer shelf to double your space; these shelves are available at home stores and kitchen centers. Place it over the first layer of food and stack bags and boxes of vegetables, frozen egg rolls, waffles, or frozen side dishes, over it. Remember to keep desserts separate from the rest of the food, so that they aren't crushed or lost in the shuffle. Try to store the packages so that you can see part of the printed label; they will be easier to identify.

- When bringing food home, place the newest food in the back of the freezer and move older products to the front, to be used first.

- Keep a plastic container in the freezer door to hold ice if your unit does not have an automatic icemaker. You can easily empty ice trays all at once into the container and then refill the trays so that you always have enough ice on hand.

Don't Get Burned—Freezer Burned, That Is...

Keep this handy frozen food storage chart in mind when filling your freezer.

Egg (raw yolks and whites)
1 year

Egg Substitute (unopened)
1 year

Butter/Margarine
(do not freeze whipped butter)
6 to 9 months

Cheese (hard)
6 weeks

Ice Cream, Sherbet (cover top with plastic wrap)
2 months

Milk
1 month

Fruits (berries, peaches, pears, etc.)
12 months

Frozen Juices
6 months

Frozen Vegetables
8 months

TV Dinners, Frozen Casseroles
3 to 4 months

Prestuffed Chicken Breasts or Pork
Don't freeze well

Raw Hamburger and Stew Meats
3 to 4 months

Ground Turkey, Veal, Pork or Lamb (or mixture)
3 to 4 months

Lean Fish (cod, haddock, sole, flounder)
6 months

Fatty Fish (perch, mackerel, salmon)
2 to 3 months

Lobster Tails
3 months

Shrimp (uncooked)
12 months

Oysters
4 months

Scallops
3 months

Ham (canned, unopened)
Don't freeze

Ham (canned, opened)
1 to 2 months

Ham (fully cooked)
1 to 2 months

Ham Slices (fully cooked)
1 to 2 months

Hot Dogs and Lunch Meats
1 to 2 months

Soups and Stews
2 to 3 months

Bacon
1 month

Sausage (raw)
1 to 2 months

Smoked Breakfast Links and Patties
1 to 2 months

Steaks
6 to 12 months

Chops
4 to 6 months

Roasts
4 to 12 months

Cooked Meat and Meat Dishes
2 to 3 months

Gravy and Meat Broth
2 to 3 months

Fresh Chicken and Turkey (whole)
1 year

Fresh Chicken and Turkey (parts)
9 months

Fried Chicken
4 months

Chicken Nuggets and Patties
1 to 3 months

As you can see, the length of time that foods can safely be frozen varies greatly. When you stock up on an item, keep in mind how long you can store it frozen before it's eaten. Purchasing items on sale, then having to dispose of them uneaten is what's known as a "false economy."

Congratulations on completing a job you've probably been putting off since you moved into your house. Now that your kitchen is reorganized and tidy, reward yourself. How? With dinner at your favorite restaurant, of course!

CHAPTER 7

The Paper Chase

It seems that the farther we advance with technology, the more we are inundated with paper. Remember when computer gurus told us we would soon be living in a paperless society? Well, guess what—it seems that the technical revolution has generated a whole new spawn of paperwork.

The vast majority of waste in recycling sites is nothing more than ordinary paper—everything from junk mail, newspapers, magazines, and phone books to the flotsam-and-jetsam paperwork of everyday life. Controlling this particular area of clutter is key to living a less stressful and simpler life. Let's tackle the paper chase together, shall we?

You've Got Mail

When you pick up your mail every day, bring it in the house to the same spot. It can be a basket in the entryway, a designated spot on the kitchen counter, or a space at your desk in the home office. Then take a few moments to go through your mail, and remember the rule to handle each piece of paper only once. Newspapers, catalogs, and magazines go to the magazine rack or a basket, where you can find them and read them at your leisure. Toss out the old catalog as you replace it with the new issue, and make sure to sort through this storage bin regularly (weekly is great) to keep it up-to-date. Toss the water, electric, or car payment into a manila folder or large envelope marked "Bills" for payment. Read personal mail, such as wedding or shower invitations, birthday cards, and the like, and enter information on your family calendar. Scan through junk mail, then toss. The big temptation here is to set down a letter, bill, or "interesting idea" from the junk mail for "later." However, later usually doesn't come! Teach yourself to clear out your mail daily, and clutter has that much less of a chance to congregate.

*C*onsider how many charge accounts you have. Do you really need four major credit cards, a gasoline card, and a card for every department store in your nearby mall? Remember that all of these cards generate reams of mail in your direction from these retailers. Simplify your life by cutting down your credit cards to just a few you can use everywhere.

Chances are you're on some mailing lists for items that no longer interest you. Take 15 minutes today to stop the accumulation of unwanted offers in the mail. You'll need to make one phone call and write a single letter to do this. To stop unwanted credit offers, dial 1–888–5–OPT–OUT at any time of day or night. Then, write to the following: DMA Mail Preference Service, PO Box 643, Carmel, NY 10512. Include your complete name, address, zip code, and a request to "activate the preference service." The Direct Marketing Association estimates that this one step will stop 75 percent of junk mail from reaching you for up to five years. Keep in mind this option may stop catalogs and promotions you would have liked to receive.

The Paper Tiger

And some ways to tame it:

- Think twice before you copy that e-mail or print that delicious recipe you want to try "someday." The great temptation of the Internet is that it makes so much information available so easily. How may times have you printed out a couple of pages to read later, and later has never come? And how many times have you printed out one page only to be flooded with six or seven? Remember: You don't have to print everything. The information will be there, on line, the next time you need it.

- Reuse paper in your printer to copy items for personal use; save the clean copy paper for items you need to send out or keep as a personal record.

- Consider using electronic or on-line banking—it cuts down dramatically on paperwork.

- Recycle or toss newspapers and magazines at least weekly. Piles of old newspapers are untidy, and a fire hazard as well.

- Store important personal papers such as your will, birth certificate, social security card, and passport in a safe place at home (a fireproof box is best) or a safe deposit box at the bank. If you store these papers at the bank, keep a list of what is in the safe deposit box on your computer or in your home files. Go through these papers twice a year to make sure they're in order. Keep a separate folder for each child in your family. In each, place their immunization record, report cards, birth certificates, social security card, and any other important information, such as allergies, doctors' names and phone numbers. This will be invaluable, especially at the beginning of each school year.

- A family calendar is a great idea. Purchase a large one and post it in an obvious place such as the kitchen. Mark down birthday parties, weddings, family parties, as invitations arrive. Keep a clothespin attached to the calendar, where you can hang the invitation or pertinent information. When the event is over, just toss.

When you control the flow of paperwork in your home, you'll feel more in control of your life, and your time is then spent the way you prefer. That means more quality time for you and your family, as well as more time for the fun things in life.

"I read about eight newspapers a day; when I'm in a town with only one newspaper, I read it eight times."

—Will Rogers

CHAPTER 8

Memories

*A*re you the one with the family photos still in their store envelopes complete with the receipt still stapled to the flap? Is your spoon collection tossed into the bottom drawer of the china cabinet? Are your miniature race cars going nowhere fast in that old broken-down box in the basement? Collections can be wonderful, but if they are stored away carelessly—or not stored at all—your precious treasures can become clutter. And who wants to inherit clutter?

Collections can also breed out of control and take over your living space. If you are allotting more space to your collections than to where you eat and sleep, it's time to pick out the few collections that mean the most to you and part with the rest.

Researchers say that most folks collect for five basic reasons:

- *Love of beauty.* There's just something soothing about contemplating a snowy white teacup with a pristine rose etched on the front.

- *A sense of satisfaction in completion.* Ask any ten-year-old boy how he feels when he rounds out his baseball card collection.

- *The thrill of the chase.* This appeals to the hunter-gatherer in all of us. Plus, it adds a little pizzazz to shopping trips, vacations, and forays to yard sales when we have a specific item in mind.

- *To go back to our roots.* Many collectibles are rich in cultural and ethnic meaning.

- *Profit.* This is usually the last reason most people acquire collections, but of course artwork, coins, and other high-end items can become quite valuable.

Almost everyone has a collection. Let's look at how to manage one without letting it turn into clutter or take over your house.

Photo Opportunity

While there are as many types of collections as there are collectors, it's a pretty safe bet that most of us have an unwieldy photo collection, so we'll start with that. Round up all of your photographs. Yes, even the ones in the junk drawer and your underwear drawer. Sit down with a trash bag nearby and sort the good from the bad and the just plain ugly . . . no, I don't mean Uncle Fred doing his weird toupee trick! Look at each photo closely. If any of them are out of focus, have red eyes, look like something from *MAD* magazine, or are missing important parts (such as heads), throw them out NOW!

If you have good quality duplicate prints, pass them on to an interested relative or friend, otherwise toss those too.

Divide photos of children into a separate pile for each child. Organize the photos, starting with the most current, and label with names, dates, and any other pertinent information on the back. Next, organize the remaining photos, starting with the most current, and label with names, dates, locations, and any other information on the back. Start with the newest photos, so that by the time you reach oldies but goodies, you'll be more selective about what to keep and what to toss. Do you really need thirty-five pictures from David's birthday? Pick out the very best ones, and pass on or toss the others. Then label the outside of envelopes containing negatives with the date and location where the photos were taken.

Now it's time to consider how you want to store your photos. You can have a photo album per child, year, or event that the children can help with, or perhaps a photo box better suits your needs. You might want to consider grouping the photos by date, or event. If you recently built a home and have all the photos as the project went along, put those in an album beginning with the lot purchase and go through to completion. Add some personal thoughts too. You'll always cherish this memory, and the kids will love looking at it. To store pictures in a photo box, wrap them in acid-free tissue or select acid-free boxes to protect your photos over time. You can find these at craft and scrapbooking stores. If you prefer albums, be sure to choose those with plastic sleeves, rather than the sticky backs to preserve the quality of your photos. If you like scrapbooks best, be sure to pick one with acid-free paper to ensure a long life for your book.

Once you have your photo albums, scrapbooks, or boxes completed, make sure you label them on the outside and store them someplace accessible, such as the bottom shelf of your bookcase. The photos are now neatly organized and out of the way, but you can enjoy them and add to them at any time. Each time you bring home new photos, review them with a critical eye and toss any bad ones. Put the others in the albums, scrapbooks, or boxes as soon as possible.

You may wish to select some of your favorite photos to arrange in a collage-type frame (frames with multiple openings). These work especially well with a theme, such as family groups, vacations, holidays, or picnics—you get the idea. When your local discount store or art supply store has a sale on collage frames, stock up on half a dozen in a size you know you can use, and arrange these together as a display. Using identical frames will unify your collections and make them stand out. Of course, you can also get creative with frames and even make your own using those you've found at thrift shops, yard sales, or even in the attic. Small beads, seashells, ribbon, or charms add whimsy and flair to your frames and personalize your photo collection.

Let's Play Post Office

You've raided the mailbox, rummaged in the wastebaskets in the post office lobby and the office, and pestered your friends to save their envelopes. Now that you have all these wonderful stamps, what should you do with them? True, an ordinary shoe box gives storage space, but you should want a nicer place to store your collection—a place to display your material, not just store it. And, on the practical side, stamps and covers (envelopes with stamps on them, used in the mail) kept in a shoe box or paper folder risk damage from dirt or creases, losing value as well as beauty.

Purchasing your first album may be a kind of experiment. If you are buying an album in person, rather than by mail, listen to the seller's advice. Good beginners' albums are available that are not too expensive, are fully illustrated to show which stamp goes where, and may even contain extra information, such as maps and facts about the countries. Buy as wisely as you can and not over your budget, and don't be too discouraged if your first album turns out to be less than perfect. You will always need places for temporary storage as you continue in the hobby. Old albums never go to waste!

With experience you will soon learn what type of storage is best for you. Using care with these collections is important

*C*ollections such as stamps or coins, which can be stored in shoe boxes or sturdy metal containers, should be reviewed every six months or so (hey, you might have something valuable in there to trade on eBay™!). Stamp and coin albums should be dusted and kept along with any relevant books and supplies, such as magnifying glasses, nearby. Avoid storing them in damp basements or hot attics. A hall closet, bedroom closet, or even an empty drawer works well.

because you can pass them on to your children or grandchildren someday, along with some sage advice from you.

Letting the Cat out of the Bag

Lots of people collect representations of animals, pigs, cows, cats, dogs . . . you name it. For these collections, you can add a shelf down about 12 inches or so from the ceiling and let the animals march around the room. For expensive collections, enclosed storage is safer.

With Six You Get Egg Roll

There are always people who collect odd things. I had a friend who loved Chinese food and collected chopsticks from restaurants all over the country. To display them, he fashioned a fortune cookie out of foam and painted it to look like a cookie, complete with a fortune tag sticking out the side. He stuck his chopstick collection into the "cookie"! What I am saying is, be imaginative . . . think out of the box, or cookie, as the case may be.

Breaking Up Is Hard to Do

Do you collect breakables such as china or porcelain? China collections such as teacups or figurines do well attractively grouped in a glass-fronted hutch, but if you don't have one of these, use your imagination instead. Clear a space on a bookshelf or cabinet, arrange a pretty piece of fabric or doily, and display your treasures on that. Keep in mind that if you have little ones around, you will want to store your breakables up high where tiny hands can't reach.

For valuable collections of porcelain and other art objects, store them in locked, glass-fronted cabinets, or if the value is especially high, you may want to put these in a safe deposit box at the bank or in a safe. Keeping them secure should be your primary concern. Documenting their existence and value is your next step. Start by making a complete list of the pieces and add pertinent information, such as date of purchase, cost, information about the artist or creator of the piece, and any other relevant information. Take a photo of the object and attach the information to it and store in a safe place.

Other Collectibles

If someone in your family collects miniature race cars or Matchbox® vehicles, think of unique ways to display them. Perhaps roaring across the shelf of a bookcase, on the lower shelf of a table, or on shelving in your family room or den created to hold these treasurers. You can even mount them on wood strips and have them racing up the walls of the collector's bedroom. It's a good idea to list the place of purchase, date, and cost of each vehicle for your records and for resale purposes; keeping the box it came in can add value.

Anyone who collects spoons from every place he or she visits knows there is a vast variety of spoon racks available. Keep in mind that open racks will allow soiling and tarnishing of the spoons and require more upkeep. Glass-fronted spoon cabinets will keep the spoons clean and reduce the upkeep considerably. Spoon collections can add a lovely decorative touch to kitchens and dining rooms. Each time you bring home a spoon, you might want to consider labeling it with the date of purchase before you place it in the rack. Use a small sticky label for this purpose, and write with a permanent felt-tipped pen to preserve the information.

It Can Happen . . .

One last collective thought . . . before you throw out Aunt Gertrude's pottery collection, make sure that it is not a collector's item and of great value. There are many books in the library and web sites that can help you determine this. I had a friend who got the surprise of her life watching an antique show on TV. They showed a porcelain piece just like the one she was thinking of donating to a rummage sale that was valued at $3,200! Now, that's the extreme, but still keep it in mind.

CHAPTER 9

*Putting on
the Ritz*

*M*ore than any other room in the house, the dining room is most often the setting for our happiest occasions, such as family dinners and birthday and holiday celebrations. What fun it is to envision a festive table spread with pretty dishes and a delicious feast, ready for our families and guests to enjoy. It can be more than a wonderful fantasy. With the right amount of organization, it can become a reality in your home.

The China Cabinet

Let's start with the china cabinet or sideboard. Remove everything, put sets of dishes in one group, crystal and stemware in another, and serving pieces such as large bowls and ladles in a third. Grouping like items together will help you find these things quickly when you need them.

The first thing I found when I started to declutter my dining room was that a lot of space was taken up with occasional dishes. You know, the Christmas dishes you use once or twice and then store again, and the serving pieces that are only used on special occasions. Take a look in your china cabinet and sideboard and you'll know what I mean. These pieces take up valuable space that you could use to store things that you use frequently and make them easier to take out and put away. And the easier things are to use in your dining room, the more you'll want to use it, whether it's for an intimate family dinner or a gathering of the whole crowd.

As you are sorting things, think about what you want to keep and what you want to discard. If you haven't used them in years, consider selling them or passing them on to other family members. Just make sure you know their value before you decide to donate them to the thrift store. Many a person has given away a valuable antique! Don't let that happen to you. It's a good idea to take your older dishes and flatware to an antique dealer first, or even check out an on-line auction site like eBay. Many older china patterns are now collectibles.

Before putting items back in the cabinet, take the time to give it a good clean. Cabinets made of wood can be washed down with ordinary tea. Brew a strong pot of tea, using 2 or 3 tea bags, and let them steep for 15 minutes or so. Cool to room temperature, and wring out a soft cloth in

*R*epair or despair—it's up to you. If you're really going to glue the handle onto that china cup, do it now. Otherwise, out it goes . . .

the tea until damp. Then wipe the shelves and buff dry with a soft, clean cloth. The tannic acid in the tea adds luster to the wood finish. For plastic or metal buffets, sprinkle about a tablespoon of baking soda onto a soft cloth and wipe down the piece. Use a clean, damp cloth to rinse; then buff with a dry cloth. For glass shelves, a solution of equal parts rubbing alcohol and water will clean and create a shine.

When you start to rearrange things, put the seldom-used pieces, such as the Thanksgiving turkey platter, Christmas candlesticks, and eggnog cups, either up high or down low in areas that are harder to reach. (You're getting the hang of this, right?) Think about how you set your table as you put things away, and group the dishes and glasses that you use together near each other. You might consider wrapping groups of dishes in plastic or plastic wrap to keep them clean. You can also purchase zippered containers that fit dishes of various sizes to store your dishes in. Look for these containers at linen stores, organizing stores, or in specialty catalogs.

For more storage space, consider using a space-saving corner cabinet or some attractive cupboards or armoires. All of these cabinets can be adapted to your needs and will enhance your room style if chosen wisely. Built-ins, of course, are a wonderful option, especially those that are floor-to-ceiling with doors and perhaps a serving top.

Before purchasing new cabinets, make sure you measure your plates, trays, and other larger pieces, so that you don't get home with a new cabinet and find that you can't close the door because the plates stick out. Measuring will also ensure that you take full advantage of every bit of shelf space in your new cabinets. For small rooms, remember that glass shelves and glass-fronted units are not only attractive, but open up the area to the eye and are easy to clean.

Sturdy pieces with doors will work well for your dining room storage. Handles on doors will also help keep the front of the cabinet clean and unmarred. Look for hanging racks for cups and stacking units for dishes and things that will allow you to take advantage of the space within the cabinet. Store things where they are easily reached by you or the kids, whoever sets the table. Make it convenient to have help.

In a small dining room, don't overlook the storage use of areas around windows and doors. These small ledges will handle glasses and other knickknacks quite easily. Areas kept available for a bar service can be cleared and used for serving pieces. Use a portable bar cart to be set up when you are ready to serve cocktails.

Linens & Things & Napkin Rings

- To store table linens from the dining room, consider hanging tablecloths and their napkins on a padded hanger or on a plain wire hanger with an empty paper towel tube slipped over the bottom bar. Storing linens this way will keep creases to a minimum and make it easy for you to select exactly what you're looking for.

- Napkin rings can be placed in a plastic bag and hung over the neck of the hanger that's holding the table-cloth.

- Hang your linens in the back of the guest closet or any other closet where you have the room.

- Storing table linens in the basement is not a good idea. Moisture and humidity can cause mold and mildew that will ruin your fine cloths.

- Linens may be stored in the attic, but be sure to store them hanging and covered with a fabric cover, such as an old sheet. Don't use plastic, which can discolor the linens over time.

Heigh-Ho, Silver

- Sterling silver or silver-plated pieces will need to be wrapped in a silver-storage cloth to slow tarnishing. Line a drawer with this cloth and slide the silver in.

- Consider divided storage trays to store silverware and keep it organized. These trays are available in an array of styles. Measure your cabinet and select accordingly.

- Large silver pieces can be wrapped directly in storage cloths, or try silver storage bags that are specially treated to retard tarnish. Look for these cloths and bags in kitchen stores, linen stores, and specialty catalogs.

- Never use rubber bands or wrap silver in plastic wrap. These will accelerate tarnishing.

Now that your dining room is clutter-free, you are ready to fulfill your fantasy of hosting a feast fit for a King—or maybe a Queen!

CHAPTER 10

The Throne Room

*N*o matter what size your bathroom is, you'll never have enough storage. Since it's also the room we most hate to clean (I've taken an informal royal survey!), it presents us with some unique challenges in conquering clutter. But start with this premise, *Less clutter means less cleaning,* and you can't go wrong.

Before you tackle this project, consider the traffic. Who uses the room—just one person, several family members, or is it a guest bath used only infrequently? Any time more than one person uses a bathroom, it's a good idea to assign each individual his or her own area for storage. This can be as simple as assigning a shelf or a portion of a shelf, grouping containers together for grooming aids, or declaring one half of the counter "his" and one half "hers." But before you start on this, let's add another person to the mix—let's bring along your QUEEN, and work through this clutter-clearing program step-by-step-by-step.

*Q*uestion: *Look around. What things in the bathroom are really working? What things do I like—what things do I hate? Am I wasting time every morning digging for essentials? Is my blow dryer tangled in its cord? How many times have I been late leaving the house because I had to search for my curling iron or razor among all of the clutter that has accumulated?*

*U*npack: You'll be familiar with this step by now. Working with one area at a time, take everything out of the medicine cabinet, remove the bottles from the side of the bath, and unpack the cabinet under the sink. Remove towels from the cupboards and toiletries from the vanity. Once you have everything emptied out, you can look it all over and decide what to keep. Be sure to work with just one area at a time, though. Otherwise you'll have an unholy mess!

*E*valuate: Think your bathroom is home to just soap and towels? Think again!

- Start with the larger things, such as towels and washcloths. Look them over to determine if any of them should become rags.

- Weed out the hot rollers you used in the '80s, your husband's sideburn trimmer that he used when he had sideburns . . . and hair, and all of those headband and hair ornaments you used when you had long hair.

- Try your blow dryers and see which one(s) work(s) the best.

- Gather up all of your prescription and over-the-counter drugs and check the expiration dates on each bottle. Discard any that are past their expiration date.

- Toss out all pill bottles that don't have labels.

- Blister-pack pills often get separated from their boxes. While the blister-pack itself often contains identifying information as to the type of drug and the expiration date, if you're in doubt, get rid of them.

- Look at creams and ointments and consider whether you actually use them anymore. If you

*M*ake sure to dispose of unwanted medications safely. Flushing them down the toilet can be bad for the environment, and simply tossing them in the trash can be deadly to children and animals. Place unwanted medication in a childproof container, then in another jar, which you should make sure to seal securely. Only then should you put the container in the garbage.

haven't used the arthritis rub you bought when your grandma visited, you probably don't need it.

- If you have six boxes of Band-Aids®, combine them. (But *never* combine bottles of pills.)
- Throw out old, dirty tensor bandages.
- Ladies, pay particular attention to your collection of cosmetics. You should know that the Food and Drug Administration recommends keeping mascara no longer than three months, because bacteria tend to multiply after that period of time. While there are no regulations in place that require the cosmetic industry to set a specific shelf life for cosmetic items, voluntary guidelines show that the stability of cosmetics varies widely after 18 months. This is especially true of "all natural" cosmetics and personal-care products, which may contain plant-derived substances conducive to bacterial growth. So check your cosmetics for changes in color or appearance, and when in doubt, toss it out!
- Suntan lotion and sunscreens do not generally have expiration dates, but it is probably a good idea to toss them after 18 months. Sunless tanning lotions can change color with age, giving you an odd-colored tan. If the color has changed, toss the product. Green tans are not attractive on most people.
- If you have kids, or live with someone who acts like one, you probably experience the tumble of rubber duckies, submarines, goggles, and boats falling off the bathtub ledges every time you take

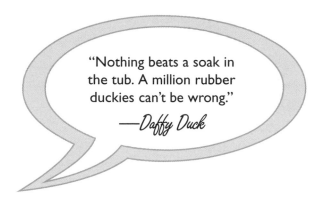

"Nothing beats a soak in the tub. A million rubber duckies can't be wrong."

—*Daffy Duck*

a shower. It's time to pare down the collection and find a dry storage space for the rest in between bath times.

*E*liminate: Now it's time to decide what stays and what goes. Need help? I suggest you throw out:

- Towels and washcloths that have holes, tears, hems coming apart—or have just seen better days—should be put in your rag container.
- Combs with missing teeth, brushes that are falling apart.
- Broken barrettes, elastic ponytail holders that have lost their snap, the hair color (Brigitte Bardot Blonde) that you can't get up your nerve to experiment with.
- If you have magazines dating back three years piling up in a basket beside the throne, it's time to throw out all but the most recent.

- Do you really need to read that bathroom joke book one more time? Now is the perfect time to say good-bye to those knock-knock jokes and create room for necessary storage.

A lot of these items can (and should) just be thrown out. However:

- You probably have a small pile of such things as a dab of nail polish in a bottle, a toothpaste tube with just a little left, some acetone polish remover with a smidgen in the bottom—you get the picture. Relegate the toothpaste and acetone to the cleaning supplies; toothpaste is great for removing grass stains. Toss in that old toothbrush too. Are there some old denture-cleaning tablets lurking in the back of the drawer? Use them to clean your toilet. Use the nail polish to label things. I have three containers of makeup that look the same from the outside. I used red nail polish to

If you have free samples and trial-size toiletries that are taking up space, why not collect them all up and give them to a local homeless shelter?

write the color numbers on the outside in big letters that I can easily see. Take an old container of
clear nail polish and store it in your nylons
drawer or desk drawer to stop runs.

- Sort out the things that can be donated to charity
  or sold at a garage sale. Make sure the items are
  clean and box them up, putting the garage sale
  items in your garage sale staging area and the
  charity donation items in a labeled box. You can
  not donate medicines or opened cosmetic products. If you found the lotion and bath gel from
  your last birthday and never liked the smell, by
  all means donate them.

*N*eaten Up: Now look around the room. It's time to
store the essentials. Nearly every area in the bathroom
can be used for storage. Think in terms of walls, doors,
floors, existing cabinets, corners, and even over the
shower and windows.

With your family's traffic flow pattern in mind, look
over the bathroom and determine which areas need
what type of storage. If you style your hair and do
makeup in one area, you'll want to store your tools
conveniently nearby. This same tactic applies to shaving supplies for the men. Since the medicine cabinet is a
poor place to store medicine (humidity is *terrible* for
all medications), let it serve as a storage cabinet for
shaving needs instead.

Those fortunate enough to have a large bathroom will benefit by adding a chest of drawers to the room. Use the largest size you can get away with, and stack towels, linens, and supplies that are not often used. You can paint or decorate the chest of drawers nicely to complement your decor. Just make sure to shellac painted surfaces, so that humidity won't cause paint to crack or peel.

- Consider a tray on the vanity for items such as cotton swabs, cotton balls, deodorants, lotions, and the like. It's far easier to move one tray when cleaning than all sorts of various containers. Look around your own home for cute and different containers. I use a wicker divided chip-and-dip tray, spray painted to match the bathroom, for my cotton balls and Q-tips®.

- Large baskets, serving trays, even glass deviled-egg trays are fun and practical to use in the bathroom for storage. I once bought some beautiful kitchen canisters at a discount store. One of the four canisters was broken, but the three that were intact matched my bath beautifully. I put some cork on the bottom so they wouldn't scratch the marble countertop and stored my styling products in one, swabs and cotton balls in another, and combs belonging to the King and I in the third. I still use them even though they no longer match the bathroom. Now the canisters do storage duty inside enclosed shelves.

- If space is at a premium, attach brackets for shelves to walls over the shower, over the door, or even over the vanity mirror. Also think in terms of plastic or wicker toilet paper holders. They store four or five rolls of toilet paper conveniently. If you have a smart cat, like the Palace Princess, keep her from spinning your toilet paper all over the room by installing it with the paper feed coming from the bottom rather than the top. That way they can't sit and spin!

- Over-the-toilet shelves look nice, but don't often hold much because of the design challenge of fitting over the toilet. A better option is a small corner cabinet that fits over the toilet. Even an étagère (a fancy name for a freestanding shelf unit!) could work well. Remember, the old adage *Out of sight, out of mind* means less cleaning required. That's why I favor cabinets with doors. Baskets inside these cabinets can organize and group things. The baskets can be any style you like—plastic strawberry baskets, wicker, metal, even shoe boxes covered with adhesive-backed paper. Be sure to clearly label the end of the box if contents aren't easily seen. Remember, *Out of sight, out of mind* doesn't give you license to hoard and overbuy. Stay organized. A medicine cabinet is not like a mountain: you don't have to use it *just because it's there*. . . .

- Make use of hooks, over-the-door hangers and over-the-door towel racks. If you have a spot for everybody's towel, there is less likelihood of them ending up in a damp heap on the floor all day. This also lessens the chance of your teenager leaving their damp towel on the bed all day! Smaller children should have hooks and racks that are easily reached.

- Don't forget to add specialty hangers to hold blow dryers and curling irons; these can be found in linen and organizing stores. They attach easily to the wall or inside a cupboard to keep the dryer handy, but neat and out of the way. Or, make your own from an ordinary plastic tubular hanger. Just loop the cord around the bottom bar, twisting firmly until the cord is secure. Tuck the plug into the last few inches of cord for a tight hold.

- Freestanding sinks are great for hiding all sorts of things when you add a decorative skirt with Velcro® tape. The skirt is easily removed for cleaning. In households with children, don't store cleaning chemicals or medicine here; stick to storing things such as blow dryers, hot rollers, or extra toilet paper or supplies.

- Consider adding roll-out shelves to your existing vanity. These shelves are mounted on rollers and pull out, instead of being stationary inside the vanity, so they make items much more accessible

and add up to more for your money, storage-
wise. These shelves also have lips on the end, so
that items don't roll off, which is an unfortunate
hazard with stationary shelves.

- Look for toothbrush holders that are covered
  (more hygienic), and try to select one that is dishwasher safe, so that it can be cleaned quickly and
  easily. Toothpaste is a good cleaning tool for
  many things, but not when it is stuck like cement
  all over the toothbrush holder.

Now that your bathroom is so cleverly organized, isn't it
time for a nice bubble bath?

CHAPTER 11

In the Bedroom

*I*deally, a bedroom should be a haven from the workaday world, a retreat where you can relax and let the cares of the day slip away. But that's hard to do if your bedroom is overflowing with clutter! Clothes on the bed, dresser drawers in disarray, and books, magazines, and odds and ends from the rest of the house will all detract from the peaceful atmosphere you want to create in your "room of rest." The important thing here is that this room function for you and your life.

A Little R&R?

Try, if you can, to arrange your room by functions, making sure you have a quiet, uncluttered area for sleeping, as well as space for your other activities. Perhaps a reading section with a cozy chair or lounge and light will appeal to you, or you may want to create a separate nook for a mini-office or a sewing or craft area. It's up to you to designate what your bedroom will be used for, and remember, it only has to be comfortable for you.

Closest to the Closet

Let's begin with the master bedroom, and here we'll talk about storage. The first place we go to store items in the bedroom, of course, is the closet. This is such a big issue I've devoted a whole chapter to it! The thing to remember about the bedroom closet is to keep in there only items that are used regularly—unless, of course, your closet is the size of Imelda Marcos's: she had room for 1,000 pairs of shoes! Most of us don't have that luxury, so for us it makes sense to keep each season's clothes in the bedroom we sleep in, and move out-of-season clothes, hats, purses, and coats to another bedroom closet, the attic, or even the garage. You can purchase metal rolling wardrobe racks for this purpose. Store out-of-season clothing on this and cover with an old sheet or large piece of clean fabric. Place dried citrus peel in the pockets to discourage moths. Remember, don't cover with plastic or store items in plastic dry-cleaning bags. This will discolor them.

Beside the Bedside

Bedside tables with drawers are great, but don't use these as a junk stash. Instead, consider what your needs are. If you like to jot things down while you're reading, for instance, stash paper and pens in your bedside table, as well as night cream, hankies, lip balm, and reading glasses. Another great option for storage is a bedside pocket to hold the book you're reading, extra socks, and a tube of hand cream—things that normally take up space in a drawer or on top of the nightstand. A bedside pocket is quite simply a pocket made of fabric with a longer piece of fabric attached that tucks in between the mattress and box spring. During the day it is covered by the bedspread, and at night it's easily reachable. You can buy these in linen stores or through specialty catalogs, or make your own to match the decor of your room.

For additional storage, consider unfinished round tables. These inexpensive tables work well by the bed, in front of a window, or next to a chair. Usually they come unassembled, with legs that screw in easily to the tabletop. You can cover them with a tablecloth that drapes to the floor. If you are handy, you might make your own covering. I once made a cloth for this type of table out of old ties that belonged to the King. It was a real conversation piece! The cloth hides a wonderful little storage nook underneath. Use yours to store extra linens, bedjackets, or books. Underneath mine I have tucked a box of paperback books that I use for reading material on trips and can leave on the plane or at the hotel when I'm done.

What Goes Where

Small items on top of dressers, chests, and nightstands should be placed on trays or in baskets or decorative hatboxes to keep them contained. Keep display items such as figurines grouped together on a wall shelf or tray on the dresser or counter. Remember, if you don't have a lot of doodads on tops of surfaces, cleaning will go quickly and your room will look restful and less cluttered.

Many of us have additional paperwork we need to store. Try placing a two-drawer file cabinet in the closet, if space permits, or next to a chair. Drape with a tablecloth and voilà! Instant table—and more storage space, to boot!

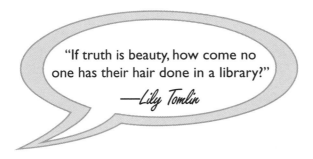

"If truth is beauty, how come no one has their hair done in a library?"

—Lily Tomlin

Shelves placed over doors or in small unused areas can keep things up off the floor and tabletops. Even small cabinets with doors can be useful when mounted above tables or headboards or placed next to dressers or chests.

What's Hidden Under *Your* Bed?

And let's not overlook that sneaky lode of storage space— underneath the bed. This is a particularly good area to use for out-of-season things such as blankets, comforters, sweaters, seasonal table linens, gift wrapping paper—just about anything you can think of (okay, it's probably not a good spot for that extra honey-glazed ham). I like to label the ends of the boxes or containers so that I don't have to open each one and look through it. Use cardboard or plastic containers; these are readily available at discount stores. Some plastic ones even have drawers that slide out, so that you don't have to pull the entire box out. If you are storing heavy items, plastic boxes will be sturdier for lightweight items, cardboard boxes are fine. If you intend to use storage boxes over an extended period of time, then plastic ones will last longer, so they are a better long-term investment.

Still need more space under the bed? Consider bed risers. These are plastic risers that hold the wheel of the bed frame and raise the bed up 6 or 7 inches. This creates a lot more space under the bed. You can purchase these in sets of four (one for each leg of the bed); double and queen-size beds will take one set, but a king-size bed will require two sets of risers. You can find these in home and health stores or linen catalogs. Do keep in mind that your bed will now be 6 inches higher; so if you are a little short in the legs yourself, you may find yourself literally climbing into bed each night!

The Quick Fix

Don't overlook the quick fixes for storage in your bedroom. I've listed a few to get you started.

- Magazine racks are useful for much more than magazines. Decorate yours to match your bedroom, and fill it with writing materials, fabrics for sewing, or filing that needs to be done.
- Plastic or metal bins can live in your closet or underneath the bed to store out-of-season clothes, books, or gifts.

- Decorative baskets can't be used enough. Great for magazines, extra towels, linens, mini-office or craft supplies, books, and so much more.

- To get the most out of your dresser space, put dividers in drawers for socks and underwear. Roll them instead of folding and they take up less room.

- Assign drawers to suit your needs; if you wear sweaters only occasionally, for instance, put them in a lower drawer. Keep the most easily reached drawers for everyday items.

- A vanity bench is another storage area that can serve a dual purpose. This is your morning "staging area" —especially useful if one or both of you have to make an early exit each day. Use the bench to lay out your clothing the evening before; you can sit on the bench as you dress, then pick up the top to stash small storage items (I use mine to hold my manila folder of monthly bills, believe it or not—it's always in the same place, and I know right where everything is).

- Wooden valets that stand about four feet high with a hanger on top are useful for laying out clothing the night before too. As well as carrying an outfit of clothing, these have a bar across the bottom that holds a pair or two of shoes. When you've finished dressing for the day, you can slip your robe or nightshirt over the valet and place your slippers on the bottom and your nightclothes are ready for you in the evening.

The Guest Bedroom

The guest or spare bedroom is a real lifesaver when you have company, but if it's so cluttered that you can't get to the bed, it won't do you much good. And what about the rest of the time when you have no guests? Then, it's wasted space. This room can be a multipurpose room instead—it's anyone's guess what's in there!

For years the King and I had a lovely big guest room that was occupied almost exclusively by the Palace Pussycat and things we didn't know where else to put. Not only was it wasted space, but I had to clean it out each time we did have guests (which usually meant I was in a hurry), so the pile in the guest room became the pile somewhere else. That wasn't the worst part, though; usually I had to clean it from top to bottom!

- Take a look at your extra room. What is it used for? Does the room now house toys for the kids or serve as a catchall for objects you can't bear to part with (like that StairMaster® you got with such good intentions last year)? Take a good look at your extra room and determine what else it could be used for.

- Most spare rooms are small, but even so they can be converted into mini music studios. These rooms are ideal practice areas to house a keyboard, violin, or other instruments. Keep these in their original cases to prevent damage from exposure to variations in humidity. When storing any of these instruments, be sure they are in a climate-controlled area of your home (not the attic or a damp basement). Properly stored and cared for instruments can be passed on from child to child, thus preserving a considerable investment. An interior walled closet is an excellent storage spot for these instruments; just remember not to stack them, as this may damage sensitive parts like strings or mouthpieces. Cube storage is ideal for musical instruments, since it contains them in one space and they can be lifted in and out of the closet with minimum possibility of damage. This also allows you to store sheet music, extra strings, guitar picks, and so on, with the instrument, so everything is in one place at practice time. When you're paying $30 for a half-hour lesson, time is money and you don't want to scramble around the house looking for the sheet music to Junior's piece for the fall recital! Follow any storage directions that come with the instruments or check with a reputable music store for advice.

- Another fine use of this space is as the hobby or sewing room. Here, a narrow table or small desk along a wall with narrow cupboards or drawers above is ideal. This will allow you to have the items you need to work with right at your fingertips, without the clutter and mess lying around you. A big plus is that you will be able to find what you need without looking through everything.

Guess Who's Coming for . . . Overnight!

Are you one of those people who say, "When you're in town, be sure you come and visit us?" Well, now is the time to pay up, because guess what—company's coming!

If you're expecting out-of-town guests, you want everything to look its best, especially the room they will be sleeping in. Of course, that means you'll have to have a bed in there! Start by looking at what you've got. A twin bed can be pushed against a wall and outfitted as a daybed very inexpensively. A daybed is actually a bed that masquerades as a sofa/sitting area. You can transform a twin bed into a daybed by placing a fitted coverlet over the mattress and arranging pillows that match across the top. These coverlet sets are found at linen and discount stores. You can still use your twin sheets to make up the bed. Full or queen size beds can also be pushed close to the wall (careful, leave enough room to walk around the bed so you can make it) and the underbed area used for storage of out-of-season clothing, gift wrapping, and so on. Under this bed is also a great spot for oversized items such as seldom-used sports equipment, or even a movie screen. You get the idea.

Before guests arrive, change the sheets and pillowcases. (Don't forget the clean blankets too!) Make the closet look its best by first being sure there is plenty of open hanging space, even if you have to remove some of your stored clothing. Put plenty of hangers in easy reach, including some for hanging trousers and skirts. A few cedar chips or a decorative sachet is a nice touch too. Air the room if it needs it, or spritz with a room spray or homemade air freshener.

Provide some drawer space so that your guests can put away their clothes and store their suitcase during the visit, or provide a luggage rack for this purpose. As a final welcoming touch, do like the classy hotels and tie several spare pillows together like a gift package with ribbon or string. Store them on the closet shelf. This not only looks nice, but also gives the pillows stability, so they will sit on the shelf better, without tumbling out every time the closet door is opened.

Organizing the spare room pays off because it allows you to use every inch of space in your home to the fullest, without stress or fuss. No need to go into panic mode when company calls; you're ready for every occasion!

CHAPTER 12

Go to Your Room

Kids' rooms are often messy, with crayons here, dolls and trucks there, and a teddy bear or two hanging around for good measure. But don't confuse messy with cluttered. Anyone who has put away the crayons, parked the trucks, and put the dolls to bed knows how easy this "mess" can be to deal with—easy, that is, if you don't have clutter. Clutter is that stuff you have to go through *before* finding your daughter's favorite pink T-shirt or your son's favorite baseball mitt. It's three odd socks, an overdue library book, and the beginning of a long abandoned finger-painted masterpiece. And it can be really irritating.

Because children are continuously growing, their rooms are often the easiest in which to

Get rid of kids' clutter and you'll be rewarded twice: with an organized kids' room now, and organized kids later!

find items to eliminate. What clothes and toys has your child outgrown? Are the days of infant-sized onesies long gone? Then it's time to throw out the stained and worn, and pass on the good. Now that Susie is five, does she really still need her infant mobile? Pack up those toys your child has deemed no longer interesting and donate them to charity. You may even enlist your child's help. We used to have a rule in my house that for every new toy, one old toy had to be donated to the children's hospital. Knowing that their toys were going to other boys and girls just like them and not the garbage dump helped my son to volunteer toys for donation with minimum hassle. Try it. They may surprise you! But please, no broken toys. These do belong in the trash.

Of course, you will want to keep a few sentimental toys and items of clothing, and some (but not all!) of their art-work. Store these in a plastic bin with a secure lid on the top shelf of their closet.

Storage and Furniture

- First, question what your child's needs are. For preschoolers up to kindergarten age, a toy box and some low shelves for books is all that is really needed.

- As your child grows, he'll need more in the way of storage. Add more shelving; a desk or table with a lamp and chair for schoolwork and projects and space for a computer are all-important.

- Teenagers may need an area for a television and/or stereo set and a phone (and teenage girls will need lots of closet space to accommodate their many trips to the mall!).

- Take a look at the height of your children, and then organize the room accordingly. Keep shelves and hooks low enough for them to reach.

- You might want to hang the hooks just a little above eye level. This will encourage kids to use the hooks and also make them obvious enough to prevent a bumped head.

Next, let's evaluate what you already have and what you need. Look at furniture options that will grow with the kids.

- Beds with storage built in underneath are particularly good, since kids of almost any age can reach them. These beds can take kids to adulthood.

- When purchasing furniture for baby, consider chests and armoires that can be used as the child grows up. This way, there's no need to purchase two sets of furniture!

- Any furniture or shelving used in kids' rooms should be solid and stable. Each piece should hold the weight of a toddler; you know how they climb. If the furniture becomes wobbly or off balance with a 20-pound bag of birdseed or cat litter on it, then it is not safe for your toddler.

- Bookshelves need to be well supported and made of sturdy material. If shelves are freestanding, be certain they are bolted securely to the wall.

Evaluate your child's needs for hanging clothes in the closet.

- Consider installing a temporary closet rod that is low enough that they can reach their clothes (even a shower curtain tension bar will work). Adjust the rod as the children grow until they can use the regular rod.

- Shelves to hold stuffed animals and things that are seldom played with can be at a higher level, leaving lower shelves for books, games, computer discs, and other things.

- When kids are small, consider placing shelves on brackets on the lower closet walls. They can eventually be removed too. This is a great place to store games.

You know the drill by now. Once you've gotten rid of the clutter (good-bye, broken Game Boy®; good-bye, one-legged doll), it's time to Neaten Up. But it's a little different this time. Now you're going to neaten up and organize in such a way as to encourage your children to keep it up for themselves. Think about it. If you pick up your kids things today, you can be darn sure you're going to have to do it tomorrow, and the day after that, and the day after that. . . . Why not teach your children to look after their own belongings? Of course, you'll have to organize their rooms so that it's easy for them to put away their own things. And, of course, you'll have to expect different things from a five-year-old and a fourteen-year-old (the five-year-old is probably going to be much easier to deal with!). But give it a try. You have nothing to lose, and, oh, so much to gain!

Here are some tips to help you organize your children's rooms so they can help keep them organized themselves:

- An over-the-door shoe bag is excellent for organizing not only shoes, but other small pieces of clothing such as socks, mittens, earmuffs, or even toys. Keep the bottom pouches filled with things the kids need to reach; save the top areas for things you can help them with, such as hair accessories and things reserved for special occasions.

- Collections such as stamps and baseball cards can fit nicely on bookshelves. Shoe boxes work well to keep things together, as do inexpensive file-card-size file boxes and clear, clean fast-food containers.

- Blocks can be stored easily in small laundry baskets or plastic bins. Mesh bags are great too.

- Toys with lots of little parts can easily get broken, and the pieces can get mislaid. Try storing small parts in Tupperware® containers or Ziploc® bags. Both come in a wonderful assortment of sizes.

- Larger toys can be stored in toy boxes or chests. Wicker hampers work well too. They are lightweight, with no heavy lids to close on little fingers, and as children grow the wickerwork can be put to work as laundry hampers.

- Dolls and their clothes and accessories can be stored in plastic under-the-bed storage boxes. The accessories won't become separated from the doll, and storage is simple, even for a child.

- Boxed games can be tied shut or have a bungee cord put around them, so that lids don't come loose and contents jumbled.

- A net hammock hung in a corner of the room is great for stuffed animals and other soft toys that don't get played with often but are too precious to give up.

Lost and Found

When I was young, I used one of my grandpa's old cigar boxes as a Lost and Found. Each time I came across a small game piece, an errant dice, or an "anonymous" part of a toy, I just tossed it into the box until I needed it—or figured out what the heck it was! The Queen Mum taught me that, and it saved us hours of searching for lost treasures. You may not have a cigar-smoking grandpa, in which case I suggest you use a shoe box or a big empty chocolate box as your Lost and Found. Try it though. You may never again have to look for the last piece of that jigsaw puzzle again.

Shared Rooms

Shared rooms offer a special challenge. Even though more than one child is living in the room, each child needs an area they can call their own. Even the tiniest members of the household are no exception. So before one of your precious children divides the room in two with the entrance squarely in his half—thereby preventing his younger sibling from coming or going—you need to step in and create areas of the room each child can call his own. You'll be saving your very sanity by following these tips:

- Separate the room. Put a bed on each side and provide individual storage for each child.

- Divide the closet evenly. If necessary, place a temporary vertical partition down the center of the closet and assign each child a side. You can divide the closet easily by tacking a piece of fabric to the shelf and letting it drop to the floor, or you can use a piece of painted lightweight wood that you cut to fit between the shelf and the floor. Assigning each child their own special-colored hangers also helps.

- In a shared room, color identification is helpful. If it's blue storage units or hangers, it belongs to Bob, and if it's red, it belongs to Mike. Color code toy storage areas, closet areas, and other furniture and accessories.

- Provide separate chests of drawers if possible; if not, assign drawers by labeling. Pick up inexpensive unfinished furniture and paint each child's furniture a different color, or divide the drawers by color.

- Teach the children to respect each other's areas, just as if they were separate rooms. It's a good life lesson.

- For a real touch of privacy, hang a lightweight roll-up plastic shade from the ceiling. When pulled down, it is a Do Not Disturb sign. When up, the kids are again happily sharing their area.

The Dreaded . . . Locker

While we're talking about kids, let's have a word about lockers. We all know how they smell . . . gym socks from the start of the school year, an apple from lunch two weeks ago, and how about those gym shoes! They are crammed full of schoolbooks that never make it to class or home, CDs, notes from friends, cookie crumbs, and there may actually be a coat and some gym clothes in there somewhere. Whoever invented the tall, narrow, dark locker knew nothing about kids and clutter. I mean, *come on;* a tiny shelf with three metal hooks and a gaping 6 feet of horror. Back when I went to school, my coat and a couple of pencils and some books fit in there pretty well; although I do remember an ugly fight with a Flutophone® one time. Nowadays kids have laptops and tons of other electronic equipment, so proper storage is essential. Here are some simple ideas to keep the kids clutter-free (and fresh smelling!) during the school year.

- Add a few stick-on hooks to hold purses, keys, gym shoes, cameras—and more.
- Hang up a small mesh bag to take in things like a hairbrush, water bottle, and Discman®.
- Pocket organizers are great—stuff them with those annoying little items that get lost at the bottom of the locker. Plastic see-through pockets are great for at-a-glance organization. Cloth pockets are better for the teenager who values her privacy.

- A couple of magnets on the back wall will hold containers for pencils and pens, and you can even hang a plastic grocery bag to fill with trash and toss out weekly. Put magnets on the back of mirrors too (all teenage girls have bad hair days).

- Grid-type stacking shelves are great for holding not just books, but electronic equipment too.

An organized locker will save you from a bag of who-knows-what at the end of the school year.

You're giving your children a priceless lesson when you teach them early to begin conquering clutter, starting with their own rooms. In doing this, they learn to take control of their own lives too. It's a win-win situation for everyone involved.

CHAPTER 13

Come out of the Closet

*N*ow let's venture into the scariest place of all: the closet. Ever go in looking for clothes to wear and wonder if you'll find the item you really need—or worse still—wonder if you'll ever come out? If empty hangers are hanging all over, crowded racks are causing clothes to wrinkle, and you seem to have to iron everything before you can wear it, well, it's time to conquer the closet. Arm yourself with some logical thinking, a sense of humor, plenty of garbage bags and boxes, and you can conquer clutter in your closet in about the same amount of time it takes you to sit through the latest Hollywood blockbuster at your local multiplex. And not only will you be pleased, but the thrift stores nearby will thank you too.

Now, onward . . . but don't think you need to venture in alone. Why not take the QUEEN with you!

Question: *What do I want from the closet? What problems do I have every time I go to the closet to select clothes? Is there an area that constantly frustrates me? Are my blouses all mixed up with my husband's shirts? Are my sweaters bunched up on the shelf or getting shoulder dimples from wire hangers? What about my shoes? Have I ever spent 10 minutes looking for that other brown shoe? Do I hang myself on a purse strap every time I reach for a skirt? What do I need to change so that I can get off to a smooth start in the morning?*

Unpack: To do the job right, you have to take everything out of the closet. If you have some rolling racks, put them to use now. If not, you can utilize the shower rod (provided it's attached firmly to the wall), the bed, and floor. Group the clothes by whom they belong to and into categories—blouses in one pile, skirts in another, slacks in still another. You get the idea.

- Remove everything from shelves and floor, sorting as you go. Make piles of keepers, "not sure," and "get rid of." In the keeper piles, try to group types of clothes together, it will save you time later.

- Clothes that need laundering or dry cleaning should go in a dirty-clothes hamper or dry-cleaning basket.

- Take the time to wash down closet walls thoroughly and vacuum the carpet or wash the floor (that way your favorite silk blouse won't get tangled in a cobweb!).

*E*valuate: Sort clothes, putting "toss" or "donate" items into appropriate containers, such as boxes or trash bags. It's a good idea to use black trash bags so that you or the family can't see your "treasures" departing. Place the clothes you are keeping on the bed or a rolling portable rack.

As you are evaluating each item, consider:

- Does it fit?
- Be tough. If you haven't worn it in a year, you probably won't ever wear it again. If you haven't been a size 6 since high school, move on and eliminate the size 6s.
- Do I need to alter this? How much will the alterations cost?
- How about repairs—can the item be repaired and still be wearable?
- Will shoe polish really take care of that huge scuff mark on the toe of my shoe?
- Give yourself permission to have a pile of "not sure" things. These are things you just can't quite make up your mind about. If, after further consideration, you are still not sure, box them up, label the box with its contents, and date it. In six

months if you haven't revisited any of the items, donate the contents or dispose of it.

- Really consider each item. Where will you wear it? When? If you can't come up with a good answer, say good-bye!

Eliminate

- Get rid of extra wire hangers. Give them back to your dry cleaner if he will take them; otherwise donate them to a nursing home or toss them.
- Anything mismatched will not likely be missed— throw out mismatched items.
- Look through your "not sure" pile one last time and make any additional judgment calls—be strong!

By now you should have boxes and bags for donating, garage sale, and trash. Remove these from the room, so that you have space to work ... and no matter now tempting it is, don't look in these containers again. If

*I*f things cannot be fixed, altered, or repaired and be really wearable, then they should be tossed. If the items are salvageable, then keep them, but take care of the problem *before* putting the item back in the closet.

they are full, tape them up and label them with where they go and get the trash bags into the trash . . . quickly! It's like pulling off a Band-Aid®, it hurts less if you just "do it"!

Neaten Up

- Determine hanger type—wire, clip, or plastic. Be consistent. A jumble of wire, plastic, and wood hangers will become tangled and be harder to separate and use—plus it just plain looks better!
- Start rehanging clothes, grouping by color and type.
- If using a double-hung system, hang trousers and skirts on the lower rack.
- Group blouses and shirts by color, and hang them over appropriate pants or skirts (this is called instant dressing!)
- Hang long clothes in areas where they won't tangle with things on the bottom of the closet floor.
- Hang or fold and store sweaters. Sweaters actually do better when folded because they don't stretch. If you prefer to hang sweaters, be sure to use padded hangers to avoid those shoulder dimples. And button them to keep their shape.
- Arrange men's ties on a tie rack or hang over a hanger. (Take a tip from a salesman friend of mine who has a vast collection of ties: after he wears one, he slips it off his neck without untying, and drapes it over a hanger in the closet. His wife has

assembled a half dozen "tie hangers" by color in the closet this way.)

- Replace purses on shelves in your storage area, grouping matching purses and shoes together.
- Use a clear plastic shoe box to capture miscellaneous items such as hairbands, scarves, and belts, and place on the shelf.
- Cover seldom-worn clothes with a cloth cover, or group them together and cover with fabric, such as an old sheet or tablecloth, to keep them clean.
- Be sure you have enough light in the closet. Consider a battery-operated light, or one that "taps" on and off as needed. This helps you to avoid leaving the house in one navy and one black shoe!

A Sentimental Journey

Now you're probably staring at a group of what I call the "sentimental keepers." These are things you don't wear or use, but can't bear to part with—so don't. Make sure they are clean (stains can oxidize over time), and pack them in a box labeled something like "sentimental favorites." Store them away, under the bed, on a top shelf, or in the attic (as long as the temperature there remains fairly consistent). You still have the items, but they're not taking up valuable space in your closet. Who knows, one day when you're baby-sitting the grandkids and run out of ideas, you may grab it for a "dress up" box. Most kids love to play this game.

No More Closet Confusion

Let's talk about storage options in your closet.

- First, consider adding extra shelving. This will give you lots of extra space for those things that you don't use often, but still need to have on hand, like handbags and totes, evening shoes, sweaters, and bathing suits.

- If you store things that tend to tip over or fall off the shelf, such as purses or stacks of sweatshirts, put them in a see-through type container such as a plastic milk crate. You want to easily see from the floor what you are looking for. If you used a closed container, have it labeled in bold print.

- I keep a set of "grab-its" in my closet. These are super-long tongs-like things on a long wooden handle that you can use to reach high above your head. Look for these in home and health stores, and catalogs. They are meant for people who lack mobility, but they're a wonderful tool to keep handy, not only in your closet, but in the kitchen, garage, and even the living room.

- Look your closet over and determine how many long items you have, such as dresses and long skirts, trousers that are hung from the cuff, bathrobes, and long coats. This will help you determine how much of your closet space to allocate to their storage. If you don't wear a lot of long things, then you will only need a small area to store them.

- If you have a lot of blouses, shirts, trousers folded over padded hangers, and other shorter things, consider adding a bar to the closet to instantly double your storage space. You don't have to run it the entire length of your closet; you can break the closet up into "long" and "short" zones. By adding double racks, you can store your slacks on the bottom and coordinating blouses on the top rack. Double racks should be installed at about 82 and 42 inches high to make the most of your closet space.

- Separate your clothing by color and you can grab an outfit at a glance when it's time to get dressed. This method also lets you know what items are in the laundry too. By adding an extra rack, you may have enough space in your closet to store sweaters hanging on padded hangers to keep them wrinkle free (although I still say sweaters are better folded—no stretching).

- No need to hang T-shirts; roll them in drawers to conserve space and deter wrinkles.

- Hooks on the back of the closet door are fine for robes and pajamas.

*T*he King thinks I should wear my dresses longer. About three years longer!

Best Foot Forward

Shoe storage is a big factor in how well you will be able to use your closet. There never seems to be enough floor space, and try as you may, shoes seem to have a life of their own. Years ago, I read in a magazine survey that shoes scattered about on the closet floor are a sign of a "creative mind." I can't tell you how many times that comforted me as I entered my closet and surveyed the whirlwind of shoes scattered on the floor. However, folks, being "creative" isn't all that much fun when you're searching for the mate to your favorite black pump at 5:30 AM! I finally solved this dilemma by adding a shelf for shoes on one wall. This keeps shoes off the floor of the closet, and again, you can see at a glance where the pair you want are kept. If there isn't space for shelving like this in your closet, purchase over-the-door shoe pockets from discount or linen stores and group your shoes together, again by color.

Get It Off Your Chest

Fitting a chest of drawers into your closet will really add space and convenience. They're a terrific place to store socks, underwear, pajamas, T-shirts, and workout clothes, as well as out-of-season items such as sweaters and bathing suits. Don't worry about the appearance of the dresser; you can use a castoff from another room, lug one home from a thrift shop or garage sale, or use Aunt Tilly's that has been gathering dust in the attic. Here's a tip if the dresser drawers smell musty: lay a slice of white bread (yes, it must be white) in a bowl and cover with undiluted white vinegar. Place one in each drawer that smells, close the drawer, and leave for 24 hours. When you open it, the smell should be gone. ODORZOUT™ is also a great odor eliminator. It absorbs stubborn odors, including smoke (in case Aunt Tilly was a smoker).

Don't Hamper Your Efforts

A hamper or a rolling three-section clothes sorter on wheels is wonderful to keep in or near the closet, if space permits. Sort your laundry by lights, darks, and hand washables as you take things off and you'll have a jump on laundry day. Keep a separate basket or nylon or canvas bag handy for dry-clean only clothes and you can easily see when a trip to the dry cleaners is necessary. Rolling sorters are great—they can be wheeled right into the laundry room.

Measure Up!

Here are some basic measurements of things usually found in your closet. (I said *usually*. This doesn't include your sophomore cheerleading uniform or the tiara you wore for your school play!) Keep these figures in mind and you'll find it easy to arrange—and rearrange—your closet. (These measurements are standards set by the American Institute of Architects.)

Did you know a standard hanger is between 17 ½ and 19 inches wide? You will need to allow a little bit of extra clearance to move the hangers in and out of the closet.

Hanging by the Numbers

Long dresses	69 inches
Robes	52 inches
Regular Dresses	45 inches
Skirts	35 inches
Trousers (cuff hung)	44 inches
Trousers (dbl. hung)	30 inches
Blouses and Shirts	28–38 inches
Men's Suits	38 inches
Women's Suits	29 inches
Coats	50–52 inches
Ties	27 inches (hung on a tie rack or over a hanger)
Dress Storage Bags	48 inches
Travel Bags	41 inches
Garment Bags	57 inches
Hanging Shoe Bags	38–72 inches

Single Rods (height)   66–72 inches

Double-Hung Rods (heights)   82 and 42 inches

When making changes to the rack system or shelving in your closet, make sure you keep these measurements in mind.

As you stand admiring your work, why not grab the camera and take a picture of that beautiful closet? Post it in your newly refurbished family scrapbook, and proudly note the date you finally conquered closet clutter!

CHAPTER 14

Putting a New Spin on the Laundry Room

*I*f you are lucky enough to have a room dedicated to laundry, you know how convenient it can be to have everything well within reach. And you also know how cluttered that laundry room can get. Read on for a few tips on how to make laundry day even less of a hassle.

First, let's get rid of that laundry room clutter. Out with that half-empty box of dye, the mismatched socks, and balls of lint that lurk in the corner of your laundry room. Ditto for the box of hardened laundry detergent. Gather up all the junk and toss it. Give the floor a good sweep and you're ready for business.

First—and perhaps most important—be sure to clear a large enough area to sort the dirty clothes into loads. (Yes, loads—you don't want to just throw a wad of clothes into the wash, or the results can be pretty scary!) Do this by sorting whites into one laundry basket, darks into another, delicates or hand washables into a third. I prefer to sort into baskets instead of on the floor because it keeps the dirty clothes in one place, not to mention makes the laundry room look much neater. If your laundry room is small, sort the clothes in a nearby room where you have space.

- To keep your laundry products in a convenient location, first assess your laundry area. Is there a shelf above the washer and dryer, or can wire shelves be installed in this area?

- A shelf above the washer or dryer is the most logical place for your laundry soap, fabric softener, dryer sheets, and spotters. Cabinets or freestanding storage along a wall work well too.

- Small washers and dryers or stackable units that are kept inside a closet can still benefit from the convenience of shelves. You should be able to squeeze out a foot or two of space to hang shelves from brackets; that's enough room for your basic laundry supplies.

- Remember, when you're thinking about shelves, up high is better than down low. First of all, it's easier to reach for a product than bend over for it, and second, it will keep chemicals out of the reach of animals and children. Just make sure you put the shelf at a height where you are not reaching too high or over your head—that could be more than inconvenient, it could be dangerous. Shoulder height or about 6 inches above shoulder height is just right for most people.

- Line up your prewash spotters, detergent, bleaches, and liquid softener near the washer. Keep your dryer fabric softener sheets near the dryer.

- I keep a special spotting basket on my laundry shelf. This is just a plastic basket the size of a shoe box where I keep my more unusual spotters, such as meat tenderizer, rust remover, nongel toothpaste, and commercial spotters. That way, when I need one of these unusual (but very effective) products, I just reach for the basket instead of rummaging around on the shelves.

- I also keep a small sewing kit in my spotting basket for making quick repairs before washing an item. (Small tears can grow in the washing machine.)

- No shelves or cabinets? Keep all of your washing supplies in a plastic laundry basket, so that you only need to reach in one place for what you need. (Plastic is better here than wicker—spills can be wiped up easily.)

- A shower curtain tension rod hung over the washer and dryer can make laundry day easier. If your wall space is too far apart to use a tension rod, you can use a pole-type curtain rod and attach it to the walls.

- Bring empty hangers from the closets on laundry day and hang them on the rod. As clothes are removed from the dryer, they can be hung immediately, so that much less ironing time is required. This also aids in sorting clothes for a quick return to the right closet.

- An over-the-door hanger is a good option if space is too tight in your laundry room for a tension rod. Keep some spare hangers here and hang clothes as you sort things out of the dryer.

- A miniature-sized wastebasket on top of your dryer is handy for cleaning the lint screen after each load, it's also a great visual reminder to do that often-forgotten job. A quick and easy way to clean this screen is to swipe it with a used dryer fabric softener sheet. Lint is picked right up and deposited in the trash neatly—no muss, no fuss. Keep an old tissue box nearby where you can store these "retired" sheets for this purpose.

- Don't overlook any storage space between the washer and dryer. Take advantage of it with a narrow rolling cart to store your laundry supplies.

- Some folks love to iron (I only like to talk about it, but I have a friend who swears it's therapeutic). If you do a lot of ironing and have the room, install an ironing board that folds flat against the wall and drops down when you're ready to use it. The iron can be stored on a shelf above where the ironing board is mounted, in a cabinet, or on the shelf with your cleaning supplies.

- No room in the laundry room, but still need an iron and ironing board handy? Consider an inexpensive

*I*f you're like me and use retired fabric softener sheets for dusting, removing burned-on food from casseroles, and keeping your sewing thread from tangling, why not keep them handy in an old tissue box on your laundry room shelf?

over-the-door ironing board holder in a nearby bedroom or den. This keeps the ironing board ready for use at a minute's notice.

Basement laundry rooms tend to get clothes scattered all over the floor. There are some creative solutions for this:

- If your home is an older one, you may very well own a laundry chute, where family members can toss their dirty clothes into a "black hole." Capture those clothes when they tumble down by using either a portable crib (very handy, as the sides are mesh and plastic, and these are resistant to dampness and mildew) or a large plastic trash barrel. Keep several empty laundry baskets nearby for sorting at laundry time.

- If your family tosses their clothes into the laundry room on a regular basis, have some baskets labeled (and color-coded) for whites, darks, and delicates.

- If you wash a lot of jeans, then be sure to label a basket just for those. That will start your sorting process before you want to start the laundry.

- When laundry rooms are located a little ways from the living areas of the house, such as in a basement or garage, it's easy to forget when a load has finished washing or drying. Solution? Set your kitchen timer or purchase a small timer to ring when it's time to get the clothes. This will save many a wrinkle, and speed up the process too.

- Last but not least, if you fold clothes on the washer and dryer or keep detergent boxes sitting on it, consider covering the top of your appliances with a towel to protect the finish from wear and tear. Sooner or later setting things on top of the appliances will remove the finish, and once the finish is gone, the rust can begin.

- Just because this is a place for washing clothes doesn't mean your laundry room should be dark and drab. You can add a throw rug (careful that it has a nonskid bottom) and a few pictures. One artist friend of mine even stenciled a beautiful garden scene in her laundry room; she figured she spent so much time in there she might as well enjoy it. The laundry room was the brightest and most cheerful spot in the whole house!

Hitting the Road with Your Laundry

If you travel to the Laundromat® or an apartment building laundry room, you will have special concerns. There are ways to make the job easier:

- Sort your clothes by loads into plastic bags before you leave home. Tall kitchen trash bags or plastic grocery bags work well for this. You can use the kitchen trash bags over and over. Pop the bags into a laundry basket, rolling bag, or whatever you transport your laundry in.

- Consider switching from liquid or powder detergent to the laundry tabs. You can drop them right in the bag as you sort the clothes, and you won't need to carry your laundry detergent with you.

- Put dryer sheets in a resealable plastic bag to avoid carrying the bulky box.

- Powdered bleach can also be carried in a resealable bag along with an appropriate-size measuring cup.

- Wire or nylon carts on wheels are handy for transporting the laundry and supplies to the laundry area. Look for ones that are collapsible and can be hung up when not in use. Of course, this will be appropriate only for those of you who have a laundry in your building. People who have to cart their laundry a couple of blocks might find a shopping buggy useful for hauling those large loads.

- Don't forget to bring your hangers, and use twist ties to hook together the hangers holding freshly hung clothes. The hangers won't become tangled or separated and will be easier to transport.

Once you get the hang of it, airing your dirty laundry isn't half bad. Follow these simple methods and you'll be onto something a lot more fun before you know it.

CHAPTER 15

Flowers in the Attic

*O*kay, so nobody really has flowers in the attic. It's not a place to be prettied with up with bouquets and doilies, and it's not a place for entertaining. But that doesn't mean your attic should hold piles of clutter either. Do you really want to fill up this premium real estate with broken furniture, long-forgotten board games, and your aunt Esther's collection of teaspoons from all the state capitals? It doesn't have to be that way.

An attic can be a great storage area as long as you keep in mind a few simple precautions and follow a few simple rules. Most important, take the time to *eliminate.* Remember: The goal is to conquer clutter, not just move it around the house. Why pack up unwanted items and then put them in the attic (or the basement or the garage) when you can deal with them once and for all? Eventually, everything that is packed is going to have to be unpacked. So why spend precious time dealing with "stuff" when you could be out enjoying yourself, spending time with your family, or working on a hobby that you really enjoy?

Remember that its radical shifts in temperature make the attic an unsuitable choice for storing many climate-sensitive items. Bugs can also be a problem, so make sure to keep insects and other pests away by spraying the attic well with a good, all-purpose, preferably poison-free organic bug spray. Pay spe-

*D*on't make clutter your hobby.

cial attention to the floor and baseboard areas. It's a good rule of thumb to vacuum the attic area down at least once a year. You might also want to try some of my own concoctions to keep bugs away:

- A mixture of 50 percent confectioner's sugar and 50 percent 20 Mule Team® Borax placed on a piece of cardboard in corners of the attic will make sure that ants feast and die. Remember, kids and pets should not ingest this mixture.

- Cockroaches can be eliminated with a mixture of 50 percent boric acid added to 25 percent nondairy creamer and 25 percent sugar. Sprinkle this mixture behind the stove and refrigerator and under the sink at the back of the cupboard. The roaches will ingest this and die. Keep this out of the reach of children and pets.

- For moths, skip the smelly mothballs, and instead, dry strips of citrus peel overnight in an oven you have warmed to 200 degrees and then shut off. Sprinkle them around clothes and into pockets of stored clothes for excellent moth protection.

Now remember, not everything can be stored safely in the attic. Follow these *do's* and *don'ts.*

DO Store the Following in the Attic:

- Dishes and pottery
- Holiday decorations
- Housewares
- Clothing—with some exceptions

DON'T Store the Following in the Attic:

- Blankets
- Stuffed animals
- Leather goods
- Fur coats

*I*tems likely to be affected by moisture and extremes in temperature should not be stored in the attic.

Let's Start with the *Do's*

- Surplus crockery should be wrapped in tissue and packed in a cardboard box. Throw in a handful of dried citrus peels to eliminate that musty odor.

- Seasonal decorations are perfect for the attic. Just make sure to store them in cardboard boxes (not plastic) to eliminate moisture buildup and avoid the possibility of mold and mildew.

- Specialty housewares such as the cake pans used for holidays and birthdays, the punch bowl with twelve matching cups, and the centerpiece you use at Easter can safely stay in the attic. Ditto for canning jars and equipment used to preserve fruits and vegetables. (Note: Don't store the rubber rings for canning in the attic, as the temperature fluctuations will cause them to dry and crack. A pantry shelf is a better option for these.)

- Winter coats, hats, scarves, mittens, and the like can be stored in the attic. So can baby dresses and com-

*R*emember to check on clothing stored in the attic at least every six months for any damage. Make a note to do this on your kitchen or office calendar.

munion dresses. Just make sure you follow a few simple precautions:

- Make sure the clothing is dry-cleaned or washed prior to storage. Food stains are often invisible to the naked eye, but they attract moths.
- Don't store your clothes in plastic bags or drop cloths; this can discolor them.
- Fine clothes should be wrapped in tissue paper.
- Hang your clothing on a portable rack, or suspend a clothesline from the rafters and use plastic hangers.
- Allow enough space between items for air to circulate.
- Cover with a clean, light-colored sheet. (In unpredictable temperature conditions, dark-colored sheets could stain your clothes.)
- And don't forget to scatter citrus peels or cedar chips. (They smell much nicer than mothballs, and work just as well at deterring pests.)

*T*o dry rinds for moth repellent, peel oranges, lemons, limes, or any other citrus fruit into strips about ½ inch wide. Heat the oven to 200 degrees and turn off. Spread the peels in a single layer on a clean cookie sheet, and leave in the closed oven until the peels are dried—usually overnight.

- Toys can easily be stored in the attic by placing them in a cabinet or box, or covering them with a plastic drop cloth or sheet. Keeping toys covered will mean less cleaning when it's time to use them again. Make sure all parts are in one place before toys are stored.
- Seasonal sports equipment such as golf clubs, skis, bikes, balls, tennis rackets, bowling balls, and so on can also be stored in the attic.
- Consider using a large plastic trash can to hold rackets, bats, mallets, and hockey sticks. This keeps things neatly contained in one place.
- Tennis balls, footballs, and soccer balls can be kept in a smaller plastic trash can.
- Golf balls and tees can be stored together in a clear plastic shoe box with a lid for easy identification. Or try storing them in mesh laundry bags hooked on the wall.

Remember that items stored in the attic are out of sight and frequently forgotten, so make a list of the equipment on hand in the attic. This way you can easily retrieve items and also save yourself from needless expenditures if Junior decides he wants to take up tennis or golf.

And Now the *Don'ts*

- Blankets, stuffed animals, leather items, and fur coats and stoles should not be stored in the attic. They're an open invitation for rodents to build a nest.

- Store blankets folded away in an underbed box or a top shelf in a closet.

- Stuffed animals should be sorted out occasionally; give those you don't need to a favorite charity. Clean stuffed animals by placing in a large plastic garbage bag with a few shakes of baking soda. Tie bag closed and shake, then remove toys. Brush them thoroughly to clean off baking soda. When you're done, just throw the bag away.

- Fur coats and stoles that have seen better days can be made over into stuffed teddy bears. Do an Internet search using keywords "recycled fur coats" for more details.

- Your attic is not the place for storing temperature-sensitive items such as CDs, books, tapes, important papers, your family photo albums, cameras, or electronic equipment. Store these things close to or in the rooms they're used in.

How to Store

You may want to install shelves in the attic and store dishes on these, covered with a plastic drop cloth. This will keep dust from collecting and make it easy to see at a glance what you have. Consider putting some old kitchen cabinets in the attic. They make great storage areas for dishes and other similar items, and your crockery will stay much cleaner when stored in an enclosed area.

Label each box carefully, so you can take down only the

boxes you want. I always tape a file card to the top and write down a list of what's inside. Keep a separate card that lists anything that might need repair before you use it, like a string of lights that doesn't work. It's an especially good idea to store all Christmas light replacement bulbs in one container; a plastic one with a lid is best. By doing this, you won't find yourself digging through the house on Christmas Eve, looking for that replacement bulb for your angel on top of the tree. Tree skirts and fabric pieces should be stored in boxes as well. Wrap them in tissue first and label the boxes for easy identification.

And, yes, you really can store flowers in the attic. Just make sure they're made of plastic or silk. Dust or clean them thoroughly before covering with an old sheet and labeling for easy reference.

CHAPTER 16

Going Down Under

G'day, mate! Going down under can be fun, unless you are referring to the basement. Basements tend to collect all of the clutter and stuff that you don't know what to do with. It just seems easier on cleaning day to grab what doesn't belong or is taking up space and stash it in the basement to be dealt with later. And let's face it, later rarely comes.

Most basements accumulate the stuff that we just can't bear to part with or don't have time to make a decision about. Over time, all of this excess clutter from the rest of the house fills the basement, robbing it of space for *useful* storage. The time has come to question what your basement requires in order to become more user-friendly and a great storage or play area. And where there's a question, there's a *QUEEN*:

Question: *What purpose do I want the basement to serve? Is it to be given over completely to storage? Is there room here for the kids to play, or for hobbies and* *crafts? How do I want to make use of this space—and who is going to use it?*

Unpack: This step is vital in the basement, since many things may have been boxed and stored there for perhaps years. Many of us who have moved several times have had this experience. After a move, three or four boxes are still filled with items that don't fit the new home and somehow end up in the basement. It's time to open those boxes and make a decision. If you can use the orange throw pillows or the Early American clock in your home, fine. If not, they go to charity. As you unpack, dispose of boxes that are not usable for storage again and get them out of your way, so that you have space to work.

Evaluate: Let's take a good look at your basement. Is there an old rocking chair with a broken seat, a pile of mildewy cushions from a patio set you no longer own, and a kitchen table minus the legs? Take stock of what you have and what you need. If they're not the same, move on to the next step. . . . During this process, evaluate the condition of your basement too. If you have leaks or other problems, this is a good time to make repairs.

Eliminate: If you don't do it now, you never will. If you haven't missed anything in those boxes since your last move, get them out of there. They are taking up precious storage space. Get rid of broken items, rusty items, anything you really don't need. When you buy a house with a basement, you don't sign a commitment to fill it up with clutter from everywhere else.

This means it's time to actually open every box and determine whether you need what is in it. If there's something stored in the basement that you haven't looked for in more than a year, eliminate it. Donate it, move it to the garage sale pile, or trash it.

Break down any empty boxes that contained electronic equipment that must be returned in its original carton for repair. Since your warranty requires that you save them, store the now-flat boxes tied together in one area.

When you're evaluating the basement, you have to do more than evaluate your clutter—you have to evaluate the basement itself, because moisture is often a problem in basements, and it's easier to prevent mildew than combat it once it begins.

*W*hile you're decluttering the basement, take the time to move the washer and dryer and check for leaky or broken hoses. Try to do this every six months.

- Portable dehumidifiers are a must in some areas. They're great at pulling excess humidity out of the air. The water collected from these is excellent for plants because it is pure, so save it to do your watering with. Keep an empty watering can or bucket nearby to transfer the water.

- Control mildewy odors by placing bowls of dry ODORZOUT™ around the basement, changing the bowls until the odor disappears. Wintergreen oil (available at the health-food store) is another wonderful deodorizer. Saturate cotton balls with the oil and place in strategic areas to combat odor.

- In areas prone to flooding, or in houses with water seepage problems, investigate whether a sump pump may control it. Once water is detected, the sump pump will turn on and immediately start removing the water. Remember that the floor area of a damp basement is not a good storage area for much of anything. Clothes will mildew, cardboard boxes will fall apart, and even

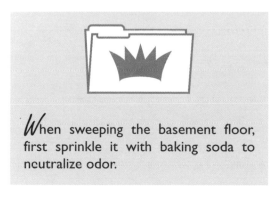

When sweeping the basement floor, first sprinkle it with baking soda to neutralize odor.

items stored in plastic boxes will take on a pungent odor from the excess humidity. So don't even try to use this as a storage space. You'll want to keep the floor area cleared out as much as possible in case of flooding or seepage.

*N*eaten Up: I always like this part best. It means you are almost done and you'll see results soon. A basement can be home to all kinds and types of storage. You can use anything and everything as storage units. Be imaginative. Look around the house, the garage, and the basement to see what you are not using efficiently, and use it for basement storage permanently.

- A closet with shelves in a basement can house a number of things. Salvaged kitchen cabinets and freestanding units such as old filing cabinets or armoires work too. Your storage options here don't have to be fancy to work.

- Sturdy coated-wire shelving is also a good choice. Here you can place items such as extra paper products, lightbulbs, or household goods in their packaging, to bring upstairs when needed. Remember to store other items on these shelves in containers, for easier cleaning.

- Keep items off the floor when storing in the basement. Start shelves and cabinets a foot or so off the ground. This will help keep dampness away from your belongings, and if you ever have a basement flood, heaven forbid, your possessions should be high and dry.

- Hanging things from wall pegboards is another good option. This provides storage for tools, extra pots and pans, and toys. Organize like items together, grouping several pegboards in a row if need be. Don't forget to check tools for rust occasionally.

- A basement is not the place to store books, photos, good wood furniture, or fabrics that can be damaged by moisture. And it's definitely not the spot for your family heirlooms or photo albums, either.

- Think "outside the box" with your basement. In locales with long winters or rainy seasons, this might be an ideal spot for a Ping-Pong® table, a StairMaster®, or even a wall-mounted television set with a mat, for following those yoga tapes you've collected. Basements also make ideal hobby and craft areas. You can purchase an old wooden kitchen table and use it to assemble a birdhouse, learn how to rubber-stamp, or tie-dye a bedspread.

Back when we were kids, we often called the basement the rumpus room. With today's hectic lifestyles, it's a relief to retreat to a room that's ready for some no-frills fun. Basements can be great stress relievers when the gang gets together for a silly game of Twister®, a craft project, or even a game of beanbag tag. And with all the clutter out of the way, who knows, you may even get to enjoy going "down under"!

CHAPTER 17

The Outer Limits

*I*s your garage loaded with broken, outgrown, unused toys and sports equipment? Are there empty containers of car wash soap, fertilizer, and pesticides taking up space? Could it be you have parts to things you don't even own anymore lying around? It's time to spruce up the garage.

Start by moving cars out of the garage, and then begin moving what is left. Use your driveway to group items together. You should come up with a few collections like this:

- Sporting equipment (golf clubs, bats, balls, tennis rackets, hockey sticks)
- Power tools—this means anything with a cord (okay, maybe not venetian blinds!)
- Regular tools
- Lawn equipment such as rakes, hoes, and clippers
- Snow shovels and blowers

- Patio furniture
- Pool supplies

Dispose of the obvious junk, like old bicycle tires, empty boxes, and dirty rags. To dispose of pesticides safely, follow the directions on the container. Some things, such as motor oil, solvents, and garden chemicals, cannot simply be tossed in the trash. Check with the company that collects your trash, and they will give you the guidelines for your state.

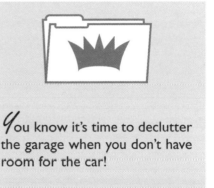

You know it's time to declutter the garage when you don't have room for the car!

Once you've cleared out the clutter, you may be left with a pile of "not sures." These could be things that need repair or something that you were going to salvage usable parts from. Now is the time to determine whether these things are worth saving. You can box and label them and if you haven't used them in another six months, trash them, or you could take the time now to remove the parts you want or to repair what needs it, and you're done. If you still have some not sures, the six month rule applies—if you haven't looked at it or used it in six months, it's out of there, no excuses!

Now that you've got the garage clear (for the first time in how many years?), why not take the opportunity to clean the floor. First sweep out all loose debris, and then mix up a bucket of hot water with some trisodium phosphate or your favorite degreasing cleaner. Wash the floor well, using an old mop, and pour the solution on, scrubbing it in with a broom. Rinse the floor well and let it dry before you start to neaten up.

It's a good idea to mark off the area that is occupied by the car or cars in your garage, so that you can visualize what storage areas are remaining. Consider the area required for opening car doors and maneuvering the car into and out of the garage. I used a piece of sidewalk chalk to mark off this space before I started.

Stow It Safely

- Decide where you can hang closed cabinets and shelving, keeping in mind that anything stored on open shelves will quickly become soiled. Consider recycling old kitchen cabinets or checking for some at yard sales. In my neighborhood, one new homeowner who didn't want the garage cabinets that came with the house gave them away free; the only catch was their new owner had to come pick them up, which he gladly did.

- Make sure you know the width of the area that you are working with so that you don't end up with shelves hanging over the area the car uses.

- If you put closed shelves at the end of the garage, you can place them high enough that you can still pull the car in underneath them. Because the shelves are closed, items will not fall out and damage the car.

These cupboards are great for sports equipment. You can even dedicate one cupboard to each sport, to keep like items grouped together. This makes it easier to get out the door on time on practice day.

- Keep one cupboard locked at all times and store in it poisonous items such as pesticides, herbicides, and dangerous tools. Keep the key in the house in a safe location.

- Large outdoor toys, lawn equipment, and patio furniture can be stored in an outdoor shed. This avoids having dirt tracked into the garage and house. If you don't have a shed, set up a corner of the garage for the lawn equipment, keeping it as far from the house access as possible and close to the garage door. This will contain the dirt in one place, and you can easily sweep it out the door.

- Place recycling containers in the garage in an area convenient to the door of the house.

- Store garden tools in a plastic 5-gallon bucket or old paint container filled with sand, to keep them clean and free of rust. Keep this near the garage door.

- Hang rakes, large shovels, and garden hoses from hooks on the wall.

- In a garage you always want to "look up." Using the garage walls and ceiling will almost double your garage space. You can build a rack that hangs from the garage ceiling to hold folding tables, chairs, luggage, and other large or unwieldy items. The employees in your local home center's building department should be able to show you how to do this. When hanging a rack from the ceiling, just remember to make sure that it is fastened properly—either to a stud or by using anchors—so that it will bear the weight of the items stored in it. (Of course, I prefer a stud!) You can also purchase ready-made racks at home centers.

- Use ceiling hooks to store bikes during the winter.
- Wall hooks can hold such things as ladders, snow shovels, brooms, and other large tools.

Re-Tool Your Tool Bench

- Tools strewn all over the workbench make it hard to get the simplest job done. First, you'll want to pick up the entire area and place everything on a bench, table, or floor conveniently nearby. Then, sort out tools according to use and place back on the bench.
- Look for a toolbox made of heavy-duty plastic. These are preferable to metal boxes, which will rust if left on a damp garage floor.
- Consider using pegboard or tool racks to hang tools over or next to the workbench too. Trace the outline of the hammers, pliers, rope, and so on, with chalk or marker so you can easily see what tool goes where.
- Install a small shelf over the workbench and arrange your containers of nails, screws, nuts, and bolts on the shelf. Or use clear plastic containers and hang from the walls. For storage, use old coffee cans, mar-

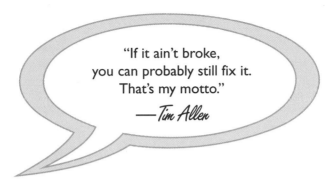

"If it ain't broke, you can probably still fix it. That's my motto."

—Tim Allen

garine tubs, or empty plastic containers. Just make sure to label them clearly, so that you don't have to fish around every time you want to find a finishing nail.

And Don't Forget

- Keep the area where you walk clear. If you have a garage service door leading outside, keep a path clear that you can use.

- Keep the area around the door leading to the house clear of things and clean. A good walk-off mat will keep you from tracking in debris.

- Consider establishing an area where you and your family can remove dirty shoes and boots before you enter the house.

- Carports or decks can also be outfitted with extra storage space by using wall hooks and ceiling racks for lawn equipment, tools, and patio furniture. Investigate purchasing a shed for the backyard to store your large outdoor items when not in use. This can be arranged just like a mini-garage.

Stand back and take a look at your efforts. I bet the neighbors are looking enviously at your garage too. Now the next time it rains or snows, you can run out to the garage and hop in the car, where it sits high and dry, instead of racing to the driveway where you used to have to park. A clutter-free garage is a great thing!

It's tempting to use glass containers such as old baby food jars to store small items, but don't! When they break, you can have shards of glass scatter all around your tools, not to mention on the garage floor, where it can easily puncture a tire.

CHAPTER 18

Do Your Homework

*W*hether you run your entire business from a home office or have just designated an area to handle work at home, the goal should be the same: create a quiet, clutter-free, stress-free environment where you can accomplish a lot in a short amount of time.

A messy, cluttered office may cause you to miss deadlines and lose information, not to mention get on your nerves. I mean, who wants to waste time looking for phone numbers when there's work to be done? Here you need to evaluate the use of your office and desk area and then make it work for you rather than against you. I've put together a few suggestions for getting yourself clutter-free and organized, but jump right in and use your imagination . . . after all, it is *your* office, so there are no rights or wrongs.

When you have a home office, it seems to be a clutter magnet. Sometimes it is in a multipurpose room, and you end up moving the sewing you need to work on later in order to balance your checkbook now. If you want to sit down and work on your novel, the mood will be gone and, trust me, so will the ideas if you have to clear a place to work. You waste precious time just looking for a place to work and another place to put all the things that are in the way. For your office to function, it needs to be properly located and have designated areas for everything.

Where to Work?

Interruptions will decrease your productivity and cause you to spend more hours working. Make sure the area you work in has a door that can be closed when it's time to go to work. A closed door means Do Not Disturb. Remember that people who work at home successfully learn to establish regular business hours and stick to them. Otherwise, they find themselves working seven days a week, many hours per day.

Here are some suggestions on choosing a designated working area in your home:

- The basement might be suitable, and certainly it might be quiet and away from the kids, but watch out for dampness, which can damage sensitive electronic equipment. A good dehumidifier is a must if you live in a damp area. Keep computers and other equipment up off the floor, and position outlets at least a foot off the floor as well. Basements can be rather drab, so you'll want to use light, bright colors to create a feeling of cheeriness. Investigate installing overhead track lights as well as good lighting near your work area to decrease eyestrain. A friend who runs a home business from her basement keeps a mini trampoline and jump rope close by. Every hour or so, she skips rope or bounces around for a few minutes. Great stress relief—and gives those tense back and neck muscles a change of pace too!

- A guest room can work well—when you don't have guests, that is. If you have a lot of weekend visitors, you might want to rethink setting up in an area that will frequently be occupied by other people.

- The family room is not a good choice because it's centrally located and noisy. Ditto for the kitchen. You can have a desk or counter area in the kitchen for bill paying and coupon clipping, but trying to work quietly in the hub of the home will be an exercise in frustration for you.

- If you are using a shared room or if space is a major concern, consider the advantages of turning a closet into a home office. This can be done quite simply by inserting a desk into a closet. Just make sure to measure the space before you make your purchase. A do-it-yourself desk can be as simple as a laminate board sitting on a pair of two-drawer file cabinets or an old table. Install hanging shelves and a bulletin board to help you organize your daily work. If you are creating one of these areas, look for computer carts that hold everything. Slide one into a closet and pull it out when you need it.

- With the luxury of a little more space, you can still hide your home office behind sliding doors at one end of a room. You can have these installed quite easily; check at your local home center for details. When you're done working, just slide the doors closed and the office is out of sight, so that the room can revert to its other use. Out of sight, out of mind.

You Want to Put It Where?

There is no right or wrong storage container for use in your office. If it works for you, it is exactly the right one; if it doesn't, it doesn't matter how cute, practical, or professional it is—it's wrong.

Get creative and have some fun here. I've used a wicker chip-and-dip tray (the divided areas house paper clips, pens, and Post-it® notes) on my desk for years.

- Divide the drawers of your desk into functional areas for pens, pencils, paper clips, staples, and other necessities. Purchase plastic or metal dividers, or make your own with small boxes or discount store finds.

- Wicker baskets with handles make great carryalls to hold computer discs and CDs.

- Stash small books and pads of paper in square metal kitchen containers from the dollar store. A friend uses an old Barbie® thermos bottle she found at a thrift store to hold pens, pencils, and letter openers.

- Purchase new or used two- or four-drawer file cabinets, or use cardboard banker's file boxes with lids.

Store files that you don't use more than once a year in the attic or basement, so that you will have more space for current things in your office files. Label drawers clearly, so you can quickly find what you need. You can also buy file boxes made of wicker and plastic, most of which have rails built in for hanging folders.

- Don't combine work files with home files.

- Keep a separate drawer for warranties, receipts, and instructions. Divide your files into categories such as *electric, water, cable, Visa®, American Express®*, and *car.*

- As you pay the bills, promptly file the receipts with the most current receipts at the front of the file.

- Keep folders for appliances and other purchases. Keep the instruction booklet and the receipt and any other information you may need in this file. You should have files that are labeled *washer, dryer, TV, stove, refrigerator,* and so on. As you throw out, donate, or replace an item, remove that instruction booklet or attach it to the piece you give away.

Conquer Computer Clutter

Take a few moments now to organize your computer files, and get rid of as much computer clutter as you can. Write down your e-mail passwords on a Rolodex® or index card and store in a handy place nearby. Include the 800 number of the technical support team for the Internet service provider you use. This way you can flip right to the card and the information you need is right at your fingertips. And consider the following to conquer that calamitous computer clutter:

- Many of us receive a barrage of e-mails from well-meaning friends—jokes, current events, craft lists, and so on. Review these e-mails regularly, and if you're getting too many, one polite little e-mail should be enough to stop the flow. You might want to try something like this:

> *As much as I like receiving these fun messages, I'm afraid that I'm just inundated with e-mails. Please remove me from your mailing list. I'll just have to trust that you'll keep me up-to-date next time we get together. Thanks for understanding.*

- Regularly review your e-mail freebies. Remember, it's not free if you have to take your free time to weed through it. How to gauge if enough is enough? Consider this:
  - Do you still receive special offers on maternity clothes, even though your youngest is in the second grade?
  - Are you getting three "joke of the day" e-mails? How many times can that chicken cross the road, anyway?

- Do you still belong to the Hamburger Helper® recipe club, but you've been a vegetarian for the past three years?

You get the idea. Now you'll have more "surf time" and less "cleanup time" when you log on.

Use things that work for you. It is your office, and the most important person to please is yourself!

CHAPTER 19

Getting It All Together

*T*he Queen Mother always told me to wear clean underwear just in case I was in an accident. Think of this as the same thing. You should always have your legal papers together and keep your family informed of the location of these documents in case of emergency. It's not morbid, and it's not tempting fate. It's just being prepared.

Keep your estate-planning documents in order, no matter how old you are. I know this seems scary—who wants to be reminded that life is short?—but it's important to protect your family and ensure that your property is handled the way you want it to be.

Having files stored on the computer is not enough. You should have backup hard copies of your will, power of attorney documents, medical insurance, and tax returns. Specific medical wishes should also be carefully spelled out: write them down and give them to the person you've designated to be your medical power of attorney. Your medical power of attorney documents should also be filed with your doctors. You should be sure that you do this every two years, or as things change. Keep the people who need to know informed of any changes. They'll thank you for it.

Store your hard copies in a fireproof box or a bank safe deposit box. Sit down and go over all of this with your family so that they clearly know your wishes and where your papers are. As part of your documents, keep records of the following information:

- Clergy name and phone number.

- Trusts, including what type, and your adviser.

- Real estate, including type, address, mortgages, bank where mortgage is held and its due date.

- Bank accounts, with bank's full name, address, telephone number, and account numbers.

- Life insurance policies, including the company name, policy number, type of policy, cash value, and the name and phone number of your agent.

- List of any 401Ks or IRAs, including account number, agent, and phone number.

- Military service information: branch, dates of service, rank, status of any pension earned, and death benefits.

- List any debts that you have. Include in this list the names of people and companies/organizations you owe money to, amounts, phone numbers, and where the original loan papers are kept.

- Social security documents and pension information.

- Death instructions: whom to call, name of funeral home, your personal wishes concerning burial information, and paperwork if you own a gravesite.

- Don't forget to include a list of persons to be contacted upon your death. Include addresses and phone numbers.

- Organ donors should make sure that they are identified on their driver's license, that the person designated to be their medical power of attorney is aware of their decision, and that family and friends are informed.

"I filled out an application that said, 'In case of emergency notify . . .' I wrote, 'Doctor.' What's my mother going to do?"

—*Steven Wright*

Make copies of your will to keep at home, but remember, only the original can be probated.

The IRS suggests that tax records be retained for three years. If you own property, keep your returns for as long as you own that property, so that when you sell it, you will know what you paid for it. Tax returns can be safely stored at home.

A quick review:

- Keep a list of where your will, power of attorney, medical power of attorney, and other important documents are stored, and make sure to give copes of this list to family members.

- Keep a list of your assets and liabilities, and be sure to update it as needed. Store this list with your important documents.

- Make a list of the names of your attorney and other legal advisers, and give a copy to family members. Keep another copy in a safe place.

- Put the name of the person who will settle your legal affairs and business on the signature card for your bank safe deposit box so that your affairs can be promptly attended to.

I know this is not fun to talk about, but it will give you peace of mind to have everything in order. This is one of the most loving acts you can perform for your family and friends.

CHAPTER 20

The Last Word

$\mathcal{S}$ome years ago, a modernist architect who was known for his simple, unornamented style coined the phrase, *Less is more*. This certainly applies to staying organized in your home. If you don't accumulate clutter, you won't have to get rid of it.

This is a wonderful theory, but how to put it into practice sure puzzles a lot of us. With the dizzying array of items available to purchase today, it's only natural to feel at times overwhelmed by "stuff." That's why clutter control starts with your purchasing decisions. Here are some things to think about before you shop:

- Think before you buy. Do you really need that? Some questions that may suggest this item is nice, but unnecessary, include:
  - Is this a new and improved version of something I already have?

- Do I really need the extra "bells and whistles"?
- What will I do with the old model?
- Is this a "single-purpose" item such as an egg poacher or hot-dog-bun warmer?
- Can some other item at home fulfill the same purpose?

- Take a careful look at "freebies"—three months of free magazines, for instance. Do you have time to read *Racing World, Hairstyle Hints,* and *Tofu Times* each month? Remember, time is money. Every free offer has a hidden "hook" too—after three months, that free magazine starts charging a subscription fee; the special trial offer membership of the auto club becomes a permanent fixture on your credit card unless it's canceled after the trial date.

- You could probably pave your driveway by now with free floppy disc and CD offers for Internet service. Review your Internet service contract every three months or so for any better offers; in between times, use the discs as Frisbees®.

- Make it a hard and fast rule that for every item of clothing you bring home, you remove an item from your closet. You will be amazed at how this not only keeps clutter from forming in your closet, but how your wardrobe will take on new life as you become more selective about the clothing you own. Many resale shops now offer consignment services that pay you in cash or trade for your clothing, so don't hesitate to make use of these stores if you don't wish to donate items to a charity. This also keeps impulse buying to a minimum.

- If you love to catalog shop, mark the page number of the item you plan to order on the front of the catalog. Wait two days and look at the item again. Generally the impulse to buy it is gone and you can trash the catalog. If not, then go ahead and order the item.

- While we're talking about impulse buying, here's a tip: When you're in one of those moods and you know a purchase is imminent, steer clear of trendy items that will lead to "buyer's remorse" before you even get home. Instead, select a basic item that fits with your current wardrobe. A white blouse or neutral-colored sweater will get a lot more use.

- Show your children the difference between a "looking day" and a "buying day." Malls and specialty stores are exciting places, full of new and unusual products, and looking is absolutely free. Think of these places as museums; they are full of interesting objects, but you don't have to own them to enjoy them. You can enjoy an hour or two in your local mall with the kids on a looking day, and end with an ice cream cone at the food court. Begin this habit early, and they won't beg and whine for every toy they see.

- Does your heart beat faster just thinking of your neighborhood warehouse store? A bargain isn't a bargain if you really don't need the item in the first place. Fourteen cans of tuna are not a great deal if you hate seafood, no matter what the price. If you must shop at a warehouse store, do so on a full stomach and with a list. When tempted to deviate from your list, promise yourself you'll try that item next time. This way, you're not denying yourself—just deferring the purchase for a little while. Try it—it works!

With a little practice, clutter control will become second nature to you. Not only will you reap the benefits of a more orderly, organized home, but you'll feel in control of your life and your finances too! Keeping your life simple is possible even in today's fast-paced world—and it's well worth the effort. As the Queen Mother often told me, "The best things in life are free." Good friends, a loving family, and a happy heart can't be bought—but there will be time to enjoy them when your life is well organized.

Resource Guide

Here I've compiled a comprehensive list of agencies and organizations that will gladly accept your donated clothing, appliances, furniture, computers, and even cars. There's even a special section on handling the sale of your collectibles.

Clothing, Household Goods, Furniture, and Appliances

Look in your Yellow Pages under "Clothes—Consignment and Retail" for a shop near you that accepts clothing in exchange for cash or credit.

You can donate your clothing, household goods, appliances, and furniture to any of the following organizations:

Salvation Army

1–800–95–TRUCK (87825)
The Salvation Army has thrift stores located throughout
North America. Call to schedule a pickup from the store near
you.

St. Vincent de Paul

A national organization with thrift stores throughout the
country. Contact your local chapter to arrange a pickup. The
phone number will be listed in the Yellow Pages under
"Social Service Organizations."

American Council of the Blind

This agency has thrift stores in most metropolitan areas. Call
1-800-866-3242 to find a store nearest you. They will provide
you with the local number to call for a pickup.

Red Cross

1-800-HELP NOW (435-7669)
This number is for clothing donations only.

Goodwill Industries

Go to *www.goodwill.org* for a list of locations near you, or
contact them at:

Goodwill Industries
9200 Rockville Pike
Bethesda, MD 20814
1-301-530-6500

Computer Donations

Any of the above organizations will gladly accept your computer donations. Don't forget that your local hospital, trade school, or area charter schools are always in need of computers too, as well as your local school district. Look in the blue pages of your phone directory under "State Government— Department of Education" for further information.

Vehicle Donations

To donate your car, contact Vehicle Donation Processing Center, Inc., a national processing agent for charities seeking vehicles. Call 1-800-269-6814, or go to *www.charityfunding.com* on the internet. They are registered with the Better Business Bureau.

Collection Sale and Donations

Collections of coins, silver, or rare objects will be gladly accepted as donations by antiques dealers (and most family members!), but if you would prefer to sell your collection, try an on-line auction site. Here are the URLs of two:

www.ebay.com
www.ubid.com

For a comprehensive list of on-line auction sites, go to *www.internetauctionlist.com.*

To learn the value of your collection, visit your local antiques dealer, check with your public library for a current price guide, or go to *www.theappraisernetwork.com* on the Internet. At this site you can post a free appraisal request, read the most commonly asked questions, and get help preparing an appraisal request.

THE ROYAL GUIDE TO
SPOT AND
STAIN
REMOVAL

This book is dedicated to my Mom and
Dad, Cecil and Florine Conway.

Because of them I can fly . . .
on very clean wings!

CONTENTS

INTRODUCTION

You're ready to leave the house in the morning when you notice a nice big coffee stain in the middle of your brand-new blouse.

That romantic candlelit dinner has left you with wax on your grandmother's tablecloth.

Your favorite pants come out of the wash with a strange black splotch in the shape of Michigan.

Junior's just come home with a first-place ribbon—and a great big grass stain.

That "absorbent, non-greasy" hand cream has just been absorbed into your skirt!

You hear: "Do you want fries with that?" and think "ketchup stain."

Stains happen! They happen to the best of us, and they happen all the time. Doesn't matter how careful you are, doesn't matter how clean. All it takes is a slip of a spoon, a wayward French fry, a leaky pen, or dirty bus seat to ruin your favorite clothes. But it doesn't have to be that way. A stain doesn't necessarily mean ruin . . . not if you approach it the right way.

The most important thing to remember about stain removal is that you have to consider the fabric as well as the stain. You can't treat silk as you would denim. You can't be as vigorous with a lace blouse as you would with a cotton tee. That's first. The second thing to bear in mind is that not all stains are created equal. Chocolate requires a different remedy from wine. The solution for ink wouldn't work on grass stains—and gum requires a treatment all its own.

That said, I'd like to encourage a little creativity in your stain removal repertoire. Don't reach for the same old product every time. Especially if it doesn't work. (Be careful of using stain removers that contain repellents, though. If the stain doesn't come out the first time, the repellent could lock it in and you could be marked for life. Not a pretty prospect.) Take a look in your cupboard. You'll be surprised at the great stain removers you'll find there, things like alcohol, baking soda, glycerin, and salt. And after you get used to using these items *as is*, you can be a little adventurous and make your own natural products. These homemade remedies are fun to concoct. They cost less than their store-bought counterparts and are better for the environment too. Give them a try. You may never go back.

So relax. Here is my *all you need to know* Royal Spot and Stain Removal Guide, straight from the Palace. Once you've read my Royal Rules of Stain Removal—and you will, won't you—you're well on your way to getting off spot free!

Royal Rules of Stain Removal

• Test the spot remover on hidden or inconspicuous areas of the fabric before you proceed.

• Approach the stain from the "wrong" side of the fabric. Put a pad of paper toweling under the offending spot as you work. This will help to blot the stain.

• Always blot, never rub! Rubbing will spread the spot and harm the fabric.

• Do not iron or apply heat to spots or stains. Heat will set the stain and you will never be able to remove it.

• If you don't know what caused the stain, start with the weakest and simplest stain removal method.

• Make sure to consider the fabric as well as the stain.

• Remember, the faster you react to a spill

or a spot, the better your chances are of removing it completely.

• Directing a blow-dryer at a freshly blotted spot will help it to dry without a ring.

• Sometimes you may still need to pretreat using your favorite laundry spotter, such as Zout®.

Part I

. . . .

STAIN REMOVERS

1

Stain Removers That Are Hiding in Your Cupboard

Some of the very best spot and stain removers are things you use every single day! These stain removers work great and they're right at your fingertips!

Alcohol: Rubbing alcohol is great for grass stains and so much more.

Ammonia: The perspiration stain fighter.

Automatic dishwasher detergent: Keep this

on hand as a bleach substitute and whitener/ brightener even if you *don't* have a dish- washer. Liquid, powder, and tablet form all work well. If you choose the tablet, make sure it has dissolved before you add clothes. Pour directly on stain, or soak.

Baking soda: Removes odors.

Club soda: My favorite *Oh my gosh, how did I do that?* spotter. Use it on any fabric or surface that can be treated with water. A slight dabbing on dry-clean-only fabrics is also permissible, just be sure to test first! Use club soda on any spill—ask the waiter for some if you're dining out—dab it on and blot it off. Club soda keeps spills from becoming stains and brings the offending spill to the surface so it can be easily removed. It's totally safe. I always make sure to have a bottle on hand.

Cream of tartar: I bet you have some of this in the kitchen cupboard, but how often do you use it? Well, here's your chance. Mix cream of tartar with lemon juice and you have a wonderful bleach for white clothes spotted with food or other stains. It's even effective on many rust stains.

Denture-cleaning tablets: The cure-all for white table linens with food stains and white cotton with stains. Dissolve one tablet per ½ cup water. Pour directly on stain or spot.

Dishwashing liquid: A wonderful spotter, used undiluted on tough stains.

Glycerin: You can remove tar, tree sap (think Christmas tree), juice stains, mustard, ketchup and barbecue sauce.

GOJO Crème Waterless Hand Cleaner®: Totally awesome for removing grease and oil, including shoe polish.

Hydrogen peroxide: 3 percent hydrogen peroxide is super for removing bloodstains, especially if they are fairly fresh. It also is a wonderful bleaching agent for stubborn stains on white clothes. Combine ½ cup of hydrogen peroxide and 1 teaspoon of ammonia for an unbeatable stain removal combination. Make sure to use 3 percent and *not* the kind you use to bleach your hair!

Lemon juice: This is nature's bleach and disinfectant. I don't know where we'd be without it. If you have spots on white clothes, apply some lemon juice and lay them in the sun. Apply a little more lemon juice prior to laundering, or prespray and launder as usual. This is really effective on baby formula stains.

Meat tenderizer: A combo of meat tenderizer (unseasoned, please, or you'll have a whole new stain!) and cold water is just the answer to protein-based stains such as blood, milk, etc.

Salt: Sprinkling salt on spilled red wine will keep the wine from staining until you can launder it. Mixed with lemon juice, salt will remove mildew stains.

Shampoo: Any brand will do. Cheap is fine. I save the small bottles from hotel/motel stays and keep them in the laundry room. Great for treating ring-around-the-collar, mud and cosmetic stains.

Shave cream: That innocent-looking can of shave cream in your bathroom is one of the best spot and stain removers available. That's because it's really whipped soap! If you have a spill on your clothes (or even your carpet), moisten the spot, work in some shave cream, and then flush it with cool water. If the offending spot is on something you're wearing, work the shave cream in and then use a clean cloth (a washcloth works fine) to blot the shave cream and the spot away. A quick touch of the blow-dryer to prevent a ring and you're on your way. The best thing about shave cream is that even if it doesn't work it won't set the stain, so the spot can still be removed later. Keep a small sample can in your suitcase when you travel. It's saved me more than once!

WD-40 Lubricant®: Check out your garage or the "fix-it" cupboard. If you don't have any, pick up a can the next time you're at the hardware store or home center. Why? Because we've all had those nasty grease stains and oil stains on clothes: Salad dressing misses the salad and gets the blouse, or grease splatters when you are cooking—or crayon/lipstick/Chap Stick® gets on your clothes! WD-40 is your answer. Spray some on, wait 10 minutes, and then work in undiluted liquid dishwashing soap and launder as usual. Works well on everything *except* silk!

White vinegar: A great spotter for suede—used undiluted. It's also a wonderful fabric softener. Just put ¼ cup white vinegar in the final rinse. (And no, you won't smell like a salad!)

It's worthwhile to keep these things on hand. As you can see, most are inexpensive *and* have other uses. They'll make you the laundry Queen—or King!—in your home.

2

Be a Spot
Hot Shot!

I love natural products, and I love things that I can make for pennies and still have them work better than the products I could buy at the store. Here are some of my favorite laundry spot removers. Use them just as you would over-the-counter products, but take note: many of them are designed to take care of specific spots and stains.

Start with a clean spray and/or squeeze

bottle, and always be sure to label any product you make. It's important to know what the bottle contains and what it was intended for. I like to include the recipe on the label too—that way I can mix up additional product with ease. Cover the label with clear packaging tape or a piece of clear adhesive sheet to protect the label from moisture.

These spotters are all intended for washable fabrics. If in doubt, test in an inconspicuous spot, such as a seam.

General All-Purpose Laundry Spotter

Combine the following to make a generic spotter that works on a wide variety of stains:

1 part rubbing alcohol

2 parts water

If you use a large spray bottle you can add 1 bottle of alcohol and 2 of the alcohol bottles filled with water. Spray this on spots and spills, wait a few minutes, and then launder as usual.

Beverage, Fruit and Grass Remover

Combine equal portions of:

     white vinegar
     liquid dishwashing soap
     water

Shake well and work the solution into the spot. Let stand a few minutes and then launder as usual.

Non-oily Stain Remover

Combine equal portions of the following ingredients:

     ammonia
     liquid dishwashing soap
     water

Shake well, and work the solution into the spot. Let stand a few minutes and flush with water. This solution works well on stains such as milk, blood, perspiration and urine. *Do not use on washable wool, silk, spandex, acrylic and acetate.*

Oily Stain Remover

Combine the following:

     1 tablespoon glycerin
     1 tablespoon liquid dishwashing soap
     8 tablespoons of water

Work the solution into grease and oil stains. Let sit a few minutes, flush with water, and launder as usual.

Again, remember all of these spotters are for washable fabrics only and none of them are for silk, wool, spandex, acrylic and acetate. When in doubt, test first!

3

Bringing Out
the Big Guns

It's time to talk about the big guns of laundry spotters. We all need them from time to time. But what's best? What really works? Read on. I've tried them all, so you won't have to!

A quick disclaimer: Remember, I am counting on you to test a small, inconspicuous area on the fabric for colorfastness *before* you use any of these spotters. Don't let laundry spotters dry. Launder soon after spotting to prevent the spot from becoming a stain. Don't let me down!

Energine Cleaning Fluid®: This is a terrific "can't be without" spotter for dry-clean-only clothes. Blot it on until the stain is gone and then blow-dry to avoid a ring.

Fels-Naptha Heavy Duty Laundry Bar Soap®: This is that old-fashioned brown bar soap that your grandmother used. It has been around 100 years—literally!—and it's a great spotter for numerous spots and stains. Wet the bar and simply rub the stain, working it in well. Let it sit a few minutes. This spotter still works even if allowed to dry on the fabric. Great for ring-around-the-collar and perspiration stains.

Ink Away™: Ink and marker can be a challenge to remove, but this product, made by the makers of Goo Gone™, really proves its worth. Follow package directions carefully and be sure to read the list of things *not* to use it on *before* you start.

Spot Shot® Instant Carpet Stain Remover: This one wins the prize for the most unusual laundry spotter, but it's *still* one of the Queen's favorite products. Yes, that's right, it's not just for carpet. It's also a great laundry prewash spotter—and boy does it work. It is safe for all colorfast washables and works in all wash temperatures. Spray the stained area thoroughly, saturating the stain. If the stain is difficult or stubborn, work it between your thumbs. Allow Spot Shot® to sit at least 60 seconds, and then launder as usual. *Do not* allow it to dry on the fabric and do not use it on silks, fabrics labeled "dry clean only" or noncolorfast fabrics. This product works on oily stains, ink, pet stains, cola, shoe polish, lipstick, blood and others. A must-have in the laundry room.

Wine Away Red Wine Stain Remover™: Don't let the name fool you, this product is much more than a red wine stain remover. It works great on Kool-Aid™, grape juice, red pop, cranberry juice, orange pop, coffee and tea, as well as red wine. I even took red food coloring out of a shirt with it. Wine Away™ is made from fruit and vegetable extracts and is totally nontoxic—I love that!

Zout® Stain Remover: This is a super-concentrated stain remover that works great on ink, blood, grease, fruit juice, grass and hundreds of other stains. A little goes a long way with this. Simply saturate the stain, work it in, wait 5 to 10 minutes, and then launder as usual.

4

Bleach 101:
Whiter Whites, Brighter
Brights

Are you one of those people who thinks that directions are what you read to find out what you did wrong? Then pay attention. I'm going to give you my dos and don'ts of bleach basics.

DO ··

• Read the directions on the container of bleach.

• Check the labels on the fabric you wish to bleach.

• Test the bleach if you are unsure. To do this with chlorine bleach, mix 1 tablespoon of chlorine bleach with ¼ cup of cold water. Find a hidden area on the piece of clothing and place a drop of the solution on it. Leave this for a minute or two and then blot to determine if there is any color change.

• To test all-fabric bleaches, mix 1 teaspoon of the bleach with 1 cup of hot water. Again, place a drop on an inconspicuous area. Wait at least 15 minutes, blot, and check for any change in the color.

• Of course if any color change takes place you won't want to use that type of bleach on that type of fabric.

• Always be sure to rinse bleach out of fabric thoroughly.

DON'TS

• Absolutely never allow undiluted chlorine bleach to come in contact with fabrics.

- Never use any kind of bleach directly on fabric without testing it first.

- Never use more bleach than called for. It can damage fabrics and is wasteful too.

- *NEVER* use chlorine bleach and ammonia in the same wash! It can generate deadly fumes.

Now let's talk about the bleaches one by one.

Chlorine Bleach

The strongest, fastest acting bleach available, chlorine bleach is very effective on cottons, linens, and some synthetics when used properly. Used improperly it can weaken cloth fibers, causing them to disintegrate. It can even cause holes. Always follow container directions with care, and never use chlorine bleach on silk, wool, spandex, acetate, fibers treated to be flame-resistant or dry-clean-only fabrics.

Most of us have had a bad experience with chlorine bleach, so use care. Never pour it on hand washables, and never pour it onto clothes that are in the washing machine. Pour it in the bleach dispenser, if your washing machine is so equipped, or into the washer while it is filling with water *before* adding the clothes. For hand washables, dilute it prior to adding the clothes and be sure to adjust the amount accordingly for the amount of water being used.

Name brands and store brands work the same, so purchase the product of your choice, or the one with the best price.

All-Fabric Bleach or Oxygen Bleach

This is a much milder form of bleach that works well on delicate fabrics or those requiring gentle care. It is slower-acting than chlorine bleach and is less effective in restoring whiteness to fabrics. It may be effective, though, through regular use. This bleach can be used on all fabrics, even silks, as long as the manufacturer's care tag does not say "no bleach." Add this bleach at the same time you add your detergent and do not pour directly on the clothes. More is not better, so measure; don't just pour.

A New Generation of Bleach

Soapworks® has come up with a new generation of bleach that is effective, user friendly, and safe for use by people with allergies and asthma. It is hypoallergenic, nontoxic, biodegradable, 100 percent natural, safe for septic tanks, contains no chemicals, no dyes and no fragrances.

This product is called Brilliant™, and it is just that! Created with hydrogen peroxide—which is the safest, natural whitener and brightener for fabrics—this bleach can be used effectively on whites and colored fabrics both. Clothes can be soaked safely for 24 hours or more without harm to either fabric or color.

Brilliant™ is also a softener, so no additional softening agent is required. Add ¼ cup to the washer as it fills with water. As with any bleach product, test in an inconspicuous area when in doubt.

Making Your Own Bleaching Agents

Yes, you *can* create your own forms of bleach with things you already have at home.

Lemon juice: Nature's bleach and disinfectant, lemon juice can be used to whiten clothes.

Take 1 gallon of the hottest water possible for the fabric you're bleaching and add ½ cup of bottled lemon juice or the slices of one or two lemons. Soak the clothes for 30 minutes or even overnight. This works especially well on white socks and underwear, and is safe for polyester fabrics. Don't use on silks, though.

Automatic dishwasher detergent: This is another wonderful bleaching agent for white clothes. Fill a bucket with the hottest possible water for the fabric you are working with, and add 2 tablespoons of any brand of automatic dishwasher detergent. Soak white clothes for 30 minutes or even overnight. Dump into the washer and launder with your detergent as usual.

To use this bleaching technique in the washer, fill the machine with water and add ¼ cup to ½ cup of automatic dishwasher detergent. Agitate for several minutes and then add clothes. Soak as directed above and then add detergent and launder as usual.

Hydrogen peroxide: This can be used to

bleach delicate items such as wool or wool blends. Soak them overnight in a solution of 1 part 3 percent hydrogen peroxide to 8 parts cold water. Launder according to care directions.

Bluing

Bluing is a whitening and brightening agent that has been around for a long, long time. Available in liquid form, bluing contains blue pigment, which actually counteracts the yellowing that occurs in some fabrics. Always dilute this with water as directed on the bottle, and never pour directly on clothes or spill on other fibers or surfaces. Look for it in the laundry aisle at the grocery store. This product will even remove the yellow from gray hair!

Part II

· ·

CLEANING GUIDE
FOR FABRIC TYPES

Yes, it's true. I really am "stain stalker." And in these next pages I am going to walk you through laundry procedures for certain fabric types and unusual items.

Acetate: This is a temperamental fabric. Do not allow it to become heavily soiled and do not use an enzyme detergent when laundering. Acetate is commonly used for curtains, brocades, taffetas, and satin. (Think evening wear.) It's also a popular lining. You can machine wash acetate in cold water or you can hand wash. Be sure not to spin or wring acetate as this will set wrinkles. Rinse extremely well and press with a cool (low setting) iron on the "wrong" side of the fabric.

Acrylic: This fabric should be laundered frequently since it can retain perspiration odors. Acrylic is usually machine washable in cool water. Check the care label. Dry flat or hang to dry, being sure to reshape the garment while it is still damp.

Angora: This wool is made from rabbit fur or goat hair. Angora sheds a lot, although if it's blended with nylon it will shed less. Wash angora in warm or cool water using a very mild soap or a little shampoo. Do not rub, twist, or lift the garment up and down in the water as this will cause stretching. Washing in a sink is best. Let the water run out and then press the liquid out of the garment. Rinse well again, pressing the water out. Roll the garment in a towel and then reshape. Dry flat out of the sun. Do not press—instead, hold a steam iron just above the garment to remove wrinkles.

Blends: Blends, such as cotton/polyester, are made from combined fibers. To launder these fabrics, follow the guidelines for the most delicate or the most prominent fiber. The most common blends are cotton/polyester, cotton/linen, and silk/polyester.

Brocades: Use care when laundering brocades. You don't want to crush or flatten the pile design. Hand wash in cool water or dry-clean according to the care label. Do not wring. Iron on the "wrong" side using a press cloth or towel between the fabric and the iron.

Canvas: A heavy, firm, very tightly woven fabric, canvas was originally made from cotton or linen, but now it comes in synthetics or blends. Machine wash canvas in cold water and tumble dry on a low setting. Test for colorfastness before washing. If it's not colorfast, have it dry-cleaned.

Cashmere: This is an expensive fiber that

comes from the undercoat of cashmere goats. Treat it with respect. Dry-clean these prizes or hand wash with care in cool water and well-dissolved gentle soap. Rinse well and do not wring. Dry flat, reshaping the garment as it dries. Iron on the "wrong" side while still damp with a cool iron, if necessary.

Chiffon: This is a very thin, transparent fabric, made from silk or synthetic fibers. Hand wash as you would silk.

Chintz: Glazed cotton, and often printed. Dry-clean this fabric unless the label states that it can be washed. Follow the care label instructions carefully.

Corduroy: Take care when washing corduroy. It wears well, but care is needed to avoid crushing and distorting the pile. Turn corduroy inside out and launder using warm water. Dry at a normal setting. Remove from the dryer while still damp and smooth the seams, pockets, etc. Hang to complete drying, and iron on the "wrong" side of the fabric. Pile may be restored by brushing gently.

Cotton: This natural vegetable fiber is woven and knitted into fabrics in all weights and textures. Hand wash lightweight fabrics such as organdy and batiste and hang to air dry. Iron when damp with a hot iron.

Machine wash light-colored and white medium to heavyweight cottons in warm water. Use cold water for bright colors that may bleed. Dry on a low dryer setting. Remove from the dryer while still damp and iron with a hot iron right away.

Damask: This is a jacquard-weave fabric. It may be made of cotton, linen, silk, wool or a blend. Hand wash lightweight fabrics and be sure to check the individual fiber listings. Dry-clean silk, wool and all heavier weight fabrics.

Denim: If you have jeans, you know this strong fabric is prone to shrinking, streaking and fading. Machine wash denim in warm water. Blue and other deep colors bleed the first several washings, so be sure to wash separately. Washing older, faded jeans with the new ones will restore some of their original color.

Dry at low settings to avoid shrinkage. Iron while damp if necessary and be aware that jeans may bleed color onto your ironing board.

Down: Down is the soft underfeather of waterfowl that is often combined with adult feathers. It is machine washable *and* dry-cleanable. Just be sure to follow the care label closely. Much of the treatment will depend on the fabric covering the down, so pay attention to manufacturer's directions.

Do not air-dry down. It dries too slowly and mold or mildew may form in the process. Dry in your dryer, using a large capacity dryer if need be. Set temperatures low (under 140 degrees), fluffing and turning the item often. Make sure to dry the item thoroughly. This can take time.

Want really fluffy duvets and pillows? Putting a clean tennis shoe or tennis ball in with the item will fluff it up!

Flannel: Flannel is actually a napped fabric, and it comes in a plain or twill-type weave. Cotton and synthetics should be washed according to the care label, but when in doubt, use cool water and mild detergent. Dry at a low dryer setting and remove flannel while damp to avoid wrinkles. You may also line-dry this fabric. Wool flannel should be dry-cleaned.

Gabardine: Firm, tightly woven twill fabric, often worsted wool, but sometimes made of cotton and synthetic fibers. We are seeing a large amount of synthetic fibers sold as gabardine in trousers and blazers for men and women. Follow your label directions—many synthetics are machine washable and dryable. If the care label says dry-clean, be sure to do so.

Lace: An extremely delicate fabric, lace may be made of cotton, linen or synthetic. Wash using a mild soap or detergent intended for delicates. Avoid rubbing since it will distort the fibers. Rinse well without wringing, shape by hand, and hang to air-dry or dry flat. Delicate lace pieces may need to be reshaped and pinned down to dry. If you must iron lace, do so over a terrycloth towel. (White is best.) Never put lace in the dryer.

Leather and suede: Generally, leather and suede are not washable. Check your care label carefully. If you have washable leather items, wash them by hand and be sure to protect them with a leather spray protectant. To clean suede, rub it with another piece of suede or a suede brush (not any other kind of brush) to restore the nap and keep it looking new.

Remember, leather needs to breathe, so do not cover it with plastic or store in a tightly enclosed area. If you are looking for a dust cover for leather or suede, use cloth—an old pillowcase is ideal.

To remove spots from leather (not for suede), try using cuticle remover. Rub it into the spot, wait 10 minutes, and then massage the area with a cloth dipped in the cuticle remover. Wipe down thoroughly.

To remove spots from suede, try dabbing with white vinegar.

Linen: A tough fabric that withstands high temperatures, linen is a favorite in hot climates. It is made of natural flax fiber, and comes in light to heavyweight fabrics. Hand wash or machine wash linen in warm water (again, read your care label). If the fabric is colorfast you may remove stains and brighten the fabric with an oxygen bleach or Brilliant Bleach™ from Soapworks®. Do not use chlorine bleach.

Iron while still damp, and to help prevent creasing you may treat with starch or sizing. Press heavyweight linens with a hot iron, and for lighter weight linen and blends (linen, plus other fibers), iron with a warm iron.

Linen is also dry-cleanable.

Mohair: An oldie but a goodie! This is fiber taken from angora goats. Follow the directions for cleaning wool.

Nylon: This is a durable synthetic fiber that comes in varying weights and is often blended with other fibers. When used alone it is machine washable in warm water. It can also be cleaned.

Dry on a low setting or hang to dry using a nonmetal hanger. Do not dry in sunlight—that will cause yellowing. Nonchlorine bleach is best for nylon.

Organdy: Think party dress! Sheer and

lightweight, organdy is actually a cotton fiber. Hand wash this and iron damp with a hot iron. Use starch as you iron to give it a crisp look. May also be dry-cleaned.

Polyester: This strong synthetic fiber won't stretch or shrink, which is probably why it's so popular. It comes in various weights and textures, and is often found blended with cotton and wool.

Wash polyester in warm water. Tumble dry and make sure not to let it sit in the dryer, because that will encourage wrinkles. Remove it immediately and you may not need to iron it. If ironing *is* necessary, make sure to use a low setting.

If the polyester is blended with another fiber, just follow the washing instructions for the more delicate fiber.

Ramie: Very similar to linen, ramie is a natural fiber made from—what else—the ramie plant! It can be used alone or blended with other fibers, such as ramie/cotton.

Machine wash in warm water, tumble dry, and iron while damp with a hot iron. Avoid twisting the fibers or they will become distorted. May be dry-cleaned also.

Rayon: This is a synthetic fiber that is sometimes called "viscose." Follow the care label directions closely, but for the very best results, have this fabric dry-cleaned. Dry-cleaning not only cleans well, but it gives rayon the crisp pressing it needs to maintain its shape and good looks.

Satin: Originally made only from silk, this shiny fabric is available in acetate, cotton, nylon, and even polyester.

Dry-clean satin made out of silk and acetate. You may wash cotton, nylon and polyester satins, as long as you follow the washing instructions for those fibers.

Seersucker: You've seen this fabric in shirts, blouses and nightwear. It has puckered stripes that are woven in during the manufacturing process. Seersucker is most frequently made of cotton, but it's also available in nylon and polyester. Be guided by the fiber content for washing and drying.

Drip-dry or tumble dry and iron on low heat if necessary.

Silk: This is a natural fiber made by the silkworm. It is a delicate fabric that requires special care to avoid damage. Check the care labels, but you may be able to hand wash crepe de chine, thin, lightweight and medium weight silk in lukewarm water with mild soap or detergent. You can also use cold water with cold water detergent.

Do not use chlorine bleach. You may use Brilliant Bleach™ by Soapworks without damaging the fibers.

Rinsing silk well is important. Rinse several times in cold water to remove all suds. Towel blot and dry flat. Do not wring or rub silk.

Iron on the "wrong" side of the fabric with a warm iron.

If your care label indicates that the garment is machine washable, follow the directions with the utmost care. Dry cleaning works best for suits, pleated silks, and silks that are not colorfast.

Do not use strong spotters or enzyme spotters on silk.

Spandex: Spandex is added to other fibers to give them stretch and elasticity. Machine wash in warm water on the delicate or gentle cycle. Do not use chlorine bleach. Do not put them in the dryer, or iron; high heat will break down spandex fibers. Line-dry or dry flat, per care label.

If you have exercise clothes containing spandex, be sure to launder each time you wear them. Body oil can break down spandex fibers.

Swimwear: After swimming in a chlorinated pool, soak your suit for 15 minutes or so in cold water with a little liquid fabric softener. Rinse in cold water, then wash in cool water with mild detergent. Rinse well again and dry in the shade. Chlorine is very hard on fabrics, weakening them and changing the color, so be sure to rinse the suit as soon as you can. Never put your suit away without rinsing it out first.

If the suit has been worn in saltwater, soak it for a few minutes in cold water to remove the salt, then wash in cold water with mild detergent. Rinse well and dry in the shade.

Fold the suit in shape once it's dry. Store in tissue or in a perforated plastic bag for winter. (A perforated bag will allow the fabric to breathe.)

Terry cloth: A toweling-type of fabric, terry cloth has a looped pile made of cotton or cotton/polyester blend. You find it in towels, of course, and even sleepwear.

Machine wash in warm or hot water. Tumble or line dry. Add softener for a softer texture.

Velour: This is a napped fabric that is available in wool, cotton, silk and synthetics. Dry-clean unless the care label indicates it can be washed and dried.

Velvet: A beautiful soft pile fabric, velvet comes in silk, rayon or cotton. Dry-clean for best results.

To raise the pile on velvet, steam from the "wrong" side over a pot of boiling water. Hold the fabric at least 12 inches from the water, and be careful not to allow the fabric to come in contact with the water. This works well for creases in the back of dresses, etc.

Wool: This is a natural fiber made from the fleece of sheep. Hand wash sweaters and other knits in cold water with cold water detergent. Rinse several times and do not wring or twist.

Towel blot and dry flat, reshaping as needed.

Part III

• •

A TO Z PALACE
SPOT AND STAIN
REMOVAL GUIDE

ACID: Acid can permanently damage fabrics, so it must be treated immediately. Neutralize acid by flushing the area with cold running water as soon as possible. Next, spread the garment over a pad of paper towels and moisten with ammonia. Dab the spot several times, then flush again with cold water. If you do not have ammonia on hand, apply a paste of cold water and baking soda, then flush with water. Repeat this several times, then launder as usual.

Do not use undiluted ammonia on wool or silk, or on any blends containing these fibers. If you have acid on silk or wool you may dilute ammonia with equal parts of cold water and apply as directed above.

ADHESIVE TAPE: Sponge adhesive tape with eucalyptus oil, baby oil, or cooking oil. Allow to soak 10 minutes or so, then work in undiluted dishwashing liquid and rinse well. Pretreat and launder as usual.

You may also consider using De-Solv-it™, Goo Gone™, or Un-Du™ to remove adhesives from fabric and hard surfaces. Un-Du™ is so great it will remove a stamp from an envelope!

ALCOHOLIC BEVERAGES: These stains will turn brown with age, so it is important to treat them as soon as possible. First, flush the area with cold water or with club soda, then sponge immediately with a cloth barely dampened with warm water and 1 or 2 drops of liquid dish soap. Rinse with cool water and dry the area with a hair dryer set on medium.

Alcohol is often invisible when it is spilled, but it can oxidize with heat and age, which makes it impossible to remove. Presoak dry alcohol stains in an enzyme solution such as Biz All Fabric Bleach™, and launder as usual.

If you spill alcohol on a dry-clean-only fabric, sponge with cold water or club soda and then take the garment to the dry cleaner as soon as possible. Make sure to point out the stain.

For beer spills, sponge with a solution of equal parts white vinegar and dishwashing liquid, then rinse in warm water.

For treating red and white wine spills, see **Wine.**

ANIMAL HAIR: Removing pet hair from clothes and bedding can be a challenge. Try using a damp sponge and wiping over clothes and bedding, etc. Rinse the sponge frequently to keep it clean. You can also remove hair by putting on rubber gloves and dipping them in water. Simply dip and wipe, dip and wipe. The hair will rinse off easily.

ANTIPERSPIRANTS AND DEODORANTS: Antiperspirants that contain aluminum chloride are acidic and may interact with some fabrics. If color changes have occurred, try sponging fabric with ammonia. Rinse thoroughly, and remember to dilute ammonia with equal portions of water when spotting wool or silk.

If you want to avoid yellow underarm stains and prevent color removal, take a bar of Fels-Naptha Soap® and work it into the underarm of clothes *before* you launder them for the first time, even if you see no visible stain. Work up a good lather between your thumbs and then launder as usual.

You can also try applying rubbing alcohol to the stain and covering the area with a folded paper towel dampened with alcohol. Keep it moist and let it sit for a few hours prior to laundering.

To treat yellowed areas that have become stiff, apply an enzyme-soaking product. Biz All Fabric Bleach™ is a good one to try. Make a stiff paste of the powder by mixing it with cold water. Rub it into the stained areas. Next, put the garment in a plastic bag and leave 8 hours or overnight. Wash in very hot water. If dealing with fabrics that can't withstand hot water, drape the underarm area over a sink and pour 1 quart of hot water through the fabric. Launder as usual.

Don't iron over a deodorant stain or you will never be able to remove it.

I have also had success soaking garments with underarm stains in a solution of 1 quart warm water and 3 tablespoons of Brilliant Bleach™. Soak up to several days if necessary. Brilliant Bleach™ is safe for whites and colorfast garments.

Last-ditch effort: Spray the stained area heavily with heated white vinegar, work in 20 Mule Team® Borax, roll up in a plastic bag and leave overnight, then launder as usual.

BABY FORMULA: For white clothes, try applying lemon juice to the stains and laying the garment in the sun. Pretreat and launder as usual.

Unseasoned meat tenderizer is also great for removing formula and baby food stains. Make a paste of the tenderizer and cool water, rub it into the stain, and let sit for an hour or so before laundering. Meat tenderizer contains an enzyme that breaks down protein stains. Just make sure to use *unseasoned* tenderizer.

Soaking colored clothes and whites in Brilliant Bleach™ is also effective, although you may have to soak for several days to achieve perfect results on difficult stains. Remember, this bleach is nonchlorine, so it's totally safe for baby things.

BARBEQUE SAUCE: See *Tomato-Based Stains.*

BERRIES (blueberries, cranberries, raspberries, strawberries): There are many complex ways to deal with berry stains, but I've had great success with one of the simplest, a product called Wine Away Red Wine Stain Remover™. Don't be fooled by the name, it works on red fruit stains and juices too.

Just spray Wine Away™ straight on the fabric and watch in amazement as it breaks down the stain. Follow the directions on the container carefully and launder immediately after use. Totally nontoxic, Wine Away™ is safe on all washable surfaces.

BEVERAGES: Blot beverage spills immediately until you have absorbed all you can, then sponge with clean, warm water and a little borax. (About ½ teaspoon borax to ½ cup of water.) Sponge and blot repeatedly and launder as usual.

Also see information under specific beverage stains.

BLOOD (fresh and dried): If you have blood all over your clothes, laundry may not be your biggest problem . . . for those little accidents try the following:

For washable fabrics, soak as soon as possible in salt water or flush with club soda. You can also make a paste of unseasoned meat tenderizer and cold water, and apply it to the stain for a few hours. Wash in cool water and detergent, by hand or machine.

Pouring 3 percent hydrogen peroxide through the stained area can be effective in many instances. The sooner you do this the more success you will have. Make sure to do this only on washable fabrics, please. Pour the peroxide through the stain, then flush with cold water, pretreat and launder as usual.

Biz All Fabric Bleach™ and Brilliant Bleach™ both work well on blood. When using Biz™, make a paste with cold water and apply to the stain, allowing it to sit for several hours. With Brilliant Bleach™, soak the garment for a significant period of time—anywhere between 1 to 24 hours. Neither of these products will harm colorfast fabrics.

For dry-clean-only fabrics, sprinkle with salt while the blood is still moist, then take to a dry cleaner as soon as possible.

Human saliva will break down fresh bloodstains, so try applying a little of your own saliva to a small spot of blood—this may do the trick.

For a quick fix for fresh bloodstains, apply cornstarch to the surface and then flush from the "wrong" side of the fabric with soapy water. Pretreat and launder as usual.

Blood on leather can be foamed away with 3 percent hydrogen peroxide. Dab on the peroxide. Let it bubble and then blot. Continue until the blood is removed. Wipe the surface with a damp cloth and dry.

BUTTER OR MARGARINE: Scrape off any solid concentration of butter with a dull edge, such as the back of a knife.

On washable fabrics, work in undiluted dishwashing liquid, wash and dry.

If the stain is old, spray it with WD-40 Lubricant® to regenerate the grease, then work in undiluted dishwashing liquid and wash in the hottest water possible for that fabric type.

Sponge silks and delicate fabrics with Energine Cleaning Fluid®. Allow to air-dry. Repeat if necessary.

Do not iron the fabric until all traces of the grease have been removed. Ironing will set the stain and make it impossible to remove.

Take dry-clean-only fabrics to the dry cleaner as soon as possible. Be sure to identify the stain and its location on the garment.

CANDLE WAX: For candle wax on clothes and table linens, place the article in a plastic bag, place the bag in the freezer, and let the wax freeze. Scrape off what you can with a dull, straight edge—the back of a knife or an old credit card works well. Lay a brown paper bag, with no writing facing the fabric, on the ironing board. (Grocery store bags work well. Just make sure that the writing is face down on the ironing board *away* from the fabric—otherwise you may transfer lettering to your garment.) Cover with a similar bag (again, with the writing *away* from the fabric) and press with a medium/hot iron, moving the paper bag like a blotter until you have absorbed every bit of wax you can. Be patient! Blot with Energine Cleaning Fluid® to remove the balance of the grease from the wax.

Wieman Wax Away™ also works beautifully on any kind of wax. Follow the directions with care.

CANDY: To remove candy from fabrics, combine 1 tablespoon of liquid dish soap with 1 tablespoon of white vinegar and 1 quart of warm water. Soak the stain in it for 15 to 30 minutes, then flush with warm, clear water. Pretreat and launder as usual.

For chocolate stains, see *Chocolate.*

CHEWING GUM: See *Gum.*

CHOCOLATE: Scrape off all that you can, then soak washable fabrics for 30 minutes in an enzyme prewash solution such as Biz™. Rub detergent into any remaining stain and work well between your thumbs. Rinse the area under forcefully running cold water. If a grease spot remains, sponge the area with dry-cleaning solution such as Energine Cleaning Fluid®. Any residual stain should come out during normal washing. If the stain is still visible after washing, soak in Brilliant Bleach™ or combine ½ cup of 3 percent hydrogen peroxide and 1 teaspoon of clear ammonia and soak the stain for 10 minutes at a time, checking every 10 minutes and resoaking if necessary. Remember, fabrics need to be tested for colorfastness before using peroxide.

For dry-clean-only fabrics, flush the stain with club soda to prevent setting, then sponge the area with Energine Cleaning

Fluid®. If the stain persists, take it to your dry cleaner.

COFFEE AND TEA (black or with sugar): Blot up all that you can and, if the garment is washable, flush immediately with cold water. Rub detergent into the stain and work well between your thumbs before laundering as usual. If the stain is still visible and you can use hot water on the fabric, spread the stain over the sink, or stretch over a bowl and tie or rubber band in place (like a little trampoline), and set the bowl in the sink. Cover the stain with 20 Mule Team® Borax and pour boiling water through it, circling from the outside of the stain until you have reached the center. Let soak 30 minutes to an hour and relaunder.

For more delicate fabrics, soak in Brilliant Bleach™.

For sturdy whites, such as knits and T-shirts, dissolve 2 denture-cleaning tablets in warm water and soak the stain for 30 minutes. Check the garment. If the stain is still visible, soak again and launder as usual.

Out at a restaurant? Dip your napkin in

water and sprinkle with salt and blot the offending stain.

For stains from lattes and cappuccinos, see *Milk.*

COLA AND SOFT DRINKS: Sponge these spills as soon as possible with a solution of equal parts alcohol and water. On washable clothes, bleach out remaining stains with an equal mixture of 3 percent hydrogen peroxide and water. Saturate stain and wait 20 minutes. If the stain is gone, launder as usual. Repeat if the stain remains. You can also soak the fabric in a solution of Brilliant Bleach™ as directed on the container.

Borax is also effective in soft drink/cola removal. Moisten the spot thoroughly and sprinkle with borax, working well between your thumbs. Flush with water and re-treat if necessary.

Getting the stain out as soon as possible is important: cola and soft drinks will discolor fabrics as they oxidize.

COLLAR STAINS: This is for those women whose husbands won't share laundry duty, the women who didn't know that the wedding ring came with a ring around the collar! It's easy to remove, though. Just use some inexpensive shampoo! Shampoo dissolves body oils so it works great on that collar ring. Keep some in a bottle with a dispenser top in the laundry room. Squirt on enough to cover the offending stain and work it in well, then launder as usual.

COPIER TONER (powder): First, carefully shake off any loose powder and brush lightly with a soft brush. An old, soft toothbrush works well. Pretreat with your favorite spotter or try Zout® or Spot Shot Instant Carpet Stain Remover® and launder as usual, using the hottest water for the fabric type. Don't rub or brush with your hand. The oil in your skin will spread and set the stain.

COSMETICS (foundation, blusher, eye shadow, eyeliner, and mascara): Bar soap such as Dove®, Caress™ and other such beauty bars work well on cosmetics spots. Wet the stain and rub with the soap, working it in well. Flush with warm water and, once stain is removed, launder as usual.

Sometimes just working in laundry detergent will be all you need. For difficult cases, add some borax to the area and work well between your thumbs.

If your garment is dry-clean-only, try some Energine Cleaning Fluid® directly on the spot. Make sure to use a cool blow-dryer to keep a ring from forming on the fabric. You'll need to take the garment to a professional cleaner if the stain doesn't come out. (See also *Makeup.*)

CRAYON AND COLORED PENCIL: Place the stained area on a pad of paper towels and spray with WD-40 Lubricant®. Let stand for a few minutes, then turn the fabric over and spray the other side. Let sit for a further 10 minutes before working undiluted dishwashing liquid into the stained area to remove the crayon and oil. Replace the paper-toweling pad as necessary. Wash in the hottest possible water for the fabric, along with your normal detergent and appropriate bleaching agent (depending on whether the clothes are white or colored). Wash on the longest wash cycle available, and rinse well.

Another way to remove crayon from washable fabrics such as wool, acrylic, linen, cotton and polyester is to lay the offending stain between two pieces of brown paper and press with a warm/medium iron. A grocery bag works well—just remember to keep any ink that may be on the bag away from the fabric. The paper works as a blotter to absorb the crayon, so keep changing it as the wax is absorbed. If any color mark remains, soak the garment in Brilliant Bleach™ or flush with Energine Cleaning Fluid®.

Note: Don't panic if the crayon has also gone through the dryer. Simply spray an old rag with WD-40 Lubricant®; then thoroughly wipe down the drum. Make sure the dryer is empty when you do this—no clothes, no crayons. Place a load of dry rags in the dryer and run through a drying cycle when you're through. This will remove any oily residue.

DYE (see also *Hair Dye*)**:** Dye stains are difficult if not impossible to remove. Try one or all of these methods.

Spread the stained area over a bowl and put a rubber band around the fabric *and* the bowl to hold the fabric taut, like a trampoline. Set the bowl in the sink with the drain in the open position to allow the water to run freely away. Turn on the cold water faucet to a nice steady drip and let it drip through the dye spot for 3 to 6 hours. Monitor the sink to be sure the water is draining. This treatment is effective in many cases.

You can also try saturating the dye spot with a combination of equal parts 3 percent hydrogen peroxide and water. Set the fabric in the sun, keeping it moist with the solution until the spot completely disappears. Rinse well and launder as usual. Use only on color-fast clothes.

If your dye problem is caused from fugitive color—that is, color that has run from one fabric to another during the wash cycle—all the bleaching in the world won't help. Try Synthrapol™ or Carbona Color Run Remover™ instead.

Quilters have used Synthrapol™ for years to remove color that runs in homemade quilts.

Make sure to read *all* the directions on the bottle prior to using.

Carbona Color Run Remover™ is extremely effective on cotton fabrics. It is not for delicates or some blends, so do read the box with care. It may also cause damage to buttons and, in some cases, zippers. You may want to remove these prior to treating.

EGG: First scrape off any solid matter. Then, soak the fabric in a glass or plastic container with any enzyme-soaking product, such as Biz Non Chlorine Bleach™. Soak for at least 6 hours or overnight. If a stain remains, work in powder detergent, rubbing vigorously between your thumbs. Rinse and wash as usual. Check the garment carefully for any remaining stain when you remove it from the washer. Don't apply heat until all of the stain is removed or the stain will become permanent.

You can also try treating the area with cool water and unseasoned meat tenderizer. Work this into the area well, and allow it to sit for a few hours, being sure to keep the area moist. Continue treating until no stain remains.

Take nonwashables to the dry cleaner as soon as possible. Quick treatment is important. Make sure you identify the stain to your cleaner so it can be treated properly and promptly.

EYELINER AND EYE SHADOW: See *Cosmetics.*

FABRIC SOFTENER SPOTS: For the greasy spots that sometimes appear on clothes after drying with dryer fabric softener sheets, dampen the spot and rub with pure bar soap and relaunder.

For spots from liquid fabric softener, rub with undiluted liquid dish soap and relaunder.

FELT TIP MARKER: See *Marker.*

FOOD DYE: Fruit juices, gelatin desserts, fruit smoothies, and frozen fruit sticks all contain food dye that can leave a nasty stain on clothes.

Treating the stain while it is still fresh is the very best thing you can do. If you are out in public and don't have access to any cleaning supplies, wet the spot with club soda or cool water and blot, blot, blot. If you are at home, then treat the spot with 1 cup of cool water to which you have added 1 tablespoon of ammonia. Once you have flushed the spot well with this solution, grab the salt shaker and rub salt into the wound . . . I mean stain! Let this sit for an hour or so, and then brush off the salt. If the stain is still visible, re-treat the same way.

You can also try stretching the fabric tight and holding it under a forceful stream of cold water. This will flush out much of the spot without spreading it. Next, rub in your favorite detergent, scrubbing vigorously between your thumbs. Rinse again in cool water. Do not apply heat to the stain until it is completely removed.

I have had great success soaking food dye spills in Brilliant Bleach™ (follow the directions for hand-soaking on the container).

If you are dealing with a red, orange, or purple stain, try Wine Away Red Wine Stain Remover™, used according to directions. Don't be fooled by the name—it is great for all red-type stains. You will be amazed!

Remember, if the stain is not removed during the spotting process, it will not come out in the laundry!

FRUIT AND FRUIT JUICE (also see *Berries*): These stains absolutely must be removed before the fabric is washed. The combination of heat and age will set fruit stains and they will be impossible to remove, even for the Queen.

Sponge or spray the area immediately with soda water or seltzer. If these products aren't available, use cold water. *Do not use hot water.* Rinse the offending spot as soon as possible while it is still wet. Rub in your favorite detergent and scrub the area between your thumbs. *Now* rinse under hot running water—as hot as the fabric can tolerate. Pull the fabric taut and allow the full force of the water to flow through the area. The stronger the flow the better.

If the stain is still visible after this treatment, make a paste of 20 Mule Team® Borax and warm water, and work it into the stained area. Let this dry and brush off. Repeat as needed. You can also try pulling the fabric tight over a bowl, using a rubber band to secure it. Sprinkle 20 Mule Team® Borax over the stain and, using the hottest water possible for the fabric type, start at the outside edge of the stain and pour the water through the borax in circles until you are pouring through the center of the stain.

Fresh fruit stains, if treated promptly, will usually come out. Quick treatment is especially important for fruits such as peach and citrus.

Old Fruit Stains: Before you can remove the stain you must reconstitute it. You can do this by applying glycerin to the area. Rub it in well and allow to soak for 30 minutes. Treat as above.

For nonwashable fabrics, gently sponge the stain with cold water as soon as it occurs and then take to a dry cleaner as quickly as possible. Be sure to identify the stain so it can be treated properly.

If the stains are red in nature, use Wine Away Red Wine Stain Remover™ as directed in the section on berry stains.

FURNITURE POLISH: Furniture polish is usually an oil-based stain, so it must be reconstituted. Restore the oil in the polish by spraying with WD-40 Lubricant®. Allow the lubricant to soak for 10 minutes, then work in undiluted dishwashing liquid. Work this in well between your thumbs to remove the grease. Flush with a forceful stream of the hottest water you can for the fabric type. Pretreat with a product such as Zout®, which is great for grease spots, and launder as usual.

You can also try cleaning the area with Energine Cleaning Fluid®, used according to can directions.

If the furniture polish has color in it, refer to the section on dye.

GLUE, ADHESIVES, MUCILAGE: Modern adhesives and glues are very hard to remove. You may have to use a special solvent. Take the garment to the dry cleaner and be sure to identify the spot.

Here's a rundown of glue types and how to remove them.

Model Glue: Can usually be removed with nail polish remover containing acetone, although you may need to purchase straight acetone at the hardware store or the beauty supply. Always test the acetone in a small area first.

Plastic Adhesives: For best results, treat these stains before they dry. Try washing in cool water and detergent. If the stain remains, bring 1 cup or so of white vinegar to a boil, and immerse the stain. Have more vinegar boiling as you treat the stain so that you can switch to the hot vinegar as soon as the first cup starts to cool. Continue reheating the vinegar and treating for 15 to 20 minutes.

Rubber Cement: Scrape off all that you can with a dull, straight edge that you can throw away. (Don't use a credit card for this—unless it's over its limit!) Treat with Energine Cleaning Fluid® as directed.

You can also try working petroleum jelly into the glue until it pills into balls that you can then scrape from the fabric. Treat the area with undiluted liquid dish soap and launder in the hottest water the fabric will tolerate.

Miscellaneous Glues: Sponge or rinse the fabric in warm water. Work in your favorite powdered detergent or liquid detergent along with some 20 Mule Team® Borax. Rub vigorously between your thumbs. Rinse and wash in the hottest water you can for the fabric type.

Remember, soap and water will remove most synthetic glue when the spot is fresh. Acetone will remove most clear, plastic cement-type glues. Make sure to test acetone in an inconspicuous area, and never use on acetate fabrics—it will dissolve them.

For old, dried glue stains, soak the fabric in a solution of boiling hot white vinegar and water. Use 2 parts white vinegar to every 10 parts of water and soak for 30 to 60 minutes. You may need to scrape off the glue as it softens. Then pretreat and launder as usual.

GRASS, FLOWERS AND FOLIAGE: There are several ways to remove grass stains from fabrics. Pick one and try it. If it doesn't completely remove the stain, try another. Don't put clothes into the dryer until the grass stain is removed.

First a word of caution: Avoid using alkalis such as ammonia, degreasers or alkaline detergents. They interact with the tannin in the grass stains and may permanently set the stain.

Okay—first, washable fabrics: Sponge on rubbing alcohol, repeating several times. If the stain persists, sponge with white vinegar and rinse. Work in your favorite laundry detergent and rinse well.

Rubbing white nongel toothpaste into grass stains will often remove them. Rub well, then rinse and wash as usual.

For jeans, apply undiluted alcohol to the area and allow to soak 15 minutes before laundering as usual.

Zout® and Spot Shot Carpet Stain Remover® also work very well on grass stains. Follow the label directions. Biz All Fabric Bleach™ made into a paste with cold water is effective in treating stubborn grass stains too.

For grass on white leather shoes, rub the grass stain with molasses and leave it on the shoe overnight. Wash the molasses off with hot soap and water, and the grass stain should be gone.

For grass on suede fabric, including shoes, rub the stain with a sponge dipped in glycerin. Then rub with a cloth dipped in undiluted white vinegar, brush the nap gently to reset, and allow to dry and brush again. Remember: test in an inconspicuous spot first.

GRAVY: With gravy you need to remove the starch used to thicken it, so you will want to soak the garment in cold water long enough to dissolve the starch. It may take several hours.

Pretreat prior to laundering with a good spotter, such as Zout®, Spot Shot Carpet Stain Remover® or Whink Wash Away Laundry Stain Remover™. Launder in the hottest possible water for the fabric type.

You can also soak the garment in Brilliant Bleach™, for days if necessary.

GREASE AND OIL (including cooking oil and salad dressing): Grease and oil must be removed thoroughly, otherwise a semitransparent stain will set and will turn dark from all the soil it attracts.

To treat a grease stain it helps to know whether it is from animal oil, vegetable oil or automotive oil.

To remove a grease stain, first remove as much of the greasy substance as possible without forcing the grease farther down into the fabric fibers. Use a paper towel to blot and absorb all the grease that you can. Next, apply a drawing agent such as baking soda, cornstarch, or talcum powder. Rub it in gently and let it sit for 15 to 30 minutes to allow the agent to absorb and draw the grease out of the fabric. Brush the powder off thoroughly and check the stain. If it looks like you can absorb more grease, repeat the process.

Next, lay the fabric over a thick rag or a heavy fold of paper towels. Working from the back of the fabric, blot with Energine Cleaning Fluid®. Change the pad under the fabric as needed and repeat if necessary.

When grease stains are stubborn, we need to fall back on the idea that grease removes grease. Spray the grease spot with WD-40 Lubricant® and let it soak for 10 minutes, then work in undiluted dishwashing liquid and work well between your thumbs. Flush with the hottest water you can for the fabric, pretreat and launder as usual. Do not use this method on silk or crease-resistant finishes.

Many grease stains will eventually turn yellow when set with age and heat. Treat these

stains by soaking in diluted hydrogen peroxide or Brilliant Bleach™. Don't use this process
unless you know that the clothes are colorfast.

Use Energine Cleaning Fluid® on dry-
clean-only fabrics, or take to a professional
dry cleaner.

For heavily soiled, greasy work clothes, try
pouring a can of original Coca-Cola® in the
washer with your detergent and launder as
usual. The combination of sugar and cola
syrup works wonders!

GUM: The best way to deal with gum is to
harden it first. Harden any item marred by
chewing gum by placing it in a plastic bag in the
freezer and leaving it overnight. Immediately
upon removing the bag from the freezer, scrape
off any gum that you can with a dull straight
edge. If all the gum is removed, treat the fabric
with an equal mixture of white vinegar and liquid dish soap. You may also try treating the area
with lighter fluid, although you must do this
outside and use extreme care, testing the fabric
first.

Sometimes rubbing the area with egg white

(*not* the yolk—no joke!) will remove the remaining residue.

If gum is still trapped, try working petroleum jelly into the fibers, and scraping off the little balls that form. Be sure to follow the directions under **Grease** in this section to remove the grease from the petroleum jelly.

Petroleum jelly will also soften old, dry gum. You want to work the petroleum jelly into the gum and then scrape off all that you can.

For those of you who ask, yes, peanut butter will work too, but it is messier. My advice is to eat the peanut butter and use the petroleum jelly!

Carbona® makes a Stain Devil for Chewing Gum Removal. It's a great little specialty spotter.

For dry-clean-only fabrics, you may freeze the fabric and scrape off what gum you can. Take it to your dry cleaner right away.

HAIR DYE: If you didn't listen to me when I told you to dye your hair naked in the backyard, then hair-dye spots may be a major problem for you. Here's what to do:

Clothing or fabrics stained with hair dye should be washed in warm water, to which you have added white vinegar and your normal detergent. Do this in a sink or container, adding about 2 tablespoons of detergent and 2 cups of white vinegar to a gallon of warm water. Let it soak for several hours.

If the stain still remains, try our favorite bleach, Brilliant Bleach™. You can soak whites and colorfast fabrics for several days if necessary, without damage. Try to avoid the hair-dye problem if you can. I suggest using the same old towel when you do your hair.

HAND CREAM: Blot off all that you can and treat with Energine Cleaning Fluid®, working from the back of the fabric. Once all of the stain is removed, launder as usual.

ICE CREAM: Yummy-yummy in the tummy—not so great on clothes! Sponge the garment as quickly as possible with cold water, club soda, or seltzer. If a stain still remains, treat it with cold water and unseasoned meat tenderizer. Let this soak on the fabric for about 30 minutes or so and then flush with cold water to see if the offending spot is gone. Pretreat with Spot Shot Carpet Stain Remover® or Zout® and launder as usual.

If a grease spot remains, treat with Energine Cleaning Fluid® working from the back of the fabric over a pad of paper towels to absorb the spot and the spotting solution.

Sometimes treating ice cream–stained fabric with a small amount of ammonia will also work. Then, of course, launder as usual.

INK: How can one little pen cause so much grief? The first line of offense is rubbing alcohol. Sponge the ink mark, or dip it into a glass of rubbing alcohol, letting it soak until the offending spot is removed. Don't be tricked into using hair spray. That may have worked in the past, but hair spray now contains a lot of oil, and that just spreads the stain.

Denatured alcohol—a much stronger version of rubbing alcohol—may be more effective. Test this first in an inconspicuous spot, as denatured alcohol may damage some fabrics.

You also can try using acetone. This too

must be tested. (And remember, *never* use acetone on acetates.)

White, nongel toothpaste rubbed firmly and vigorously into the stain may work. After this method be sure to pretreat and launder as usual.

Often just soaking ink stains in milk will dissolve them.

Turpentine is effective on very challenging ink stains. Working over a pad of paper towels, tap the spot on the back of the fabric using the back of a spoon or an old toothbrush. Don't rub. Work in undiluted dishwashing liquid prior to laundering, and wash in the hottest water possible for the fabric type. Dispose of all paper, etc., saturated with turpentine immediately—outside, please.

Some inks only respond to solvents, so you may need to use Energine Cleaning Fluid®.

On leather, remove ballpoint ink by rubbing with cuticle remover or petroleum jelly. You may need to leave it on the stained area for several days to achieve success.

On vinyl, believe it or not, the best thing is for you to be so mad that you could spit!

Saliva will remove ballpoint ink from vinyl—as long as you are quick. Apply generously and wipe with a soft cloth. For old stains, apply glycerin, let it soak for 30 minutes or so, and then attempt to wash the stain away with a wet soft cloth rubbed over a bar of soap.

KETCHUP: See *Tomato-Based Stains.*

KOOL-AID™: Flush the spot as quickly as possible with club soda and then hold under forceful running water. If a stained area still remains, soak in Brilliant Bleach™ until the stain is removed. This may take hours or days, depending on the fabric and the stain. Soak only white or colorfast clothes in Brilliant Bleach™.

For red, grape, fruit punch, and other red Kool-Aid™ flavors, treat with Wine Away Red Wine Stain Remover™ for instantaneous stain removal.

LIPSTICK: Lipstick is actually an oily dye stain. Water, heat or wet spotters will only spread it and make the problem worse and set the stain.

Rub in vegetable oil, WD-40 Lubricant® or

mineral oil and let it sit on the spot for 15 to 30 minutes. Next sponge the area with a little ammonia—sudsy or clear is fine.

Now, before you launder, work in undiluted liquid dish soap to be sure you have removed all of the oil.

Another method I have had real success with is GOJO Crème Waterless Hand Cleaner™. Look for this at hardware stores and home centers. Work it into the lipstick, rubbing between your thumbs vigorously. Launder as usual. This method is great for the smear of lipstick on cloth table napkins.

In an emergency, try spraying the spot with a little hair spray. Let this sit for a few minutes and then wipe gently with a damp cloth. Test this method in an inconspicuous spot first.

You will also find that Zout®, Spot Shot Carpet Stain Remover® and Whink Wash Away Laundry Spotter™ are generally effective on lipstick.

For really stubborn, old stains, try moistening with denatured alcohol, then treat with undiluted liquid dish soap.

If you are getting dressed and you accidentally get lipstick on your clothes, try rubbing the stain with white bread. (Yes, it has to be white!)

MAKEUP (oily foundation, powder, cream blush, cover creams): Sprinkle baking soda on the makeup smudge, then brush the area with an old wet toothbrush until the makeup is removed. Nongel white toothpaste scrubbed with a toothbrush is also effective.

Liquid dish soap or shampoo will generally remove makeup stains. Work the product into the stain vigorously between your thumbs.

For stubborn makeup stains use nonoily makeup remover, pretreat and launder as usual. (See also *Cosmetics.*)

MARKER, WASHABLE: Rinse the stain from the fabric with cold water until no more color can be removed. Place the fabric on paper towels and saturate the back of the fabric with alcohol, using a cotton ball to blot the stain. Replace the paper towels as needed as they absorb the color. Work in Fels-Naptha Soap® until the spot is well lathered and wash in hot water with laundry detergent and fabric appropriate bleach. Rinse in warm water.

MARKER, PERMANENT: First of all, permanent usually means permanent. But before you give up and throw in the towel—or blouse, or pants, or whatever—here are some things to try.

Fill a glass with denatured alcohol (use a size appropriate to the stain) and dip the stained area into the alcohol, allowing it to soak. If it appears that the marker is being removed, continue the process.

If the stain appears stubborn, try scrubbing the marker spot with an old toothbrush, white, nongel toothpaste, and some baking soda. Give it a really good scrubbing. Rinse. If the marker stain is almost gone, soak in a cup of warm water and 2 denture-cleaning tablets for whites, and Brilliant Bleach™ for colorfast clothes. This will require some time, but the stain all comes out, so it's worth it.

If the marker is still there, scrub with Lava™ soap prior to trying the denture-cleaning tablets or bleach.

Good luck. And look out for those big black permanent markers and those Sharpies™. They're great pens, but they're murder on clothes! I can't even tell you how many times I have "accidentally" written on my clothes during a book signing with a Sharpie™ in my hand!

MAYONNAISE: See *Grease.*

MEAT JUICES: Once dry, meat juices are very tough to remove, so it's important to react quickly. Sponge the area immediately with cold water (not hot—it will set the stain), or with club soda. Next, apply unseasoned meat tenderizer and cold water, working the mixture in well. Let it sit for 30 to 60 minutes. Pretreat and launder as usual, but be sure to use *cool* water.

On dry-clean-only fabrics, sponge with cold water and take to a professional cleaner.

MEDICINES: It would be impossible to list all the medicines on the market. But this section should give you an idea of what to look out for, as well as what to do for each family of medicine.

Alcohol: Medicines containing alcohol stain quickly. Treat these stains as you would spilled alcohol.

Iron: Iron or medicines containing iron products should be treated as rust.

Oily Medicines: Oily medicines should be treated with a degreasing product. I have had great luck with Soapworks At Home All-Purpose Cleaner™, used undiluted. Work it in well and then rinse.

You can also treat these stains as you would an oil or grease stain.

Syrups: Cough syrup or children's medicines can usually be removed with water. Soak the fabric with cool water as soon as possible. Running cold water full force through the fabric can be helpful, and you may also want to try working in Fels-Naptha®, or soaking the stain in Biz Non Chlorine Bleach™ or Brilliant Bleach™. If the syrup is red, use Wine Away Red Wine Stain Remover™. (See, I told you not to be fooled by its name! It is murder on red stains!)

MILDEW: Mildew is a fungus that grows and

flourishes in warm, humid, dark conditions, like the shower, the basement, etc. The best way to avoid mildew is to ensure that things are totally dry *before* you put them away. Invisible spores can quickly grow to huge proportions, especially on natural materials such as cotton, wool, leather, paper, wood, etc.

Air needs to circulate to keep mildew from forming, so do not crowd clothes into closets.

Store clothing only after it has been cleaned and dried thoroughly.

If you are storing things such as leather purses, belts, shoes, even suitcases, clean them well, then set them in the sun for an hour or so. Do not store things in plastic as this caters to damp conditions.

If you smell a damp or musty smell coming from a closet, suspect mildew immediately and act quickly to dry it out. Even allowing a fan to blow in the closet overnight can make a huge difference by drying and circulating the air.

Okay—here's what to do if you already have mildew stains on fabrics. First, try working some Fels-Naptha Laundry Bar Soap® into the area and laundering. If stains remain and the fabric will tolerate chlorine bleach, soak it in 1 gallon of cold water to which you have added 2 to 3 tablespoons of chlorine bleach.

Moistening white or colorfast clothes with lemon juice, sprinkling them with salt and laying the garment in the sun may also remove mildew. If in doubt, test this method first.

Leather presents a different challenge. Take the item outside and brush off all the powdery mildew that you can with a soft brush. Wipe the leather with equal parts of rubbing alcohol and water, or try massaging cuticle remover into the area. After 10 minutes, wipe vigorously with a soft cloth.

Wash leather with a complexion bar soap such as Dove® or Caress™ and buff dry—do not rinse.

Remember: with mildew, the best defense is a good offense, so try to keep it from occurring.

MILK/CREAM/WHIPPING CREAM/HALF AND HALF: Rinse fabric under a cold, forceful stream of water from the faucet. Treat with unseasoned meat tenderizer and cool water. Allow to soak for 30 minutes; then flush with cool water again. If greasy-looking marks remain, treat with Energine Cleaning Fluid®, working from the back of the fabric over a heavy pad of paper towels. Launder as usual.

Treat washable fabrics stained from milk by flushing with cool water before working in detergent and a little ammonia. Wash in cool water and air-dry.

For dry-clean-only fabrics, take to a professional as soon as possible and identify the stain when you drop off the item.

MUD: The key word here is *dry.* Let mud dry. Never treat a wet mud stain other than lifting off any solid pieces with a dull straight edge. Once mud has dried, take the vacuum cleaner and vacuum the area with the hose attachment. You'll achieve the greatest suction that way. This may be a two-person job: one to hold the fabric, one to hold the hose.

Rub the cut side of a potato over the mud stain and launder as usual.

For stubborn stains, sponge with equal portions of rubbing alcohol and cool water. For red mud stains, treat with a rust remover (see *Rust*). Rubbing 20 Mule Team® Borax into a dampened mud stain will often remove it.

Spraying with Spot Shot Carpet Stain Remover® prior to laundering is also helpful.

MUSTARD: The word makes me shiver! This is a terrible stain to attempt (notice I said *attempt*) to remove.

The turmeric in mustard is what gives mustard its distinctive bright yellow color—it's also what would make it a darn good dye!

Remove as much of the mustard as possible, using a dull straight edge. Next, flex the fabric to break the grip of the embedded residue on the fabric fibers. Apply glycerin (hand cream section, drugstore) and let it sit at least an hour. Pretreat and launder as usual.

If the fabric is white or colorfast, soak the stain in hydrogen peroxide for 30 minutes. Again, Brilliant Bleach™ may remove the stain after a lengthy soaking.

For white clothes, dissolve a denture-cleaning tablet in ½ cup of cool water and allow the stained area to soak.

Things to avoid: Ammonia and heat. They will both set the stain and you will never get it out.

Kind of makes you think that ketchup and relish are all you need on that hotdog, doesn't it!

MYSTERY STAINS: These are spots and spills that you have no idea where they came from. The unknowns. Here's what to do:

• Blot with cool water (hot water sets stains).

• Blot with a sponge or cloth dampened with water and a teaspoon or so of white vinegar (not for cotton or linen).

• Blot with a sponge or cloth dampened with water and a teaspoon or so of clear ammonia (again, not for cotton or linen).

• Blot with rubbing alcohol diluted 50/50 with cool water.

• Sponge with a solution of Brilliant Bleach™ and water.

NAIL POLISH: Okay, if you had polished your nails naked in the backyard you wouldn't be reading this, would you? Stretch the fabric over a glass bowl and make a little trampoline by securing the fabric with a rubber band. Drip acetone-based polish remover through the stain with a stainless steel spoon (not silver) and tap the stain with the edge of the spoon. Continue dripping the acetone through the fabric until the polish is removed. This requires time and patience. If you run out of either, walk away and come back later. Straight acetone, purchased at the hardware store or beauty supply, may work faster, but be sure to test an area first.

If a color stain remains after the polish is removed, dilute hydrogen peroxide (50 percent peroxide, 50 percent water), apply to the stain, and set the fabric in the sun, keeping it moist with the peroxide solution. Do this only for white or colorfast clothes.

Do not use acetone on silk or acetates, and always test the acetone on an inconspicuous area prior to beginning.

Nonwashable fabrics should be dry-cleaned.

ODORS: Eliminate odors, don't use a perfumed cover-up. I like ODORZOUT™ odor eliminator because it absorbs odors and removes them permanently—without leaving any telltale smells behind. It is nontoxic and safe for all surfaces, and it can be used wet or dry. It is also safe for the environment and a little goes a long way. Keep some on hand. It's great for just about any odor you're likely to come across, such as smoke, mildew, mold, feces, urine, food odors, any kind of odor. Do not use a perfumed cover-up.

OIL (also see **Grease and Oil):** Blot up all oil quickly. Avoid rubbing or you will force the oil farther into the fibers. Pretreat washable fabrics with your favorite spot remover, or use one recommended for oily stains in this book. Launder in the hottest possible water for the fabric.

Nonwashables should be dry-cleaned.

OINTMENT (A and D ointment, Desitin, zinc oxide): Anyone who has had a baby will be familiar with this problem stain. Use hot water and detergent, rubbing the fabric against itself to remove the oil. If the stain remains, treat as indicated in the section on *Grease and Oil*.

For zinc oxide, soak the garment in white vinegar for 30 minutes after treating as above, then launder as usual.

PAINT, LATEX: Treat this stain immediately for best results. It is important to remove paint *before* it dries, so keep the stain wet if you can't work on it right away.

Flush the paint from the fabric with a forceful stream of warm water. Next, treat the stain with a solution of liquid dish soap and water, or laundry detergent and water. Work it into the stained area, soaping and rinsing until the stain is removed. Do this as many times as necessary. If the fabric is color-fast, you can also work in some automatic dishwasher detergent and let it soak on the fabric for 5 to 10 minutes before laundering as usual.

You can also try a product aptly named

OOPS!™ Just follow the directions on the can closely.

On fabrics such as cotton and polyester, try spraying the garment with oven cleaner and letting it sit about 15 to 30 minutes before flushing with plenty of water. Use *extreme* care with this method and use it at your own risk. Some fabrics cannot tolerate the oven cleaner, but if the garment is ruined by the paint, it is worth a try. Also use care where you spray the oven cleaner and what you set the fabric on afterward.

PAINT, OIL-BASED: Get busy and remove this spill ASAP. You're out of luck if it dries. If you must go to the store for products, keep the spill moist: *Do not allow oil-based paint to dry.*

Check the paint can and use the thinner recommended by the manufacturer. Sometimes thinner for correction fluid will also work. Remember to test an area first with these two methods.

I fall back on turpentine when all else fails. Work the turpentine into the spill, and once the paint is removed, work in GOJO Crème Waterless Hand Cleaner™. That will take out the oiliness from the turpentine. Remember to dispose of turpentine soaked rags or paper towels outside, as soon as possible.

When working on a paint spill, work from the back of the fabric over a thick pad of paper towels. Tap the stained area with an old toothbrush or an old spoon as you work to force the paint out.

Now that you have removed the stain, saturate it with detergent and work in vigorously. Cover the area with the hottest water you can use for the fabric, and let it soak overnight. Scrub again, between your thumbs, and launder as usual.

PENCIL: Okay, how easy is this? Take a nice, clean, soft eraser, and gently rub the offending mark away! Just be sure the eraser is clean, or you will create a large stain. If the spot is stubborn, sponge with Energine Cleaning Fluid®.

PERFUME: Follow the directions in the section on *Alcoholic Beverages.* A few words to the wise: The best time to put it on is right before you put on your clothes, not after. And never spray perfume directly on your clothes. This will damage them. The combination of alcohol and oil is death to fabrics.

PERSPIRATION STAINS: These stains are really the pits. Perspiration will weaken fabrics, so treat vulnerable areas with care and treat those invisible perspiration problems right after you wear a garment for the first time—*before* you toss it in the washer.

Moisten the underarm area—or any other spot where perspiration stains are a problem—and work in a lather of Fels-Naptha Soap®. Once you've worked up a good lather, toss the garment in the machine and launder as usual.

Working Biz Activated Non Chlorine Bleach™ into the stained fabric is also effective. Just make sure to wet the offending area first!

Always treat perspiration areas on a garment *prior* to laundering. If odor is present, apply warm water to the area and work in 20 Mule Team® Borax. Let sit 30 minutes or so, then launder.

If you already have stains, try dampening the fabric with warm water and working in laundry detergent and Biz™. Let that soak about 30 minutes and launder as usual.

I have found that soaking garments (whites or colors) in Brilliant Bleach™ from Soapworks® is very effective for removing underarm stains.

You can also try to clean existing stains with heated white vinegar. Spray it on the fabric and then work in 20 Mule Team® Borax. This works well on odor as well as stains.

If the fabric has changed color, try spraying with sudsy ammonia, let sit about 15 minutes, then launder as usual.

Bear in mind that yellowed or discolored fabric may be damaged. The garment may not be salvageable.

Treat everything prior to washing for the first time and do try switching brands of antiperspirant. Never wear shirts or blouses more than one day if you have a perspiration problem. You may find that wearing natural fibers such as cottons will be less of a problem than polyester and polyester blends. If your problem is serious you may want to try underarm shields. They trap moisture before it can reach the fabric. They can be removed and thrown away each day, and can't be seen through the garment. Look for them in lingerie stores and in catalogs. Also check out the section in this stain removal guide on *Antiperspirants and Deodorants.*

PURPLE OR BLUISH COLOR ON SYNTHETIC FIBERS: Sometimes synthetic fibers will develop a purple tinge after repeated laundering. Remove it with Rit Color Remover™ and launder as usual.

RUST: On white fabrics, saturate with lemon juice and sprinkle with salt, then lay in the sun. (No, not you—the fabric!) If the rust is stubborn, apply the lemon juice and salt, and pour water through the stain. Use boiling water if the fabric will tolerate it; otherwise use hot. Check the care label.

You can also cover the stained area with cream of tartar, then gather up the edges of the fabric and dip the spot in hot water. Let stand 5 to 10 minutes and then launder as usual.

There are good commercial rust removers on the market. Try Whink Rust Remover®, Magica®, and Rust Magic®. Be sure to read directions carefully when using commercial rust removers. Some cannot be used on colored fabric, so check carefully.

SAP, PINE TAR: See *Tar.*

SCORCH MARKS: Sorry to say, but severe scorch marks cannot be removed.

Light scorch marks may be treated with a cloth dampened with 1 part 3 percent hydrogen peroxide and 3 parts water. Lay the cloth over the scorch mark and press with a medium/hot iron. Do not iron off of the cloth or you will scorch the fabric again. Make sure to try this method first in a small, inconspicuous space.

If the scorch is still visible, moisten the spot with the diluted peroxide and lay it in the sun.

Very light scorch marks may also be removed by wetting them with water and laying the garment in the sun.

If the scorch mark has appeared on white clothes, saturate the scorched area with lemon juice and lay it in the sun. Keep it moist with the lemon juice until the stain is removed.

For white cottons, sometimes boiling in ½ cup of soap and 2 quarts of milk will remove the stain. Try this at your own risk. Some fabrics may not tolerate boiling.

For light scorches you can also rub the fabric with the cut side of a white onion (not a red onion—it will stain) and then soak the fabric in cold water for several hours. Launder as usual.

Remember: scorching weakens fibers, so use care and always relaunder the item once the scorch mark has been removed.

SHOE POLISH: Work laundry detergent into the fabric immediately and rinse. For persistent stains, sponge with alcohol. Use undiluted alcohol on white clothes, and 1 part alcohol to 2 parts water on colored fabrics. Rinse again, or try using turpentine after first testing in an inconspicuous spot.

Shoe polish has an oily base containing dye. Using the wrong things such as water, heat, or wet spotters will spread and set the stain.

Work in vegetable oil or WD-40 Lubricant® and let it sit for 15 minutes. Sponge on a little ammonia (not on silk, please), then work in undiluted dishwashing liquid and launder as usual.

Energine Cleaning Fluid® may also help to eliminate the final stained area.

If you have any discoloration remaining from the dye in the shoe polish, soak the fabric in Brilliant Bleach™ until the stain is removed.

If the shoe polish stain is old and heavy, you may need to treat it with petroleum jelly. Cover the polish and work in the petroleum jelly, let it soak for 30 to 60 minutes, and then scrape off all that you can of the polish and the petroleum jelly. Work in undiluted dishwashing liquid and flush with a forceful stream of hot water. Pretreat and launder as usual.

Liquid Shoe Polish: Blot up all that you can from the fabric. Do not rub—this will spread the stain. Do not apply water. Instead, saturate with alcohol—undiluted for whites, diluted as above for colors. Continue to flush with alcohol, work in your favorite laundry detergent, and then rub vigorously to remove all trace of the stain.

SILK SPOTS: Spots on silk are hard to remove and must be handled with care.

Dry-cleaning solvent may spot-clean silk, but you're likely to be left with a ring on the fabric. Make sure to use the blow-dryer on the spot to avoid that telltale ring.

For unusual or heavy stains, take to a professional. Too much rubbing can remove the color from silk.

SILLY PUTTY®: First of all, let gravity do the work for you. Lay the fabric over a bowl and let the Silly Putty® simply drop off. You'll only have to clean up what's left!

Scrape off the balance of any Silly Putty® with a dull edge, such as an old credit card or knife back. Spray with WD-40 Lubricant® and let stand a few minutes. Scrape again, removing all the Silly Putty® that you can. Continue to do this, changing from the dull straight edge to cotton balls. If any stain remains, saturate a cotton ball with rubbing alcohol, blot the stain, and rinse. Work in liquid dish soap and launder as usual in the hottest water you can for the fabric type.

If you don't have WD-40 Lubricant®, use petroleum jelly instead.

SOFT DRINKS: See *Cola and Soft Drinks.*

SOOT: Launder clothing in the hottest possible water for the fabric with your normal detergent, ½ cup of 20 Mule Team® Borax and ½ cup of Arm and Hammer Washing Soda™.

STICKERS: Heat white vinegar and apply it, undiluted, directly to the fabric. Allow the vinegar to soak until the sticker can be peeled back with ease.

TAR: Lift off as much solid matter as possible using a plastic (disposable) knife. Spread the stained area over a heavy pad of paper towels and apply glycerin to the fabric, tapping it with the back of an old toothbrush or plastic spoon. Change the paper towels as they absorb the tar. Finally, once you have removed all the tar you can, work in some turpentine or eucalyptus oil. Flush the stained area with alcohol, or work in undiluted liquid dish soap. Pretreat and launder as usual. Spot Shot Carpet Stain Remover® is a good spotter for this.

Dried Tar: Warm the glycerin or some olive oil and spread over the area, allowing it to soak until the tar is loosened. Then proceed as above.

Nonwashables should be taken to the dry cleaner as soon as possible.

TEA: See *Coffee and Tea.*

TOMATO-BASED STAINS (ketchup, spaghetti sauce, tomato sauce, barbecue sauce, etc.): Flush these stains well with cool water as soon as possible. Make sure you apply water to the back of the fabric. Apply white vinegar and then flush again with a forceful stream of water.

Apply Wine Away Red Wine Stain Remover™ per package directions.

URINE: Fresh urine stains are fairly easy to remove. First rinse well, flushing with lots of cool water. Presoak using an enzyme powder or Biz All Fabric Bleach™. Then launder as usual.

You may also soak urine-stained fabric in salt water, then rinse and launder as usual.

If the color of the fabric has changed due to the urine, sponge the area or spray with clear ammonia, then rinse and launder as usual.

For Old Urine Stains: Soak in clear hot water for an hour—the hotter the better. Add detergent and wash as usual, then rinse. Use the appropriate bleach for the fabric type, or Brilliant Bleach™ if you prefer.

See also the treatment mentioned under **Odors.**

VOMIT: Shake off or scrape what you can over the toilet. Flush the fabric from the "wrong" side with cool water, using a force ful stream. Once you have removed solid matter and excess liquid, make a paste of liquid laundry soap and 20 Mule Team® Borax and vigorously scrub the fabric. Rinse with salt water, pretreat and launder as usual.

Quick treatment is important to avoid stains from foods and stomach acid.

See also the treatment mentioned for **Odors.**

WINE: Never serve red wine without having white wine; nearby! And always tend to the stain *as soon as you can!*

For red wine spills, dilute the spot with white wine; then flush with cool water and apply salt.

If no white wine is available, sprinkle heavily with salt and flush with club soda or cool water.

Applying a paste of 20 Mule Team® Borax and water usually works.

For red wine spills and other red stains, keep Wine Away Red Wine Stain Remover™ on hand. It is totally nontoxic and works so fast on red wine and red stains that even I am still amazed. The directions are simple and easy. Blot up the spill, apply the Wine Away™, and watch the red stain disappear. Blot with a wet cloth. You'll thank me many times for this one!

YELLOW SPOTS AND STAINS: These stains are common on white clothes and linens. Denture-cleaning tablets will generally remove these stains. Fill a basin with water and add 1 or 2 tablets. Allow the tablets to dissolve and then soak the fabric until the yellow is removed.

RESOURCE GUIDE

ACETONE: A great spotter, but be careful. It is exceedingly strong and can damage fibers. Look for this at hardware stores, home centers and beauty supply stores.

ACT NATURAL CLOTHS®: See Euronet USA.

BIZ® ACTIVATED NON CHLORINE BLEACH: A great all-purpose powdered bleach. Look for it in the laundry aisle at grocery stores and discount stores.

BORAX: Better known as 20 Mule Team® Borax Laundry Additive. This can be found in the detergent aisle.

BRILLIANT BLEACH™: See Soapworks®.

CARBONA® COLOR RUN REMOVER: Removes fugitive color from fabrics. Available in grocery and discount stores.

CARBONA® STAIN DEVILS: A great series of spotters that target specific stains, like gum, blood, milk, etc.

CLEAR AMMONIA: There are two types of ammonia, clear and sudsy (sometimes called "cloudy"). Clear doesn't contain soap and should be used where suggested for that reason.

CLEAN SHIELD® SURFACE TREATMENT (formerly Invisible Shield®): This is such a wonderful product—just the name gives me goose bumps! It turns all of those hard-to-clean surfaces in your home (the exterior of the washing machine and dryer, any surface that is not wood or painted) into nonstick surfaces that can be cleaned with water and a soft cloth. No more soap scum or hard-water deposits! It never builds up so it won't make surfaces slipperier, and it's nontoxic too! Call 1-800-528-3149 for a supplier near you.

CUSTOM CLEANER®: Try this if you're looking for a do-it-yourself dry-cleaning kit to freshen and spot-clean clothes. I love it. Custom Cleaner® works on all kinds of spots and has a very pleasant, clean scent. Look for this at grocery stores and discount stores.

DENATURED ALCOHOL: This is an industrial alcohol reserved for heavy-duty cleaning. Don't use it near an open flame, and make sure to dispose outside the home any rags that were used to apply it. Launder or clean anything that you treat with it as soon as possible. Look for this in cans at hardware stores and home centers.

DE-SOLV-IT CITRUS SOLUTION™: Available in home centers, hardware stores, etc., De-Solv-It Citrus-Solution™ has a multitude of uses both inside and out. Great for laundry.

ENERGINE CLEANING FLUID®: A great spotter. Look for this at the hardware store, the home center, and even in some grocery stores (usually on the top shelf with the laundry additives).

EPSOM SALTS: Usually used for medicinal

purposes, but handy for laundry too. Look for this in the drugstore.

EURONET USA: Makers of ACT Natural® Microfiber Cloths. These easy-to-use cloths have been scientifically proven to kill germs and bacteria. They even come with a warranty. I never travel without a cloth, and I keep one in my desk and briefcase to quickly clean up any of those little spills on clothes. Call 1-888-638-2882 or visit www.euronetusa.com

FELS-NAPTHA HEAVY-DUTY LAUNDRY BAR SOAP®: You'll find this wonderful laundry spotter and cleaner in the bar soap section of the grocery store. It's usually on the bottom shelf covered in dust, because nobody knows what to use it for!

FRESH BREEZE LAUNDRY SOAP®: See Soapworks.

GLYCERIN: Look for glycerin in drugstores in the hand cream section. Always purchase plain glycerin, *not* the type containing rose-water.

GOJO CRÈME WATERLESS HAND CLEANER®: Not just a hand cleaner, GOJO is great for laundry too. Look for it at home centers and hardware stores.

HYDROGEN PEROXIDE: Make sure to choose 3 percent—the type used for cuts, *not* the type used to bleach hair. (That's too strong and will remove color from fabric.)

MEAT TENDERIZER: Great for spotting protein stains. Use the unseasoned variety, please, or you will have a whole new stain to deal with. Store brands work fine.

NAIL POLISH REMOVER: I caution you to use non-acetone polish remover first. It's much less aggressive than acetone polish remover.

NONGEL TOOTHPASTE: This is just a fancy name for old-fashioned plain white toothpaste. Gels just don't work, so don't even try.

ODORZOUT®: A fabulous, dry, 100 percent natural deodorizer. It's nontoxic, so you can use it anyplace you have a smell or a stink. Also available in a pouch for shoes, laundry hampers, etc. Call 1-800-88STINK, or visit their website at www.88stink.com

PUREX® LAUNDRY DETERGENT: Available wherever detergents are sold.

RETAYNE®: Used *before* you launder colored clothes for the first time, it will help retain color. Available wherever quilting supplies are sold.

RUST REMOVER: These are serious products, so follow the directions carefully. Look for products like Whink® and Rust Magic® at hardware stores and home centers.

SHAVING CREAM: The cheaper brands work fine for spotting. Cream works better than gel.

SOAPWORKS®: Manufacturer of wonderful nontoxic, user-friendly and earth-friendly cleaning, laundry, and personal care products. Try their Fresh Breeze Laundry Powder®, originally designed for allergy and asthma sufferers. Also try their Brilliant Bleach™. Believe me, it *is* brilliant! Call 1-800-699-9917 or visit their website at www.soapworks.com

SOOT AND DIRT REMOVAL SPONGE: These big brick erasers are available at home centers and hardware stores, usually near the wallpaper supplies. Clean them by washing in a pail of warm water and liquid dish soap, rinse well, and allow to dry before using again.

SPOT SHOT INSTANT CARPET STAIN REMOVER®: My all-time favorite carpet spotter is a wonderful laundry spotter too! Available most everywhere, or call 1-800-848-4389.

SYNTHRAPOL®: Great for removing fugitive color. Available wherever quilting supplies are sold.

UN-DU™: Removes sticky residue from fabric and hard surfaces. Look for it at office supply, home centers and hardware stores.

WASHING SODA: I like Arm and Hammer® Washing Soda, which can be found in the detergent aisle at the grocery store along with other laundry additives. No, you cannot substitute baking soda; it's a different product!

WD-40 LUBRICANT®: Fine spray oil for lubricating all kinds of things, WD-40® is wonderful for regenerating grease so that it can be removed from clothes. Look for this at the hardware store, home center, and even the grocery store.

WIEMAN'S WAX AWAY™: Removes candle wax from fabrics and hard surfaces. Look for it at grocery stores and discount stores.

WINE AWAY RED WINE STAIN REMOVER™: This unbelievably good product can be found at Linens 'n Things, or wherever liquor is sold. Call 1-888-WINEAWAY for a store near you.

ZOUT STAIN REMOVER®: A very versatile laundry pre-spotter, Zout® is thicker than most laundry spotters, so you can target the spot. It really works! Buy it in grocery stores, discount stores, etc.

Your Personal Tips and Hints

Your Personal Tips and Hints

Your Personal Tips and Hints

Your Personal Tips and Hints

Your Personal Tips and Hints

Your Personal Tips and Hints

Your Personal Tips and Hints

Your Personal Tips and Hints

Your Personal Tips and Hints

Your Personal Tips and Hints

Your Personal Tips and Hints